T0257265

Data Structure and Algorithms Using C++

Scrivener Publishing
100 Cummings Center, Suite 541J
Beverly, MA 01915-6106

Publishers at Scrivener
Martin Scrivener (martin@scrivenerpublishing.com)
Phillip Carmical (pcarmical@scrivenerpublishing.com)

Data Structure and Algorithms Using C++

A Practical Implementation

Edited by

Sachi Nandan Mohanty

ICFAI Foundation For Higher Education, Hyderabad, India

and

Pabitra Kumar Tripathy

Kalam Institute of Technology, Berhampur, India

Scrivener
Publishing

WILEY

This edition first published 2021 by John Wiley & Sons, Inc., 111 River Street, Hoboken, NJ 07030, USA and Scrivener Publishing LLC, 100 Cummings Center, Suite 541J, Beverly, MA 01915, USA
© 2021 Scrivener Publishing LLC
For more information about Scrivener publications please visit www.scrivenerpublishing.com.

Wiley Global Headquarters
111 River Street, Hoboken, NJ 07030, USA

For details of our global editorial offices, customer services, and more information about Wiley products visit us at www.wiley.com.

Limit of Liability/Disclaimer of Warranty
While the publisher and authors have used their best efforts in preparing this work, they make no representations or warranties with respect to the accuracy or completeness of the contents of this work and specifically disclaim all warranties, including without limitation any implied warranties of merchantability or fitness for a particular purpose. No warranty may be created or extended by sales representatives, written sales materials, or promotional statements for this work. The fact that an organization, website, or product is referred to in this work as a citation and/or potential source of further information does not mean that the publisher and authors endorse the information or services the organization, website, or product may provide or recommendations it may make. This work is sold with the understanding that the publisher is not engaged in rendering professional services. The advice and strategies contained herein may not be suitable for your situation. You should consult with a specialist where appropriate. Neither the publisher nor authors shall be liable for any loss of profit or any other commercial damages, including but not limited to special, incidental, consequential, or other damages. Further, readers should be aware that websites listed in this work may have changed or disappeared between when this work was written and when it is read.

Library of Congress Cataloging-in-Publication Data

ISBN 978-1-119-75054-3

Cover image: Pixabay.Com
Cover design by Russell Richardson

Set in size of 11pt and Minion Pro by Manila Typesetting Company, Makati, Philippines

Contents

Preface

Welcome to the first edition of *Data Structures and Algorithms Using C++*. A data structure is the logical or mathematical arrangement of data in memory. To be effective, data has to be organized in a manner that adds to the efficiency of an algorithm and also describe the relationships between these data items and the operations that can be performed on these items. The choice of appropriate data structures and algorithms forms the fundamental step in the design of an efficient program. Thus, a deep understanding of data structure concepts is essential for students who wish to work on the design and implementation of system software written in C++, an object-oriented programming language that has gained popularity in both academia and industry. Therefore, this book was developed to provide comprehensive and logical coverage of data structures like stacks, queues, linked lists, trees and graphs, which makes it an excellent choice for learning data structures. The objective of the book is to introduce the concepts of data structures and apply these concepts in real-life problem solving. Most of the examples presented resulted from student interaction in the classroom. This book utilizes a systematic approach wherein the design of each of the data structures is followed by algorithms of different operations that can be performed on them and the analysis of these algorithms in terms of their running times.

This book was designed to serve as a textbook for undergraduate engineering students across all disciplines and postgraduate level courses in computer applications. Young researchers working on efficient data storage and related applications will also find it to be a helpful reference source to guide them in the newly established techniques of this rapidly growing research field.

Dr. Sachi Nandan Mohanty and
Prof. Pabitra Kumar Tripathy
December 2020

Introduction to Data Structure

1.1 Definition and Use of Data Structure

Data structure is the representation of the logical relationship existing between individual elements of data. In other words the data structure is a way of organizing all data items that considers not only the elements stored but also their relationship to each other.

Data structure specifies

- Organization of data
- Accessing methods
- Degree of associativity
- Processing alternatives for information

The data structures are the building blocks of a program and hence the selection of a particular data structure stresses on

- The data structures must be rich enough in structure to reflect the relationship existing between the data, and
- The structure should be simple so that we can process data effectively whenever required.

In mathematically   **Algorithm + Data Structure = Program**

Finally we can also define the data structure as the "Logical and mathematical model of a particular organization of data"

Sachi Nandan Mohanty and Pabitra Kumar Tripathy. *Data Structure and Algorithms Using C++: A Practical Implementation*, (1–14) © 2021 Scrivener Publishing LLC

1.2 Types of Data Structure

Data structure can be broadly classified into two categories as Linear and Non-Linear

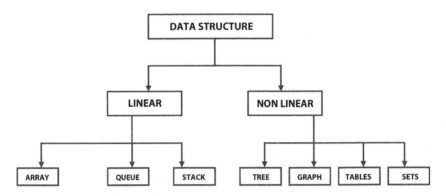

Linear Data Structures

In linear data structures, values are arranged in linear fashion. Arrays, linked lists, stacks, and queues are the examples of linear data structures in which values are stored in a sequence.

Non-Linear Data Structure

This type is opposite to linear. The data values in this structure are not arranged in order. Tree, graph, table, and sets are the examples of non-linear data structure.

Operations Performed in Data Structure

In data structure we can perform the operations like

- Traversing
- Insertion
- Deletion
- Merging
- Sorting
- Searching

1.3   Algorithm

The step by step procedure to solve a problem is known as the **ALGORITHM**. An algorithm is a well-organized, pre-arranged, and defined computational module that receives some values or set of values as input and provides a single or set of values as out put. These well-defined computational steps are arranged in sequence, which processes the given input into output.

An algorithm is said to be accurate and truthful only when it provides the exact wanted output.

The efficiency of an algorithm depends on the time and space complexities. The complexity of an algorithm is the function which gives the running time and/or space in terms of the input size.

Steps Required to Develop an Algorithm

- Finding a method for solving a problem. Every step of an algorithm should be defined in a precise and in a clear manner. Pseudo code is also used to describe an algorithm.
- The next step is to validate the algorithm. This step includes all the steps in our algorithm and should be done manually by giving the required input, perform the required steps including in our algorithm and should get the required amount of output in a finite amount of time.
- Finally implement the algorithm in terms of programming language.

Mathematical Notations and Functions

❖ **Floor and Ceiling Functions**
Floor function returns the greatest integer that does not exceed the number.
Ceiling function returns the least integer that is not less than the number.

$\lfloor no \rfloor$ denotes the floor function

$\lceil no \rceil$ denotes the ceil function

Ex :

$\lfloor 5.23 \rfloor = 5$ $5.23 \lceil = 6 \rceil$

❖ **Remainder Function**

To find the remainder "mod" function is being used as

A mod B

❖ **To find the Integer and Absolute value of a number**

INT(5.34) = 5   This statement returns the integer part of the number

INT(- 6.45) = 6   This statement returns the absolute as well as the integer portion of the number

❖ **Summation Symbol**

To add a series of number as a1+ a2 + a3 +............+ an the symbol Σ is used

$$\sum_{i=1}^{n} a_i$$

❖ **Factorial of a Number**

The product of the positive integers from 1 to n is known as the factorial of n and it is denoted as n!.

0! = 1

Algorithemic Notations

While writing the algorithm the comments are provided with in [ ].

The assignment should use the symbol ": =" instead of "="

For Input use Read : variable name

For output use write : message/variable name

The control structures can also be allowed to use inside an algorithm but their way of approaching will be some what different as

Simple If

```
If condition, then:
        Statements
[end of if structure]
```

If...else

```
If condition, then:
      Statements
Else :
      Statements
[end of if structure]
```

If...else ladder

```
If condition1, then:
      Statements
Else If condition2, then:
      Statements
Else If condition3, then:
      Statements
.............................................

.............................................

.............................................
Else If conditionN, then:
      Statements
Else:
      Statements
[end of if structure]
```

LOOPING CONSTRUCT

```
Repeat for var = start_value to end_value by
step_value
      Statements
[end of loop]

Repeat while condition:
      Statements
[end of loop]
      Ex : repeat for I = 1 to 10 by 2
            Write:  i
            [end of  loop]
```

OUTPUT

```
1 3 5 7 9
```

1.4   Complexity of an Algorithm

The complexity of programs can be judged by criteria such as whether it satisfies the original specification task, whether the code is readable. These factors affect the computing time and storage requirement of the program.

Space Complexity

The space complexity of a program is the amount of memory it needs to run to completion. The space needed by a program is the sum of the following components:

- A fixed part that includes space for the code, space for simple variables and fixed size component variables, space for constants, etc.
- A variable part that consists of the space needed by component variables whose size is dependent on the particular problem instance being solved, and the stack space used by recursive procedures.

Time Complexity

The time complexity of a program is the amount of computer time it needs to run to completion. The time complexity is of two types such as

- Compilation time
- Runtime

The amount of time taken by the compiler to compile an algorithm is known as compilation time. During compilation time it does not calculate for the executable statements, it calculates only the declaration statements and checks for any syntax and semantic errors.

The run time depends on the size of an algorithm. If the number of instructions in an algorithm is large, then the run time is also large, and if the number of instructions in an algorithm is small, then the time for executing the program is also small. The runtime is calculated for executable statements and not for declaration statements.

Suppose space is fixed for one algorithm then only run time will be considered for obtaining the complexity of algorithm, these are

- Best case
- Worst case
- Average case

Best Case

Generally, most of the algorithms behave sometimes in best case. In this case, algorithm searches the element for the first time by itself.

For example: In linear search, if it finds the element for the first time by itself, then it behaves as the best case. Best case takes shortest time to execute, as it causes the algorithms to do the least amount of work.

Worst Case

In worst case, we find the element at the end or when searching of elements fails. This could involve comparing the key to each list value for a total of N comparisons.

For example in linear search suppose the element for which algorithm is searching is the last element of array or it is not available in array then algorithm behaves as worst case.

Average Case

Analyzing the average case behavior algorithm is a little bit complex than the best case and worst case. Here, we take the probability with a list of data. Average case of algorithm should be the average number of steps but since data can be at any place, so finding exact behavior of algorithm is difficult. As the volume of data increases, the average case of algorithm behaves like the worst case of algorithm.

1.5   Efficiency of an Algorithm

Efficiency of an algorithm can be determined by measuring the time, space, and amount of resources it uses for executing the program. The amount of time taken by an algorithm can be calculated by finding the number of steps the algorithm executes, while the space refers to the number of units it requires for memory storage.

1.6   Asymptotic Notations

The asymptotic notations are the symbols which are used to solve the different algorithms and the notations are

- Big Oh Notation (**O**)
- Little Oh Notation (**o**)
- Omega Notation (**Ω**)
- Theta Notation (**θ**)

Big Oh (O) Notation

This Notation gives the upper bound for a function to within a constant factor. We write $f(n) = O(g(n))$ if there are +ve constants $n0$ and C such that to the right of $n0$, the value of $f(n)$ always lies on or below $Cg(n)$

Omega Notation (Ω)

This notation gives a lower bound for a function to with in a constant factor. We write $f(n) = \Omega g(n)$ if there are positive constants $n0$ and C such that to the right of $n0$ the value of $f(n)$ always lies on or above $Cg(n)$

Theta Notation (θ)

This notation bounds the function to within constant factors. We say $f(n) = \theta g(n)$ if there exists +ve constants $n0$, $C1$ and $C2$ such that to the right of $n0$ the value of $f(n)$ always lies between $c1g(n)$ and $c2(g(n))$ inclusive.

Little Oh Notation (o)

$F(n) = o(g(n))$ iff $f(n) = O(g(n))$ and $f(n) \;!= \Omega g(n)$.

Introduction

An important question is: How efficient is an algorithm or piece of code? Efficiency covers lots of resources, including:

CPU (time) usage
Memory usage
Disk usage
Network usage

All are important but we will mostly talk about CPU time
Be careful to differentiate between:

Performance: how much `time/memory/disk/`... is actually used
when a program is running. This depends on the machine, compiler, etc.,
as well as the code.

Complexity: how do the resource requirements of a program or algorithm
scale, i.e., what happens as the size of the problem being solved gets larger.
Complexity affects performance but not the other way around. The time
required by a method is proportional to the number of "basic operations"
that it performs. Here are some examples of basic operations:

```
one arithmetic operation (e.g., +, *).
one assignment
one test (e.g., x == 0)
one read
one write (of a primitive type)
```

Note: As an example,

O(1) refers to constant time.
O(n) indicates linear time;
$O(n^k)$ (k fixed) refers to polynomial time;
O(log n) is called logarithmic time;
$O(2^n)$ refers to exponential time, etc.

*$n^2 + 3n + 4$ is $O(n^2)$, since $n^2 + 3n + 4 < 2n^2$ for all n > 10. Strictly speaking,
$3n + 4$ is $O(n^2)$, too, but big-O notation is often misused to mean equal to
rather than less than.*

1.7   How to Determine Complexities

In general, how can you determine the running time of a piece of code?
The answer is that it depends on what kinds of statements are used.

1. Sequence of statements

```
statement 1;
statement 2;
    ...
statement k;
```

Note: this is code that really is exactly k statements; this is **not**
an unrolled loop like the N calls to *addBefore* shown above.)
The total time is found by adding the times for all statements:

```
total time = time(statement 1) + time
(statement 2) + ... + time(statement k)
```

If each statement is "simple" (only involves basic operations) then the time for each statement is constant and the
total time is also constant: O(1). In the following examples,
assume the statements are simple unless noted otherwise.

2. **if-then-else statements**

```
if (cond) {
    sequence of statements 1
}
else {
    sequence of statements 2
}
```

Here, either sequence 1 will execute, or sequence 2 will execute.
Therefore, the worst-case time is the slowest of the two possi-
bilities: max(time(sequence 1), time(sequence 2)). For example, if sequence 1 is O(N) and sequence 2 is O(1) the worst-case
time for the whole if-then-else statement would be O(N).

3. **for loops**

```
for (i = 0; i < N; i++) {
    sequence of statements
}
```

The loop executes N times, so the sequence of statements also
executes N times. Since we assume the statements are O(1), the
total time for the for loop is N * O(1), which is O(N) overall.

4. **Nested loops**

```
for (i = 0; i < N; i++) {
    for (j = 0; j < M; j++) {
        sequence of statements
    }
}
```

The outer loop executes N times. Every time the outer loop
executes, the inner loop executes M times. As a result, the
statements in the inner loop execute a total of N * M times.
Thus, the complexity is O(N * M). In a common special case

where the stopping condition of the inner loop is `j < N` instead of `j < M` (i.e., the inner loop also executes N times), the total complexity for the two loops is $O(N^2)$.

5. **Statements with method calls:**
   When a statement involves a method call, the complexity of the statement includes the complexity of the method call. Assume that you know that method *f* takes constant time, and that method *g* takes time proportional to (linear in) the value of its parameter *k*. Then the statements below have the time complexities indicated.

   ```
   f(k);  // O(1)
   g(k);  // O(k)
   ```

   When a loop is involved, the same rule applies. For example:

   ```
   for (j = 0; j < N; j++) g(N);
   ```

   has complexity (N^2). The loop executes N times and each method call g(N) is complexity O(N).

Examples

Q1. What is the worst-case complexity of the each of the following code fragments?

Two loops in a row:

```
for (i = 0; i < N; i++) {
    sequence of statements
}
for (j = 0; j < M; j++) {
    sequence of statements
}
```

Answer: The first loop is O(N) and the second loop is O(M). Since you do not know which is bigger, you say this is O(N+M). This can also be written as O(max(N,M)). In the case where the second loop goes to N instead of M the complexity is O(N). You can see this from either expression above. O(N+M) becomes O(2N) and when you drop the constant it is O(N). O(max(N,M)) becomes O(max(N,N)) which is O(N).

Q2. How would the complexity change if the second loop went to N instead of M?

A nested loop followed by a non-nested loop:

```
for (i = 0; i < N; i++) {
    for (j = 0; j < N; j++) {
        sequence of statements
    }
}
for (k = 0; k < N; k++) {
    sequence of statements
}
```

Answer: The first set of nested loops is $O(N^2)$ and the second loop is $O(N)$. This is $O(max(N^2,N))$ which is $O(N^2)$.

Q3. A nested loop in which the number of times the inner loop executes depends on the value of the outer loop index:

```
for (i = 0; i < N; i++) {
    for (j = i; j < N; j++) {
        sequence of statements
    }
}
```

Answer: When i is 0 the inner loop executes N times. When i is 1 the inner loop executes N-1 times. In the last iteration of the outer loop when i is N-1 the inner loop executes 1 time. The number of times the inner loop statements execute is N + N-1 + ... + 2 + 1. This sum is N(N+1)/2 and gives $O(N^2)$.

Q4. For each of the following loops with a method call, determine the overall complexity. As above, assume that method f takes constant time, and that method g takes time linear in the value of its parameter.

```
a. for (j = 0; j < N; j++) f(j);
b. for (j = 0; j < N; j++) g(j);
c. for (j = 0; j < N; j++) g(k);
```

Answer: a. Each call to f(j) is $O(1)$. The loop executes N times so it is N x $O(1)$ or $O(N)$.

b. The first time the loop executes j is 0 and g(0) takes "no operations." The next time j is 1 and g(1) takes 1 operations. The last time the loop executes j is N-1 and g(N-1) takes N-1 operations. The total work is the sum of the first N-1 numbers and is $O(N^2)$.

c. Each time through the loop g(k) takes k operations and the loop executes N times. Since you do not know the relative size of k and N, the overall complexity is O(N x k).

1.8   Questions

1. What is data structure?
2. What are the types of operations that can be performed with data structure?
3. What is asymptotic notation and why is this used?
4. What is complexity and its type?
5. Find the complexity of $3n^2 + 5n$.
6. Distinguish between linear and non-linear data structure.
7. Is it necessary is use data structure in every field? Justify your answer.

Review of Concepts of 'C++'

2.1 Array

Whenever we want to store some values then we have to take the help of a variable, and for this we must have to declare it before its use. If we want to store the details of a student so for this purpose we have to declare the variables as

```
char  name [20], add[30] ;
int roll, age, regdno ;
float total, avg ;
         etc......
            for a individual student.
```

If we want to store the details of more than one student than we have to declare a huge amount of variables and which are too much difficult to access it. I.e/ the programs length will increased too faster. So it will be better to declare the variables in a group. I.e/ name variable will be used for more than one student, roll variable will be used for more than one student, etc.

So to declare the variable of same kind in a group is known as the Array and the concept of array is used for this purpose only.

Definition: The array is a collection of more than one element of same kind with a single variable name.

Types of Array:

The arrays can be further classified into two broad categories such as:

- One Dimensional (The array having one boundary specification)
- Multi dimensional (The array having more than one boundary specification)

Sachi Nandan Mohanty and Pabitra Kumar Tripathy. *Data Structure and Algorithms Using C++: A Practical Implementation*, (15–48) © 2021 Scrivener Publishing LLC

2.1.1   One-Dimensional Array

Declaration:

Syntax :

> Data type variable_name[bound] ;

The data type may be one of the data types that we are studied. The variable name is also same as the normal variable_name but the bound is the number which will further specify that how much variables you want to combine into a single unit.

> Ex : int roll[15];

In the above example roll is an array 15 variables whose capacity is to store the roll_number of 15 students.

> And the individual variables are
> roll[0] , roll[1], roll[2], roll[3] ,................,roll[14]

Array Element in Memory

The array elements are stored in a consecutive manner inside the memory. i.e./ They allocate a sequential memory allocation.

For Ex : int x[7];

Let the x[0] will be at the memory address 568 then the entire array can be represented in the memory as

x[0]	X[1]	X[2]	X[3]	X[4]	X[5]	X[6]
568	570	572	574	576	578	580

Initialization:

The array is also initialized just like other normal variable except that we have to pass a group of elements with in a chain bracket separated by commas.

Ex : int x[5]= { 24,23,5,67,897 } ;

In the above statement x[0] = 24, x[1] = 23, x[2]=5, x[3]=67,x[4]=897

Retrieving and Storing Some Value From/Into the Array

Since array is a collection of more than one elements of same kind so while performing any task with the array we have to do that work repeatedly. Therefore while retrieving or storing the elements from/into an array we must have to use the concept of looping.

Ex: Write a Program to Input 10 Elements Into an Array and Display Them.

```
#include<iostream.h>
      void main()
      {
      int x[10],i;
      ;
      cout<<"\nEnter 10 elements into the array";
            for(i=0 ; i<10; i++)
                 cin>>x[i];
      cout<<"\n THE ENTERED ARRAY ELEMENTS ARE :";
            for(i=0 ; i<10; i++)
                 cout<<"    "<<x[i];
      }
```

OUTPUT
```
Enter 10 elements into the array
12
36
89
54
6
125
35
87
49
6
THE ENTERED ARRAY ELEMENTS ARE  :   12    36
89   54    6 125    35   87   49    6
```

2.1.2   Multi-Dimensional Array

The array having more than one boundary specification is known as multi dimensional array. The total number of elements to be stored in side a multi dimensional array is equals to the **product of its boundaries**.

But we do use the two dimensional array to handle the matrix operations. The two dimensional array having two boundary specifications.

Declaration of Two-Dimensional Array

The declaration of the two dimensional array is just like the one dimensional array except that instead of using a single boundary we have to use two boundary specification.

SYNTAX

data_type variable_name[boundary1][boundary2];

Ex : int x[3][4];
In the above example x is the two dimensional array which has the capacity to store (3x4) 12 elements. The individual number of elements are

x[0][0]	x[0][1]	x[0][2]	x[0][3]
x[1][0]	x[1][1]	x[1][2]	x[1][3]
x[2][0]	x[2][1]	x[2][2]	x[2][3]

INITIALIZATION

The array can also be initialized as like one dimensional array.

Ex: int x[3][4] = {{3,5,7,8}, {45,12,34,3}, {56,89,56,23}};

OR

int x[3][4] = {3,5,7,8,45,12,34,3,56,89,56,23};
After the above initialization

x[0][0]=3	x[0][1]=5	x[0][2]=7	x[0][3]=8
x[1][0]=45	x[1][1]=12	x[1][2]=34	x[1][3]=3
x[2][0]=56	x[2][1]=89	x[2][2]=56	x[2][3]=23

Processing of a Two-Dimensional Array

While processing a two-dimensional array we have to use two loops.

Example : WAP to input a 3 x 3 matrix and find out the sum of lower triangular elements.

```
#include<iostream.h>
     void main()
        {
        int mat[3][3],i,j,sum=0;
```

$$\left(\begin{array}{ccc} A[0][0] & A[0][1] & A[0][2] \\ A[1][0] & A[1][1] & A[1][2] \\ A[2][0] & A[2][1] & A[2][2] \end{array} \right) \left(\begin{array}{ccc} 5 & 7 & 9 \\ 2 & 6 & 8 \\ 12 & 24 & 7 \end{array} \right)$$

The sum will be
A[0][0]+A[1][0]+A[1][1]+A[2][0]+A[2][1]+A[2][2]
That means in each case the value of 'i' >= 'j'
So the condition will be   if(i>=j) { sum=sum
+ a[i][j] }
The result will be sum = 5+2+6+12+24+7 = 56

/* INPUT THE ARRAY */

```
for(i=0 ; i<3 ; i++)
      for(j=0 ; j<3 ; j++)
         {
   cout<<"\nEnter a number";
   cin>>mat[i][j];
         }
```

/* LOGIC TO SUM THE LOWER TRIANGULAR ELEMENTS */

```
for(i=0 ; i<3 ; i++)
    for(j=0 ; j<3 ; j++)
       {
       if(i>=j)
          sum=sum+mat[i][j];
       }
```

/* PRINT THE ARRAY */

```
cout"\nTHE  ENTERED MATRIX IS\n";
for(i=0 ; i<3 ; i++)
   {
     for(j=0 ; j<3 ; j++)
         {
   cout<<"   "<<mat[i][j];
         }
   cout<<"\n";
   }
   cout<<"\nSum of the lower triangular matrix is"<<sum;
   }
```

OUTPUT
Enter a number 5
Enter a number 7
Enter a number 9
Enter a number 2
Enter a number 6
Enter a number 8
Enter a number 12
Enter a number 24
Enter a number 7

THE ENTERED MATRIX IS

5	7	9
2	6	8
12	24	7

Sum of the lower triangular matrix is 56

2.1.3   String Handling

The string is a collection of more than one character. So it can also be called as a character array. The approaching to the string/character array is somewhat different compare to the normal array due to its speciality nature.

The speciality is that the string always terminates with a NULL ('\0') character. So while accessing the string there is no need to use the loop frequently(We may access it as a array with the help of loop).

When we will access it with the loop (like int, float etc. array) than the NULL character will not be assigned at the end of it, so while printing it we are bound to use the loop again. If we want to convert the character array to a string so we have to assign the NULL character at the end of it, manually.

Representation of a string and a Character Array

Let char x[10]="India";   /* Representation of a string*/

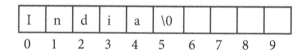

char x[10] = {'I','n','d','i','a'};   /* Character Array */

I	n	d	i	a					
0	1	2	3	4	5	6	7	8	9

Declaration of a Character Array

The declaration of the string/character array is same as the normal array, except that instead of using other data type the data type 'char' is used.

Syntax : Data_type var_name[size] ;

Ex: char name[20];

Initialization of a String

Let char x[10]="India";   /* Representation of a string*/

I	n	d	i	a	\0				
0	1	2	3	4	5	6	7	8	9

char x[10] = {'I','n','d','i','a'};   /* Character Array */

Example: Wap to Input a string and display it.

```
#include<iostream.h>
    void main()
    {
    char x[20];
    cout<<"\nEnter a string";
    gets(x);
    cout<<"\n THE ENTERED STRING IS "<<x;
    }
```

OUTPUT

Enter a string Hello
THE ENTERED STRING IS Hello

OR

This process of Input is not preferable because forcibly we are bound to input the 10 characters, not less than 10 or above 10 characters.

```cpp
#include<iostream.h>
    void main()
    {
        char x[20];
            int i;
    cout<<"\nEnter a string";
    for(i=0;i<10;i++)
    cin>>x[i];

    x[i]='\0'; /* CONVERTING THE CHARACTER ARRAY
TO STRING */
    cout<<"\n THE ENTERED STRING IS "<<x;
    }
```

OR

```cpp
#include<iostream.h>
    void main()
    {
    char x[20];
int i;
    cout<<"\nEnter a string";
gets(x);
cout<<"\n THE ENTERED STRING IS ";
        for(i=0; x[i] !='\0';i++)
        cout<<x[i];
    }
```

OUTPUT

Enter a string Hello

THE ENTERED STRING IS Hello

NOTE : If we want to scan a string as individual characters then we have to use the loop as `for(i=0; str[i] !='\0';i++)`

This is fixed for all the strings after input it.

Example – 2

Write a program to input a string and count how many vowels are in it.

```
#include<iostream.h>
void main()
    {
  char x[20];
int i,count=0;
cout<<"\n Enter a string";
gets(x);
    cout<<"\n The entered string is"<<x;
for(i=0; x[i]!='\0';i++)
    if(toupper(x[i])=='A'    ||    toupper(x[i])=='E'
||   toupper(x[i])=='I'   ||   toupper(x[i])=='O'  ||
toupper(x[i])=='U')
   count++;
cout<<"\n The string"<<x<< "having"<<count<<"num-
bers of vowels";
}
```

OUTPUT

Enter a string Wel Come
The entered string is Wel Come
The string Wel Come having 3 numbers of vowels.

Example :

Write a program to find out the length of a string.

```
#include<iostream.h>
void main()
  {
  char x[20];
int i,len=0;
  cout<<"\n Enter a string";
    gets(x);
for(i=0;x[i]!='\0';i++)
    len++;
cout<<"\n THE LENGTH OF"<<x<<"IS"<<len;
  }
```

OUTPUT
Enter a string hello India
THE LENGTH OF hello India IS 11

OR

```
#include<iostream.h>
void main()
 {
 char x[20];
int i;
  cout<<"\n Enter a string";
   gets(x);
for(i=0;x[i]!='\0';i++)  ;
cout<<"\n THE LENGTH OF"<<x<<"IS"<<len;
 }
```

OUTPUT
Enter a string hello India
THE LENGTH OF hello India IS 11

String Manipulation

The strings cannot be manipulated with the normal operators, so to have some manipulation we have to use the help of certain string handling functions. 'C'-language provides a number of string handling functions amongst them the most popularly used functions are

    a. Strlen()
    b. Strrev()
    c. Strcat()
    d. Strcmp()
    e. Strcpy()
    f. Strupr()
    g. Strlwr()

These functions prototypes are declared inside the header file **string.h**
❖ **Strlen()**
Purpose : Used to find out the length of a string.
Syntax : integer_variable = strlen(string);

❖ **Strrev()**
  Purpose : Used to find out the reverse of a string.
  Syntax : strrev(string);

❖ **Strcat()**
  Purpose: Used to concatenate(Join) two strings. It will append the source string at the end of the destination. The length of the destination will be the length of source + length of destination
  Syntax: strcat(destination,source);

❖ **Strcmp()**
  Purpose: Used to compare two strings.
  Process: The string comparison always starts with the first character in each string and continuous with subsequent characters until the corresponding characters differ or until the end of a string is reached.

This function returns an integer value that is

< 0 if s1 < s2
== 0 if s1 == s2
>0 if s1 > s2

ASCII VALUES
A = 65   a = 97
0 = 48

The string comparison is always based upon the ASCII values of the characters.
  Syntax : integer_variable = strcmp(s1,s2);

❖ **Strcpy()**
  Purpose : To copy a string to other.
  Syntax : strcpy(destination,source);

❖ **Strupr()**
  Purpose : To convert all the lower case alphabets to its corresponding upper-case.
  Syntax : strupr(string);

❖ **Strlwr()**
  Purpose : To convert all the upper case alphabets to its corresponding lower-case.
  Syntax : strlwr(string);

2.2   Function

Definition: One or more than one statements combined together to form a block with a particular name and having a specific task.

The functions in 'C' are classified into two types as

    a.   Library Function or Pre defined function
    b.   User defined function

The library functions are already comes with the 'C' compiler(Language). Ex : printf(), scanf(), gets(), clrscr(), strlen() etc.

The user defined functions are defined by the programmer when ever required.

2.2.1   User Defined Functions

We will develop the functions just comparison with the library functions, i.e/ All the library functions can be categorized into four types as

    1. integer variable = strlen(string/string variable)
         [The strlen() takes a string ,find its length and returns it to a integer variable]
    2. gets(string variable);
         [the gets() takes a variable and stores string inside that which will be entered by the user]
    3. character variable = getch();
         [The getch() does not take any value/variable but it stores a character into the character variable which will be entered by the user]
    4. clrscr();
         [This function does not take argument and not return also, but it does its work that means it clears the screen]

So by studying the above four types of functions we concluded that by considering the arguments taken by the function and the values returned by the functions the functions can be categorized into four types as

    1. The function takes argument and also returns value.
    2. The function does not take argument but returns value.
    3. The function takes argument but not return value.
    4. The function does not take argument and also not return values.

Parts of a Function

A function has generally three parts as

1. Declaration (Specifies that how the function will work, it prepares only the skeleton of the function)
2. Call [It call the function for execution]
3. Definition [It specifies the work of the function i./ it is the body part of the function]

2.2.2   Construction of a Function

1. **Function takes argument and also returns value.**
   DECLARATION
   Return_type   function_name(data type, data_type, data_type, ...);

   Ex: int sum(int,int);

   CALL
   Variable = function_name(var1,var2,var3,.................);

   Ex: x = sum(a,b);

   Where a,b,x are the integer variables

   DEFINITION
   Return_type   function_name(data_type var1, data_type var2,...........)
   {
           Body of the function ;
   Return(value/variable/expression);
   }

   Ex:
   ```
       int sum(int p, int q)
        {
            int z;
            z = p+q;
            return(z);
        }
   ```

2. **Function does not take argument but returns value.**
   DECLARATION
   Return_type function_name();
           Or

Return_type function_name(void);
   Ex : int sum();

CALL

 Variable = function_name();
   Ex : x = sum();

Where x is an integer.

DEFINITION

 Return_type function_name()

```
        {
                Body of function;
                Return (value/variable/expression);
        }
```

Ex:

```
    int sum()
        {
            int a,b;
            cout<<"\nEnter 2 numbers";
            cin>>a>>b;
            return(a+b);
        }
```

3. **Function takes argument but not returns value**
   DECLARATION
   void function_name(data type1,data type2,...............);

   Ex : void sum(int,int);

CALL

function_name(var1,var2,var3............);

   Ex : sum(x,y);

Where x and y is an integer.

DEFINITION

Void function_name (data_type1 v1, data_type2 v2,.........)

```
        {
                Body of function ;
        }
```

Ex:

```
    void sum(int x, int y)
        {
                    cout<<"\nSum = "<<x+y;
        }
```

4. **Function does not take arguments and not returns value.**
   DECLARATION
   void function_name(void);
   >   Ex : void sum();

   CALL
   function_name();

   >   Ex : sum();

   DEFINITION

```
    Void function_name ()
    {
          Body of function ;
    }
```

Ex:

```
   void sum()
   {
int x,y;
cout<<"\n Enter two numbers";
cin>>x>>y;
          cout<<"\nSum = "<<x+y;
   }
```

ARGUMENTS : Based upon which the function works.

RETURN TYPE: The value returned /given by the function to its calling part.

WAP TO FIND OUT THE SUM OF TWO NUMBERS

Category – 1

```
    #include<iostream.h>
    void main()
    {
int sum(int,int);
int x,y,z;
cout<<"\n Enter two numbers";
cin>>x>>y;
z = sum(x,y);
cout<<"\n Addition of"<<x<<"and"<<y<<"is"<<z;
}
int sum(int p, int q)
{
int r;
r = p+q;
return(r);
}
```

OUTPUT
```
Enter two numbers 5
6
Addition of 5 and 6 is 11
```

Category – 2

```
#include<iostream.h>
void main()
    {
int sum();
int z;
z = sum();
cout<<"\n Addition is"<<z;
    }
int sum()
    {
int x,y;
cout<<"\n Enter two numbers";
  cin>>x>>y;
  return(x+y);
    }
```

OUTPUT
```
Enter two numbers 5
6
Addition is 11
```

Category – 3

```
#include<iostream.h>
void main()
    {
void sum(int,int);
int x,y;
cout<<"\n Enter two numbers";
cin>>x>>y;
    sum(x,y);
    }
void sum(int   p,int q)
    {
        Cout<<"\n Addition
of"<<p<<"and"<<q<<"is"<<p+q;
    }
```
OUTPUT
```
Enter two numbers 5
6
Addition of 5 and 6 is 11
```

Category – 4

```
#include<iostream.h>
void main()
    {
void sum();
sum();
    }
void sum()
    {
  int x,y;
  cout<<"\n Enter two numbers";
    cin>>x>>y;
  cout<<"Addition of"<<x<<"and"<<y<<"is"<<x+y;
    }
```

OUTPUT
```
Enter two numbers 5
6
Addition of 5 and 6 is 11
```

2.2.3 Actual Argument and Formal Argument

Those arguments kept inside the function call is known as actual argument and those arguments kept inside the function definition is known as the formal arguments (Because these are used to maintain the formality just to store the values of the actual arguments).

Ex:

```
#include<iostream.h>
void main()
    {
int sum(int,int);
int x,y,z;
cout<<"\n Enter two numbers";
cin>>x>>y;
z = sum(x,y); /* Here x and y are called as the
actual argument*/
    cout<<"\n Addition of"<<x<<"and"<<y<<"is"<<z;
    }
int sum(int  p, int q) /* Here p and q are called as the formal
argument */
    {
int r;
r = p+q;
return(r);
    }
```

OUTPUT
```
Enter two numbers 5
6
Addition of 5 and 6 is 11
```

If a function is to use arguments, it must declare variables that accept the values of the arguments. These variables are called the **formal parameters** of the function.

The formal parameters behave like other local variables inside the function and are created upon entry into the function and destroyed upon exit.

While calling a function, there are two ways that arguments can be passed to a function:

Call Type	Description
Call by value	This method copies the actual value of an argument into the formal parameter of the function. In this case, changes made to the parameter inside the function have no effect on the argument.
Call by pointer	This method copies the address of an argument into the formal parameter. Inside the function, the address is used to access the actual argument used in the call. This means that changes made to the parameter affect the argument.
Call by reference	This method copies the reference of an argument into the formal parameter. Inside the function, the reference is used to access the actual argument used in the call. This means that changes made to the parameter affect the argument.

By default, C++ uses **call by value** to pass arguments. In general, this means that code within a function cannot alter the arguments used to call the function and above mentioned example while calling max() function used the same method.

2.2.4 Call by Value and Call by Reference

When a function is called by its value then that function call is known as call by value.

When a function is called by its reference/address then that function call is known as call by reference.

Difference Between Call by Value and Call by Reference

In call by value if the value of the variable is changed inside the function than that will not effect to its original value, because the value of the actual parameters are copied to the formal arguments so there is no interlink between them.

But in call by reference if the value of the variable is changed inside the function then that will be effected to its original value, because in call by reference the addresses of the actual arguments are copied to the formal arguments that's why there is a interlink between them. So any change made with the formal argument then that will effect to the actual value.

Ex:

Call by value

```
#include<iostream.h>
void main()
{
int x=5,y=6;
void change(int,int);
cout<<"\n X="<<x<<"and Y="<<y;
change(x,y);
cout<<"\n X="<<x<<"and Y="<<y;
}
void change(int a,int b)
{
a=a+5;
b=b+5;
cout<<"\n X="<<a<<"and Y="<<b;
}
```

OUTPUT

```
X = 5 and Y=6
X=10 and Y=11
X=5 and Y=6
```

Call by REFERENCE

```
#include<iostream.h>
void main()
{
int x=5,y=6;
void change(int *,int *);
```

```
    cout<<"\n X="<<x<<"and Y="<<y;
    change(&x,&y);
    cout<<"\n X="<<x<<"and Y="<<y;
     }
   void change(int *a,int *b)
        {
        *a=*a+5;
        *b= *b+5;
   cout<<"\n X="<<*a<<"and Y="<<*b;
        }
```

OUTPUT
```
 X = 5 and Y=6
 X=10 and Y=11
 X=10 and Y=11
```

2.2.5   Default Values for Parameters

When you define a function you can specify a default value for each of the last parameters. This value will be used if the corresponding argument is left blank when calling to the function.

This is done by using the assignment operator and assigning values for the arguments in the function definition. If a value for that parameter is not passed when the function is called, the default given value is used, but if a value is specified this default value is ignored and the passed value is used instead. Consider the following example:

```
#include <iostream>

int sum(int a, int b=20)
{
  int result;

  result = a + b;

  return (result);
}

int main ()
{
  // local variable declaration:
  int a = 100;
  int b = 200;
  int result;
```

```
// calling a function to add the values.
result = sum(a, b);
cout << "Total value is :" << result << endl;

// calling a function again as follows.
result = sum(a);
cout << "Total value is :" << result << endl;

return 0;
}
```

When the above code is compiled and executed, it produces following result:

Total value is :300
Total value is :120

2.2.6 Storage Class Specifiers

The storage class specifiers are the keywords which are used to declare the variables. Without the help of storage class specifier we cannot declare the variables but till now we declare the variables without using the storage class specifier. Because by default the c-language includes the variable into 'auto' storage class.

'C++'-language supports four storage class specifiers as auto, static, extern, register

AUTO

Initial Value	: **Garbage value**
Storage Area	: **Memory**
Life	: **With in the block where it is declared**
Scope	: **Local**

STATIC

Initial Value	: **Zero**
Storage Area	: **Memory**
Life	: **With in the block where it is declared**
Scope	: **The value of the variable will persist between different function calls**

EXTERN

Initial Value	: **Zero**
Storage Area	: **Memory**
Life	: **The variable can access any where of the program**
Scope	: **Global**

REGISTER

Initial Value   : **Garbage**
Storage Area   : **CPU Memory**
Life   : **With in the block where it is declared**
Scope   : **Local**

Difference between STATIC and AUTO

```
#include<stdio.h>
        void main()
         {
        void change();
        change();
        change();
        change();
         }
        Void change()
         {
        auto int x=0;
          printf("\n X= %d",x);
        x++;
         }
```

OUTPUT
 X=0
 X=0
 X=0

```
#include<stdio.h>
        void main()
         {
        void change();
        change();
        change();
        change();
         }
        Void change()
         {
        static int x;
          printf("\n X= %d",x);
        x++;
         }
```

OUTPUT
 X=0
 X=1
 X=2

2.3 Pointer

The pointer is a variable which can store the address of another variable. Whatever changed with the value of the variable with the help of the pointer that will directly effect to it.

2.3.1 Declaration of a Pointer

Like other variables the pointer variable should also be declared before its use

SYNTAX

Data_type *variable_name;
Example: int *p;

2.3.2 Initialization of a Pointer

Initialization means to assign an initial value, since the pointer can store only the address so during its initialization we have to assign an address of another variable.

Ex: int *x,p;
X=&p;   /* INITIALIZATION */

NOTE : After declaration of the pointer variable, if we write simply the variables name than it will represent to address and *variable will represent to value. But in C++ always we have to use *variable since it deals with object.

```
Example : (IN C)
WRITE A PROGRAM TO INPUT A NUMBER AND DISPLAY IT.
    #include<iostream.h>
    void main()
    {
    int *p,x;
    p=&x;
    printf("\n Enter a number");
    scanf("%d",&x);
```

INSIDE MEMORY

P   X

| 1087 | 5 |

P=&X

732   1087 P = 1087, *P=5

X=5 AND &X = 1087

```
printf("\n THE VALUE OF X (THROUGH POINTER) IS %d",*p);
    printf("\n THE VALUE OF X IS %d",x);
    }
```

OUTPUT
```
Enter a number 5

THE VALUE OF X(THROUGH POINTER) IS 5
THE VALUE OF X IS 5
```
(IN C++)

WRITE A PROGRAM TO INPUT A NUMBER AND DISPLAY IT.

```
#include<iostream.h>
void main()
 {
int *p,x;
p=&x;
cout<<"\n Enter a number";
cin>>*x;
```

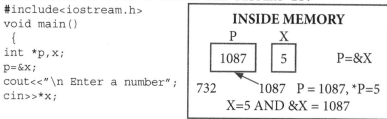

```
cout<<"\n THE VALUE OF X(THROUGH POINTER) IS "<<*p;
cout<<"\n THE VALUE OF X IS"<<*x;
         }
```

OUTPUT
```
Enter a number 5

THE VALUE OF X(THROUGH POINTER) IS 5
THE VALUE OF X IS 5
```

2.3.3   Arithmetic With Pointer

In general the arithmetic operations include Addition, Subtraction, Multiplication, and Division. But in case of pointer we can perform only the addition and subtraction operations. That means when we perform an addition/subtraction operation with the pointer then it shifts the locations because pointer means an address. If we add one to the integer pointer then it will shift two bytes (int occupies two bytes in memory), so for float 4 bytes, char 1 byte, long double 4 bytes and accordingly it will shift the positions.

Ex: Let int *p,x ;

P=&x;

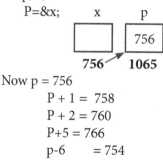

Now p = 756
$$P + 1 = 758$$
$$P + 2 = 760$$
$$P+5 = 766$$
$$p-6 \quad = 754$$

NOTE : Pointer means the address so we can perform any type of operation with *p (value at address)

2.3.4   Passing of a Pointer to Function

As like normal variables we can also pass a pointer to the function as its argument.

DECLARATION
   Return_type function_name(data_type *, data_type *,............);

CALL
   Variable = function_name(ptrvar, ptrvar, ptrvar,.........);

DEFINITION
   Return_type function_name(data_type *var, data_type *var,............)
      {
      body of function ;
      return(value/var/exp) ;
      }

Example:
WRITE A PROGRAM TO FINDOUT THE FACTORIAL OF A NUMBER

```
#include<iostream.h>
void main()
   {
long int fact(int *);
int *n;
long int f;
cout<<"\n Enter a number";
cin>>*n;

f=fact(n);
cout<<"\n Factorial Is"<<f;
   }
long int fact(int *p)
   {
   int i;
long int f=1;
   for(i=1;i<=*p;i++)
        f*=i;
   return(f);
   }
```

> When the function f=fact(n) is called then the address which is inside the pointer variable n that will copied to the pointer variable p(formal argument) So in this case what ever changes made with 'p' that will directly effect to 'n'

```
OUTPUT
  Enter a number 5
  Factorial is 120
```

2.3.5   Returning of a Pointer by Function

Declaration

Return_type * function_name(data type,data type...............);

CALL

Ptr_Variable = function_name(var1,var2,............);

DEFINITION

Return_type* function_name(data_type v1,................................)
{
body of function
return(pointer_var);
}

EXAMPLE
WRITE A PROGRAM TO FINDOUT THE FACTORIAL OF A NUMBER

```
#include<iostream.h>
void main()
  {
long int * fact(int *);
int n;
long int *f;
cout<<"\n Enter a number";
cin>>n;
f=fact(&n);
cout<<"\n Factorial Is %ld"<<*f;
    }
long int * fact(int *p)
  {
  int i;
long int f=1;
  for(i=1;i<=*p;i++)
       f*=i;
  return(&f);
  }
```

OUTPUT
Enter a number 5
Factorial is 120

2.3.6   C++ Null Pointer

It is always a good practice to assign the pointer NULL to a pointer variable
in case you do not have exact address to be assigned. This is done at the
time of variable declaration. A pointer that is assigned NULL is called a
null pointer.

The NULL pointer is a constant with a value of zero defined in several
standard libraries, including iostream. Consider the following program:

```
#include <iostream>

using namespace std;

int main ()
{
    int  *ptr = NULL;

    cout << "The value of ptr is " << ptr ;

    return 0;
}
```

When the above code is compiled and executed, it produces the following result:

```
The value of ptr is 0
```

On most of the operating systems, programs are not permitted to access
memory at address 0 because that memory is reserved by the operating
system. However, the memory address 0 has special significance; it signals
that the pointer is not intended to point to an accessible memory location.
But by convention, if a pointer contains the null (zero) value, it is assumed
to point to nothing.

To check for a null pointer you can use an if statement as follows:

```
if(ptr)    // succeeds if p is not null
if(!ptr)   // succeeds if p is null
```

Thus, if all unused pointers are given the null value and you avoid the
use of a null pointer, you can avoid the accidental misuse of an uninitialized pointer. Many times uninitialized variables hold some junk values and
it becomes difficult to debug the program.

2.4   Structure

A structure is a collection of data items(fields) or variables of different data types that is referenced under the same name. It provides convenient means of keeping related information together.

DECLARATION

```
struct tag_name
       {
       Data type member1 ;
       Data type member2;
       .............................
       .............................
       .............................
       };
```

The keyword struct tells the compiler that a structure template is being defined, that may be used to create structure variables. The tag_name identifies the particular structure and its type specifier. The fields that comprise the structure are called the members or structure elements. All elements in a structure are logically related to each other.

Let us consider an employee data base, which consists of the fields like name, age, and salary, so for this the corresponding structure declaration will be

```
struct emp
 {
char name[25];
int age;
float salary;
 };
```

Here the keyword struct defines a structure to hold the details of the employee and the tag_name emp is the name of the structure.

Over all struct emp is a user defined data type.

So to use the members of this structure we must have to declare the variable of struct emp type and the structure variable declaration is as same as the normal variable declaration which takes the form as

struct tag_name variable_name;

Ex : struct emp e;

Here e is a structure variable which has the ability to hold name, age, and salary and to access these individual members of the structure the way is

Structure_variable . member_name;

i.e/ To access name,age,salary the variable will be e.name,e.age,e.salary

Example: WAP TO INPUT THE NAME,AGE AND SALARY OF A EMPLOYEE AND DISPLAY.

```
#include<iostream.h>
struct emp //CREATION OF STRUCT EMP DATA TYPE
        {
        char name[25];
        int age;
        float salary;
        };
void main()
   {
struct emp e;             //Declaration of the
structure variable
cout<<"\n Enter the name,age and salary";
gets(e.name);             //Input the name
cin>>e.age>>e.salary;     // Input the age
and salary

cout<<"\n NAME IS "<<e.name;    //Display name
cout<<"\n AGE IS "<<e.age;      //Display age
cout<<"\n SALARY IS "<<e.salary;  //Display salary


   }
```

OUTPUT

Enter the name ,age and salary

H.Narayanan

56

72000

NAME IS H.Narayanan

AGE IS 56

SALARY IS 72000.000000

The above discussed structure is usually used in 'C' but the 'C++' provides its structure with a little bit modification with the structure of 'C' that is in C++ we may also store the member functions as a member of it.

Ex: WAP TO INPUT A NUMBER AND DISPLAY IT by using FUNCTION

No doubt that this program is not efficiently used with the structure because the structure is used when there is a requirement to handle more than one element of different type. But in the above program only single variable is to be used but for easy understanding the difference of structure in 'c' and structure in 'c++' this one is better.

IN 'C'

```c
#include<stdio.h>
struct print
   {
int x;
   } ;
void main()
   {
struct print p;
void display(struct print);
printf("\n Enter the number");
scanf("%d",&p.x);
display(p);
   }
void display(struct print p)
   {
printf("THE ENTERED NUMBER IS %d",p.x);
   }
```

OUTPUT

Enter the number 23

THE ENTERED NUMBER IS 23

IN C++

```cpp
#include<iostream.h>
struct print
   {
int x;
void display( )//Arguments are not required
because both x and display() are in the same scope
   {
cout<<"\n Enter the number";
cin>>x;
cout<<"THE ENTERED NUMBER IS "<<x;
```

```
    }
  } ;
void main()
    {
    print p;//In C++ to declare the structure vari-
    able struct is not mandatory
    p.display();
    }
```

OUTPUT
Enter the number 23
THE ENTERED NUMBER IS 23

Observe that the C++-structure is better than the C-Structure but it has also some limitation. That means the above program can also be written as

---

Inside the void main() instead of calling the function as p.display() we may also replace it as
cout<<"Enter the number";
cin>>p.x;
cout<<"THE ENTERED NUMBER IS"<<p.x;

Which is not a small mistake it can make frustrate to the programmer that even if the programmer provides a function to does the work but instead of using that we are using according to our logic. Here the importance of the designer is Nill and this happens since the structure allow all of its members to use any where of the program. But if the data member 'x' will not allowed to use inside the main() then we are bound to use the function which is provided by the programmer.

So Finally the main drawback is that structure does not allow any restriction to its members.

To overcome this problem C++ implements a new, abundantly used data type as "class" which is very much similar to the structure but it allows the security of members i.e/the programmer has a control over its members.

NOTE: C++ structure also provides data hiding and encapsulation but other properties like the Inheritance, Polymorphism are not supported by it. So to overcome this C++ introduces the **CLASS.**

2.4.1   The typedef Keyword

There is an easier way to define structs or you could "alias" types you create. For example:

```
typedef struct
{
   char   title[50];
   char   author[50];
   char   subject[100];
   int    book_id;
}Books;
```

Now you can use *Books* directly to define variables of *Books* type without using struct keyword. Following is the example:

Books Book1, Book2;

You can use **typedef** keyword for non-structs as well as follows:

typedef long int *pint32;

pint32 x, y, z;
x, y, and z are all pointers to long ints

UNION

The UNION is also a user defined data type just like the structure, which can store more than one element of different data types. All the operations are same as the structure. The only difference between the structure and union is based upon the memory management i.e/ the structure data type will occupies the sum of total number of bytes occupied by its individual data members where as in case of union it will occupy the highest number of byte occupied by its data members.

Example 7.11

Write a program to demonstrate the difference between the structure and Union.

```
#include<iostream.h>
struct std
   {
   char name[20],add[30];
```

```
    int roll,total;
    float avg;
   };
union std1
   {
   char name[20],add[30];
   int roll,total;
   float avg;
   };
 void main()
  {
   struct std s;
   union std1 s1;
cout<<"\nThe no.of bytes occupied by the structure
is"<<sizeof(struct std));
cout<<"\nThe no.of bytes occupied by the union
is"<<sizeof(union std1));
  }
```

OUTPUT

```
     The no.of bytes occupied by the structure is 58
     The no.of bytes occupied by the structure is 30
```

NOTE: While using UNION we have used the values of the variables immediately before entering any value to any member. Because the union shares a single memory area for all the data members.

2.5   Questions

1. What are the advantages of unions over structures?
2. What is a pointer and its types?
3. What is the difference between Library functions and User-defined functions?
4. What is the difference between call by value and call by reference.
5. What is the difference between array and pointer?
6. Is it better to use a macro or a function?
7. What is a string?
8. Discuss different types of storage class specifiers.
9. Discuss local and global variables.
10. Is it of benefit to use structure or array? Justify your answer.

Sparse Matrix

3.1 What is Sparse Matrix

In computer programming, a matrix can be defined with a two-dimensional array. Any array with 'm' columns and 'n' rows represents a mXn matrix. There may be a situation in which a matrix contains more number of ZERO values than NON-ZERO values. Such matrix is known as sparse matrix.

Sparse matrix is a matrix which contains very few non-zero elements.

When a sparse matrix is represented with two-dimensional array, we waste lot of space to represent that matrix. For example, consider a matrix of size 100 X 100 containing only 10 non-zero elements.

In this matrix, only 10 spaces are filled with non-zero values and remaining spaces of matrix are filled with zero. That means, totally we allocate 100 X 100 X 2 = 20000 bytes of space to store this integer matrix, and to access these 10 non-zero elements we have to make scanning for 10,000 times.

3.2 Sparse Matrix Representations

A sparse matrix can be represented by using TWO representations, such as

1. Triplet Representation
2. Linked Representation

Method 1: Triplet Representation

In this representation, we consider only non-zero values along with their row and column index values. In this representation, the 0th row stores total rows, total columns, and total non-zero values in the matrix.

Sachi Nandan Mohanty and Pabitra Kumar Tripathy. Data Structure and Algorithms Using C++: A Practical Implementation, (49–58) © 2021 Scrivener Publishing LLC

For example If a Matrix

7	0	0	1	0	2
0	1	9	0	0	0
0	0	0	7	0	0
0	0	0	0	0	0
8	0	0	0	0	0
0	0	3	0	0	0

Sparse Matrix of the Above array is

6	6	8
0	0	7
0	3	1
0	5	2
1	1	1
1	2	9
2	3	7
4	0	8
5	2	3

The elements arr[0][0] and arr[0][1] contain the number of rows and columns of the sparse matrix respectively. The element arr[0][2] contains the number of non zero elements in the sparse matrix.

The declaration of the sparse matrix takes the form

Data type sparse[terms + 1][3];

Where the term is the number of non zero elements in the matrix.

Method 2: Using Linked Lists

In linked list, each node has four fields. These four fields are defined as:

- **Row:** Index of row, where non-zero element is located
- **Column:** Index of column, where non-zero element is located
- **Value:** Value of the non zero element located at index – (row,column)
- **Next node:** Address of the next node

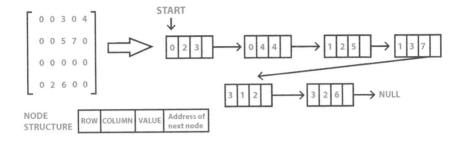

| NODE STRUCTURE | ROW | COLUMN | VALUE | Address of next node |

3.3   Algorithm to Represent the Sparse Matrix

STEP-1   Input the array of mXn elements.
STEP-2   [COUNT THE NUMBER OF NON ZERO ELEMENTS]
  REPEAT For I = 1 to m
    REPEAT For j = 1 to n
      If arr[i][j] !=0 THEN:
        Count := count+ 1
        [END OF IF]
      [END OF LOOP]
    [END OF LOOP]
STEP-3   SP[0][0] := m
  SP[0][1]:=n
  SP[0][2] := COUNT
STEP-4   K:=1
  REPEAT For I = 0 to m
   REPEAT For j = 0 to n
   If arr[i][j] !=0 THEN:
    Sp[k][0] := I
     Sp[k][1]:=j
    Sp[k][2] := arr[i][j]
    K:=k+1
     [END OF IF]
     [END OF LOOP]
    [END OF LOOP
STEP-5   REPEAT For I = 1 to k+1
    REPEAT For j = 1 to 3
    Print sp[i][j]
        [END OF LOOP]
        [END OF LOOP
STEP-6   EXIT

3.4   Programs Related to Sparse Matrix

Program for Array Representation of Sparse Matrix

```cpp
#include<iostream>
#include<iomanip>
using namespace std;
//driver program
int main()
  {
    int arr[10][10],i,j,row,col,count=0,k=0,sp[15][3];
    //ask user about the numbe o3f ows and columns sparse matx
    cout<<"\nENTER HOW MANY ROWS AND COLUMNS";
    //read row and col
    cin>>row>>col;
    //loop to read the normal matrix
      for(i=0;i<row;i++)
        for(j=0;j<col;j++)
          {
            cout<<endl<<"Enter a number";
            cin>>arr[i][j];
          }
          //loop to print the normal matrix that read from user
          cout<<"\nTHE ENTERED ARRAY ELEMENTS ARE\n";
          for(i=0;i<row;i++)
          {
            for(j=0;j<col;j++)
              cout<<setw(4)<<arr[i][j];
            cout<<endl;
          }
//loop to count the number of non zero elements in the matrix
      for(i=0;i<row;i++)
        for(j=0;j<col;j++)
            if(arr[i][j]!=0)//condition for non zero elements
                  count++; //increase the count

    //set the first row of sparse matrix
sp[0][0]=row;
    sp[0][1]=col;
    sp[0][2]=count;

    k=1;//k points to second row of sparse matrix
    //loop to fill theother rows of sparse matrix
      for(i=0;i<row;i++)
        for(j=0;j<col;j++)
            {
              if(arr[i][j]!=0)
                {
                    sp[k][0]=i;
```

```
                sp[k][1]=j;
                sp[k][2]=arr[i][j];
                k++;
            }
        }
        //print the sparse matrix
    cout<<"\nTHE SPRASE MATRIX IS\n";
      for(i=0;i<=count;i++)
      {
      for(j=0;j<3;j++)
        cout<<"   "<<sp[i][j];
      cout<<endl;
      }
    }
```

OUTPUT

```
ENTER HOW MANY ROWS AND COLUMNS4
3
Enter a number0

Enter a number
0

Enter a number0

Enter a number0

Enter a number3

Enter a number0

Enter a number5

Enter a number0

Enter a number6

Enter a number0

Enter a number0

Enter a number8
THE ENTERED ARRAY ELEMENTS ARE
    0    0    0
    0    3    0
    5    0    6
    0    0    8
THE SPRASE MATRIX IS
    4    3    4
    1    1    3
    2    0    5
    2    2    6
    3    2    8
```

Transpose of a Sparse Matrix

```cpp
#include<iostream>
#include<iomanip>
using namespace std;
int   main()
 {
    int arr[10][10],i,j,row,col,count=0,k=0,sp[15]
    [3],tran[10][3];

      //ask user about the numbe o3f ows and columns sparse matx
    cout<<"\nENTER HOW MANY ROWS AND COLUMNS";
    //read row and col
    cin>>row>>col;
    //loop to read the normal matrix
      for(i=0;i<row;i++)
       for(j=0;j<col;j++)
          {
            cout<<endl<<"Enter a number";
            cin>>arr[i][j];
          }
          //loop to print the normal matrix that read from user
          cout<<"\nTHE ENTERED ARRAY ELEMENTS ARE\n";
          for(i=0;i<row;i++)
          {
          for(j=0;j<col;j++)
             cout<<setw(4)<<arr[i][j];
             cout<<endl;
          }


//loop to count the number of non zero elements in the matrix
      for(i=0;i<row;i++)
         for(j=0;j<col;j++)
            if(arr[i][j]!=0)//condition for non zero elements
                    count++; //increase the count

    //set the first row of sparse matrix
sp[0][0]=row;
    sp[0][1]=col;
    sp[0][2]=count;

      k=1;//k points to second row of sparse matrix
      //loop to fill theother rows of sparse matrix
        for(i=0;i<row;i++)
          for(j=0;j<col;j++)
              {
                if(arr[i][j]!=0)
```

```
            {
                sp[k][0]=i;
                sp[k][1]=j;
                sp[k][2]=arr[i][j];
                k++;
            }
        }
        //print the sparse matrix
cout<<"\nTHE SPRASE MATRIX IS\n";
    for(i=0;i<=count;i++)
            {
    for(j=0;j<3;j++)
        cout<<"   "<<sp[i][j];
    cout<<endl;
            }
    /*TRANSPOSE*/
    tran[0][0]=col;
    tran[0][1]=row;
    tran[0][2]=count;
    k=1;
        for(i=0;i<col;i++)
          for(j=1;j<=count;j++)
            {
            if(sp[j][1]==i)
                {
                tran[k][0]=sp[j][1];
                tran[k][1]=sp[j][0];
                tran[k][2]=sp[j][2];
                k++;
                }
            }
            cout<<"\nTRANSPOSE OF THE SPRASE MATRIX
            IS\n";
        for(i=0;i<=count;i++)
        {
          for(j=0;j<3;j++)
           cout<<setw(5)<<tran[i][j];
           cout<<endl;
        }
}
```

OUTPUT

```
ENTER HOW MANY ROWS AND COLUMNS4
3
Enter a number0

Enter a number0

Enter a number2

Enter a number3

Enter a number0

Enter a number0

Enter a number0

Enter a number9

Enter a number0

Enter a number8

Enter a number0

Enter a number0
THE ENTERED ARRAY ELEMENTS ARE
    0    0    2
    3    0    0
    0    9    0
    8    0    0
THE SPRASE MATRIX IS
    4    3    4
    0    2    2
    1    0    3
    2    1    9
    3    0    8
TRANSPOSE OF THE SPRASE MATRIX IS
    3    4    4
    0    1    3
    0    3    8
    1    2    9
    2    0    2
```

3.5 Why to Use Sparse Matrix Instead of Simple Matrix?

- **Storage:** There are lesser non-zero elements than zeros and thus lesser memory can be used to store only those non-zero elements.
- **Computing time:** Computing time can be saved by logically designing a data structure traversing only non-zero elements.

3.6   Drawbacks of Sparse Matrix

Memory Drawbacks of a Sparse Matrix

Every element of a program array takes up memory and a sparse matrix can end up taking unnecessary amounts of memory space. For example, a 10×10 array can occupy 10 x 10 x 1 byte (assuming 1 byte per element) = 100 bytes. If a majority of these elements say 70 of 100, are zeroes, then 70 bytes of space is essentially wasted. Sometimes large sparse matrices are too big to fit into memory.

Computational Drawbacks of a Sparse Matrix

Performing algorithmic computations (like matrix multiplication, for example) takes up a lot of unnecessary time for each zero computation. Anything multiplied by zero is zero, but this operation still has to be performed which is seen as a waste of computational time.

A sparse matrix can be compressed and memory reduction can be achieved by storing only the non-zero elements. However, this will also require programming additional structures to recover the original matrix when elements have to be accessed, but overall a compressed sparse matrix can ultimately increase computational speed.

Sparse matrices are very common in machine learning algorithms. Now that your question 'what is sparse matrix' is answered, let's understand some examples and its uses.

3.7   Sparse Matrix and Machine Learning

As mentioned earlier, sparse matrices are a common occurrence in Machine Learning algorithms.

1. In Data Storage

Activity count arrays often end up being a sparse matrix. For example:
(a) In a movie application like Netflix, the array that stores the check of which movies are watched and not watched in a catalog.
(b) In e-commerce programs, data that represents the products purchased and not purchased by a user.
(c) In a music app, the count of songs listened and not listened to by a user.

2. In Data Preparation

Sparse matrices are often seen in encoding schemes, which are used for data preparation.

Examples:

(a) One-hot encoding, which is used to represent categorical data as sparse binary vectors.

(b) Count encoding, which is used in the representation of the frequency of words in a document.

(c) TF-IDF encoding, which is used in representing frequency scores of words in the vocabulary.

3. Machine Learning Study Areas

Sometimes, machine learning study areas require the development of specialized methods to address sparse matrices as input data. Examples are:

(a) Natural Language Processing when working with text documents

(b) Recommendation systems for product catalog programs.

(c) In Computer Vision when scanned images have a lot of dark or black pixels.

Different Methods of Sparse Matrix Representation & Compression

Storing a sparse matrix as is takes up unnecessary space and increases computational time. There are ways for sparse matrix representation in a 'compressed' format, which improves its efficiency.

3.8   Questions

1. What is a sparse Matrix?
2. Write some implementation areas of sparse matrix.
3. How to represent sparse matrix.
4. Differentiate with suitable example about the representation of sparse matrix.
5. Is it more beneficial to use sparse matrix than dense matrix? Explain your answer.
6. What are the limitations of sparse matrix?
7. Specify a few limitations of sparse matrix.

Concepts of Class

4.1 Introduction to CLASS

Like structure the class is also a user defined data type or Abstract Data Type (which derives/combines the properties of different data types into a single unit), which combines both the data members and member functions into a single unit. The Object oriented properties like Data encapsulation and Data Hiding is fully supported by the class.

Like structure the class has also its declaration and before its use we must have to declare it. The declaration of the class is very simple except that all the members of the class can be arranged in different sections (block) to achieve the data hiding.

The main purpose of C++ programming is to add object orientation to the C programming language and classes are the central feature of C++ that supports object-oriented programming and are often called user-defined types.

A class is used to specify the form of an object and it combines data representation and methods for manipulating that data into one neat package. The data and functions within a class are called members of the class.

When you define a class, you define a blueprint for a data type. This does not actually define any data, but it does define what the class name means, that is, what an object of the class will consist of and what operations can be performed on such an object.

Sachi Nandan Mohanty and Pabitra Kumar Tripathy. *Data Structure and Algorithms Using C++: A Practical Implementation*, (59–90) © 2021 Scrivener Publishing LLC

4.2   Access Specifiers in C++

As the name specifies these are the controllers of the members for a class. To achieve the properties of the OOPs the class provides three different Access Specifiers such as

- Private
- Public
- Protected

These are also known as Member Access Control.

PRIVATE:
The members which are declared with in the private group they are not allowed to use outside of the class only the members of the class can share it which is the data hiding.

PUBLIC:
The members which are declared with in this category are allowed to use any where of the program.

PROTECTED:
This section is as same as the private category if used in single classes. The only difference to private is that, these members can be transferred to the derived classes incase of Inheritance.

4.3   Declaration of Class

```
class class_name
      {
private :
      data members;
      member functions();
public :
      data members;
      member functions();
protected:
      data members;
      member functions();
      };
```

Member Function

A member function of a class is a function that has its definition or its prototype within the class definition like any other variable. It operates on any object of the class of which it is a member, and has access to all the members of a class for that object.

Example :

```
class print
        {
private:
        int x;
public :
        void display()
        {
                cout<<"\n Enter the number";
                cin>>x;
                cout<<"THE ENTERED NUMBER IS "<<x;
        }
};
```

The function display() is kept in the public section because by using this only one can print the value of x but x is in the private category so any one want to display a number is bound to use the display(). This is the benefit of the class.

Difference between the class and structure

Class	Structure
The Keyword class is used	The Keyword struct is used
It provides the inheritance, polymorphism	It does not provide these concepts
By default the members of class are private.	By default the members of structure are public.
Data abstraction is supported	Not supported

Declaration of an OBJECT

The object is an instance of a class. Through the object one can use the members of the class.

Syntax : class_name object_name;

Accessing the members of a class

The members of a class can be accessed with the help of the objects like the structure. That means **object_name.member_name;**

Difference between PRIVATE, PUBLIC, AND PROTECTED in programmatically way.

Example

```
        class differ
         {
        private :
                int x;
        public :
        int y;
        protected:
                int z;
         };
    void main()
    {
    differ obj;         //Declaration of the object
        cout<<"Enter a number for x";
        cin>>obj.x;   //Error, because x is private
        cout<<"Enter a number for y";
        cin>>obj.y;   //No Error, Since Y is public
        cout<<"Enter a number for z";
        cin>>obj.z;   //Error, because z is protected
    }
```

4.4   Some Manipulator Used In C++

The C++ allows some manipulator functions which are used for to have some extra formatting during the output. Out of them most commonly used manipulator functions are

- endl
- setw()
- setfill()
- dec
- oct
- hex
- setprecision()

These manipulators are defined inside the <iomanip.h> so before its use we must have to include<iomanip.h>

endl

This manipulator allows a new line. It does the same work as "\n".

Ex : cout<<"HELLO"<<endl<<"WEL COME";

OUTPUT

    HELLO
    WEL COME

setw()

This manipulator is used to allow some gap in between two numbers.

Ex : int x=5,y=4

    cout<<x<<setw(5)<<y;

OUTPUT

    5_ _ _ _ 4 (_ indicates the white space)

setfill()

This manipulator is used to allow to fill the gap by a character which is provided by the setw() manipulator.

Ex :

    int x=5,y=4;
    cout<<setfill('$');
    cout<<x<<setw(5)<<y;

OUTPUT

    5$$$$4

Dec,oct,hex

These manipulators are used to display the integer in different base values.

Dec : Display the number in integer format

Oct : Display the number in Octal format

Hex : Display the number in Hexadecimal format

Ex :

```
void main()
  {
int  x = 14;
cout<<"DECIMAL "<<dec<<x;
cout<<endl<<"OCTAL"<<oct<<x;
cout<<endl<<"HEXADECIMAL"<<hex<<x;
  }
```

OUTPUT

    DECIMAL 14
    OCTAL 16
    HEXADECIMAL e

Setprecision()

This manipulator is used to controls the number of digits to be displayed after the decimal place of a floating point number.

Ex :

```
float x=5.23456;
cout<<setprecision(2)<<x;
cout<<endl<<setprecision(0)<<x;
cout<<endl<<setprecision(6)<<x;
```

OUTPUT

```
5.23
5.23456
5.23456
```

4.5 Defining the Member Functions Outside of the Class

We already know that a class consists of different data members and member functions and when we provide the definitions of the member functions inside the class then the class became a complex and it also difficult to handle the errors.

So it will be better to declare the member functions inside the class but provide the definitions outside of the class. To achieve this the Scope Resolution Operator is used.

The process to define the member functions outside of the class is

Return_type class_name :: function_name(data_type var1,data_type var2......)

```
{
Body of function ;
Return(value/variable/expression;
}
```

4.6 Array of Objects

Like other normal variable the objects can also be used as an array and the declaration is also as same as the normal array.

Declaration

```
Class_name object[size];
```

Example

Write a program to input the detail of 5 students and display them.

```
class student
        {
    char name[20],add[30];
    int roll,age;
      public :
    void input();
    void print();
        };

void student :: input()
    {
cout<<endl<<"Enter the name and address";
gets(name);
gets(add);
cout<<endl<<"Enter the roll and age";
cin>>roll>>age;
    }

void student :: print()
    {
cout<<endl<<"NAME IS "<<name;
cout<<endl<<"ADDRESS"<<add;
cout<<endl<<"AGE IS "<<age;
cout<<endl<<"ROLL IS"<<roll;
    }

void main()
   {
student obj[5];
int i;
for(i=0;i<5;i++)
   {
obj[i].input();
   }
for(i=0;i<5;i++)
  {
 obj[i].print();
  }
 }
```

4.7   Pointer to Object

If the object is a pointer then the members of the class can be accessed by using the indirection operator as

```
Object_name -> member_name;
```

Ex : **WAP to check a number as prime or not**

```cpp
#include<iostream.h>
class prime
   {
private:
   int x;

public :
      void input();
         void check();
       };
void prime :: input()
   {
 cout<<"Enter the number";
cin>>x;
   }
void prime :: check()
   {
int i;
for(i=2 ; i<=x;i++)
 {
  if(x%i==0)
     break;
 }
if(i==x || x==1)
  cout<<"PRIME";
else
 cout<<"NOT PRIME";
}

void main()
   {
prime *p;
p->input();
p->check();
   }
```

4.8   Inline Member Function

C++ provides a facility to use the keyword inline for its conventional users. C++ provides an inline function where the compiler writes the code for the function directly in the place where it is invoked, rather than generating the target function for a function and invoking it every time it is needed.

When a normal function calls it always shift the control from its call to definition part which will take more extra time in executing a series of instructions for shifting the control, saving registers, returning the value to the calling function and arranging the values.

To avoid this we may replace the task with macros as

For ex : #define min(a,b) (a<b ? a:b)

This saves the overhead of a function call by simply replacing the expression

min(a,b) (a<b ? a : b) textually in the program

The major drawbacks of the macro is that they are not really functions and therefore the usual error checking does not occur during compilation.

So to avoid this C++ introduces a new feature called as Inline function which is expanded in line when it is invoked. That is when a function calls then the compiler replaces its call with the function definition. Generally the inline is used for those functions which having smaller in size. The inline is not a command. It is a request to compiler and whether the function will be treated as inline or not that depends upon the compiler even if we mention the inline.

In C++ when we define the member functions of a class inside the body then by default these will treated as Inline but when we will define the functions outside of the body of class then we have to define the function as inline explicitly.

> When we define the member function inside a class then by default the C++ compiler will treat it as inline but when we provide the definition of a function outside of a class then we may also set it as Inline by the keyword **inline**.

inline   return_type   class_name   ::   function_name(data_type var.................)

```
  {
 Body of function;
Return(value/variable/expression);
  }
```

Example
WAP to find out the GCD of two numbers

```
#include<iostream.h>
class GCD
  {
private :
   int a,b;
public :
   void input();
   void find();
  };

inline void GCD :: input()
  {
 cout<<endl<<"Enter two numbers";
 cin>>a>>b;
 }
inline void GCD :: find()
  {
int r;
  if(a<b)                 //Makes a as greater than b
    {
       r=a;
       a=b;
       b=r;
    }
  r = a%b;
   while(r!=0)
     {
    a = b;
    b = r;
    r = a%b;
     }
cout<<"GCD"<<b;
  }
void main()
  {
 GCD obj;
obj.input();
obj.find();
  }
```

Syntax :

```
       inline return_type function_name(argument list....)
           {
               Body of function;
               Return(value/variable/expression);
           }
```

There are some restrictions to use the inline such as

- If a function having a static variable
- If a function having loop, switch or goto statement, conditional statement
- If a function is recursive
- If a function having return statement.

4.9   Friend Function

In normal circumstance we may hide/protect the data members by declaring them in Private. But the friend can access any of the members of the class, regardless of their access specification. The keyword **friend** makes a function as a non member of the class even if its declaration is inside the class.

The friend function can be declared at any where of the class. Since it is a non member of the class so we must have to pass an object as its argument to extract the members of the class.

Syntax

friend return_type function_name(data_type var,...........);

The keyword friend can be studied in four different ways as

- Simple friend function
- Friend with inline substitution
- Granting friendship to another class
- Two or more class having same friend function.

4.9.1   Simple Friend Function

```
      #include<iostream.h>
class a
 {
  private:
     friend void display(a obj);
     int x;
 };
   void display(a obj)
      {
       cout<<"Enter a number";
       cin>>obj.x;
```

```
        cout<<"The value is "<<obj.x;
      }
 void main()
   {
     a obj;
     display(obj);
   }
```

OUTPUT
Enter a number 23
The value is 23

Question : The friend function is declared inside the class so how it became the non_member of the class ?

Ans : No doubt the friend function is declared in side the class but it does not follow the properties of a member of the class that means if we try to extract the member of a class then it must be accessed with the help of the object as
    Object_name .member_name but the friend function is called as a normal function inside the main()
    Second thing is that as a member of a class if we want to provide the definition outside of the class then we must have to use the scope resolution operator but here we define the friend function as a normal function.
    So from the above discussion we came to know that even of the friend function is declared inside the class but it is not a member of the class.

4.9.2 Friend With Inline Substitution

```
        #include<iostream.h>
 class a
   {
   private:
       int x;
   public:
 friend void display(a obj);
   };

     inline void display(a obj)
        {
        cout<<"Enter a numer";
        cin>>obj.x;
        cout<<"The value is "<<obj.x;
        }
```

```
void main()
  {
    a obj;
    display(obj);
    }
```

4.9.3   Granting Friendship to Another Class (Friend Class)

In this methodology a class can grant its friendship to another class. For example Let us consider two classes as A and B. Let A grants friendship to B then B has the ability to access the members of the class A but reverse is not true.

Syntax

```
class A
  {
friend class B;
private :
        data member ;
        member function();
public :
        data member ;
        member function();

protected :
        data member ;
        member function();
    };
class B
  {
        private :
              data member ;
              member function();
          return_type function_name (A obj);
        public :
              data member ;
              member function();
          return_type function_name (A obj);
        protected :
              data member ;
              member function();
          return_type function_name (A obj);
    };
```

Example

```
#include<iostream.h>
#include<iomanip.h>
```

```
#include<stdio.h>
class std
 {
 friend class mark;
 private:
   char name[20],add[20];
   int age,roll,m[5],total;
   float avg;
 public:
   void input();
  };
class mark
  {
  public:
      void result(std obj);
  };
void std :: input()
  {
  total=0;
    cout<<"Enter the name and address";
    gets(name);
    gets(add);
    cout<<"Enter the age,roll";
    cin>>age>>roll;
    cout<<"Enter the marks in 5 subjects";
      for(int i=0;i<5;i++)
        {
        cin>>m[i];
        total=total+m[i] ;
        }
      avg= float(total)/5;
  }
void mark :: result(std obj)
  {
   cout<<endl<<"NAME IS "<<obj.name;
   cout<<endl<<"ADDRESS "<<obj.add;
   cout<<endl<<"AGE IS  "<<obj.age;
   cout<<endl<<"ROLL IS "<<obj.roll;
   for(int i=0;i<5;i++)
   cout<<endl<<"MARK "<<i+1<<" IS "<<obj.m[i];
   cout<<endl<<"TOTAL IS "<<obj.total;
   cout<<endl<<"AVERAGE IS "<<obj.avg;
        if(obj.avg>=50)
          cout<<endl<<"P A S S";
          else
          cout<<endl<<"F A I L";
   }
void main()
 {
  std obj;
```

```
   mark obj1;
   obj.input();
   obj1.result(obj);
 }
```

4.9.4   More Than One Class Having the Same Friend Function

A friend function can also be used for different classes. For this if N –No of classes want to keep a friend function as common than we must have to declare N-1 classes as forward declaration.

```
class name1 ;
class name2 ;
..........................
..........................
..........................
class nameN-1 ;

class nameN
   {
private :
        data member;
        member function();
public:
        data member;
        member function();
   friend return_type function_name(name1 obj1,name2 obj2...
nameN objn);
protected :
        data member;
        member function();
   };

class name1
   {
private :
        data member;
        member function();
public:
        data member;
        member function();
   friend return_type function_name(name1 obj1,name2 obj2...
nameN objn);
protected :
        data member;
        member function();
   };
```

....

....

....

```
class nameN-1
  {
private :
      data member;
      member function();


public:
      data member;
      member function();
   friend return_type function_name(name1 obj1,name2 obj2...
nameN objn);
protected :
      data member;
    member function();
  };
```

Example

```
   #include<iostream.h>
class A;
class B;
class C
 {
 private:
    int x;
 public:
    void input();
    friend void average(A obj,B obj1,C obj2);
 };
class A
  {
    private:
       int y;
    public:
      void input();
      friend void average(A obj,B obj1,C obj2);
  };
class B
  {
    private:
       int z;
    public:
      void input();
      friend void average(A obj,B obj1,C obj2);
```

```
 };
void C :: input()
 {
  cout<<"Enter a number";
  cin>>x;
 }
void A :: input()
 {
  cout<<»Enter a number»;
  cin>>y;
 }
void B :: input()
 {
  cout<<"Enter a number";
  cin>>z;
 }

void average(A obj,B obj1,C obj2)
   {
      float avg;
      avg = float(obj2.x + obj.y + obj1.z)/3;
    cout<<"AVERAGE OF "<<obj2.x<<"  "<<obj.y<<"  "<<obj1.z<<"
    IS "<<avg;
   }
void main()
 {
    A obj;
    B obj1;
    C obj2;
    obj.input();
    obj1.input();
    obj2.input();
  average(obj,obj1,obj2);
 }
```

4.10   Static Data Member and Member Functions

The static is a storage class specifier which is generally used for the declaration of the variable it having a speciality compare to other normal variables that is it maintain the consistency of the value of the variable even if it is out of the scope of the function. In C++ we may use the **static** with the members of the class. When we declare a data member as static then the initialized value of the variable is **ZERO** and it will create a single copy of the variable for all the objects and that will be shared by all the objects. The scope of the static variable is local but it works as like a global variable.

The static data members allocated memory during the compilation time where as the nonstatic data members allocate the memory during compilation time.

Before the main function we must have to define a static data member as

```
data_type class_name :: variable;
        or
data_type class_name :: variable = value;
```

Difference between normal and static data members

```
class demo
   {
private:
       int    x;
   };
void main()
   {
demo obj,obj1,obj2;
......................
......................
       }
```

In the above case the 3 copies of the data_member 'x' will be created for the three objects obj,obj1,obj2. So if we will change the 'x' through obj then that will not affect the 'x' of obj1 and also obj2.

```
class demo
      {
    private:
        static int   x;
      };
int demo :: x;
  void main()
     {
  demo obj,obj1,obj2;
......................
......................

      }
```

In this case instead of creating three copies it will create a single copy of the data_member 'x' for all the objects and that will be shared by the objects. So if we change the value of the data_member through obj than that will be effect to obj1 and obj2.

Example

```
         #include<iostream.h>
class demo
 {
private:
    static int x;
public:
  void change();
  void display();
 };
 void demo :: display()
  {
    cout<<x;
  }
void demo :: change()
 {
  x++;
 }
int demo :: x=5;
void main()
 {
  demo obj,obj1,obj2;
  obj.display();
  obj1.display();
  obj2.display();
   obj.change();
  obj.display();
  obj1.display();
  obj2.display();
 }
```

OUTPUT   555666

The keyword static can also be used with the member function. The speciality with the function is that it can only use the static data members and can be called by the class name as

   class_name :: function_name();

```
#include<iostream.h>
class demo
 {
  static int x;
  public :
    static void print();
  };
void demo :: print()
 {
 cout<<endl<<++x;
```

```
 }
 int demo :: x=5;
void main()
 {
 demo obj;
 demo :: print();
 obj.print();
 }
```

OUTPUT   6   7

4.11   Constructor and Destructor

4.11.1   Constructor

The constructors are the special member functions which are used for the initialization. It is special because it is working and way of representing is totally different from the normal functions. We cannot initialize the data members inside the private section and generally we arrange the data members inside the private section. So if we want to initialize the member than we have to do this inside a member function, which is not preferable because to have an initialized value we have to call a member function. So it will be better to initialize the data members whenever the class members will gets activated for use i.e. when the objects are being created. To achieve the C++ provides the constructors for its conventional programmers.

The constructors are the special member functions which are called automatically whenever an object is being created.

Certain rules we have to follow which using the constructor such as

- The name of the constructor is same as the class name.
- The constructors do not have any return type not even void.
- They cannot be inherited.
- The keywords like virtual, const, volatile, static cannot be used.

The constructors are of four types such as

- Empty Constructors
- Default constructors
- Parameterized Constructors
- Copy constructors

4.11.1.1   Empty Constructor

The name itself designates that the constructors whose body part is absent is called as empty constructors. These constructors are not used.

Syntax :
```
constructor_name()
{
}
```

4.11.1.2   Default Constructor

In default constructor we have to initialize the data members by assigning some value to them and whatever the value may be assigned that will be fixed for all the objects that means by default the objects members will store the values which is given inside the default constructors.

Syntax :
```
constructor_name()
{
data_member = value;
data member  = value;
..............................
..............................
data member = value;
  }
```

Example
```
  #include<iostream.h>
class hello
  {
 private:
      int x;
 public :
    hello();
   void display();
   };
hello :: hello()
  {
 x=5;
   }
void hello :: display()
  {
 cout<<endl<<x;
   }
```

```
void main()
  {
 hello obj,obj1,obj2;   //constructors are called
obj.display();
obj1.display();
obj2.display();
  }
```

OUTPUT

5

5

5

4.11.1.3   Parameterized Constructors

When we want to initialize the data members according to the values given by the user then we have to choose the parameterized constructors. In this type some parameters should have to pass during the creation of the objects.

Syntax :

constructor name(data type V1, data type V2............... data type Vn)

```
        {
        Member1 = V1;
        Member2 = V2;
        Member3 = V3;
        .....................
        .....................
        .....................

        Membern = Vn;
                }
```

During the creation of object the format would be

```
        class_name obj(v1,v2,.....vn);
```

Example

```
#include<iostream.h>
#include<conio.h>
#include<iomanip.h>
class fibo
  {
private:
    int a,b,c,n;
```

```
public :
   fibo(int);
   void generate();
 };
fibo :: fibo(int x)
   {
     a=0;
     b=1;
     c=a+b;
     n=x;
   }
void fibo :: generate()
    {
     cout<<"THE FIBONACCI SERIES NUMBERS ARE";
     cout<<endl<<a<<setw(4)<<b;
     for(int i=3;i<=n;i++)
        {
        c=a+b;
         cout<<setw(4)<<c;
         a=b;
         b=c;
         }
    }
void main()
  {
     int n;
     cout<<"Enter how many digits U want to print";
     cin>>n;
    fibo obj(n);
    clrscr();
       obj.generate();
  }
```

OUTPUT

Enter how many digits U want to print **8**

```
THE FIBONACCI SERIES NUMBERS ARE
0   1   1   2   3   5   8   13
```

4.11.1.4   Copy Constructor

The copy constructor is a special type of constructor where the data members are initialized by the object. So when there is a need that the initialization should be by the object than use the copy constructor. The format is same as the parameter constructor except that the argument of the constructor should be always the object.

Since the data members are initialized by the object so before that the object should have to be initialized so while using the copy constructor we have to use either the default constructor or parameterized constructor. Because due to this the data members of the object first will be initialized and then with the help of the object again the data members are initialized. Since the data member get the same value two times so this constructor is so named.

SYNTAX

constructor name(class name &object);

Example

```
        #include<iostream.h>
#include<conio.h>
#include<iomanip.h>
class fibo
 {
private:
   int a,b,c,n;
public :
   fibo(int);
   fibo(fibo &obj);
   void generate();
 };
 fibo :: fibo(fibo &obj)
     {
   a=obj.a;
   b=obj.b;
   c=obj.c;
   n=obj.n;
     }
fibo :: fibo(int x)
   {
     a=0;
     b=1;
     c=a+b;
     n=x;
   }
void fibo :: generate()
   {
     cout<<"THE FIBONACCI SERIES NUMBERS ARE";
     cout<<endl<<a<<setw(4)<<b;
     for(int i=3;i<=n;i++)
       {
       c=a+b;
       cout<<setw(4)<<c;
```

```
        a=b;
        b=c;
        }
    }
void main()
  {
    int n;
    cout<<"Enter how many digits U want to print";
    cin>>n;
    fibo obj(n);
      obj.generate();     }
```

OUTPUT

Enter how many digits U want to print 8

```
THE FIBONACCI SERIES NUMBERS ARE
0   1   1   2   3   5   8   13
```

4.11.2   Destructor

A destructor is also a member function of the class which is used for the destruction of the objects which are created by a constructor. That is this is used for the de-allocation purpose. The declaration of the destructor is as same as the constructor except that the destructor is declared with the tiled(~) symbol and it does not have any return type as well as it does not have any argument.

The destructors are also called automatically. The keyword "virtual" cam be used with destructor.

Ex :

```
#include<iostream.h>
#include<conio.h>
class demo
   {
   public:
     demo()
        {
         cout<<"CONSTRUCTOR IS CALLED";
        }
       void input()
        {
         cout<<endl<<"HELLO";
        }
      ~demo()
        {
         cout<<endl<<"DESTRUCTOR IS CALLED";
         getch();
        }
```

```
    };
void main()
 {
    demo obj;
    obj.input();
 }
```

OUTPUT

```
CONSTRUCTOR IS CALLED
HELLO
DESTRUCTOR IS CALLED
```

4.12   Dynamic Memory Allocation

Allocation of memory for a variable during run time is known as DYNAMIC MEMORY ALLOCATION.

Need of Dynamic Memory Allocation

When there is a requirement to handle more than one element of same kind then the concept of array is being implemented. During the declaration of an array we must have to mention its size which contradicts the flexibility nature of an array, because if we specifies the boundary point of an array then that array will be stipulated for that much amount of data, if the amount of data exceeds the boundary then the array fails to handle it and on the other hand if we specify a large volume of boundary for the array then, it does not matter that it will recover the first drawback but it will lead to memory loss, because some portion of memory is utilized from a huge block so the remaining unused memory is blocked and that is not used by any other program. But as a better programmer, he/she should be conscious about the memory, that means how a task can be completed with a minimum amount of memory.

So to avoid this it will be better to reserve the memory according to the user choice/requirement and this is only possible during the runtime.

To have a dynamic memory allocation C++ allows a new operator as "new" and for the deallocation purpose it provides "delete" operator which does the same work as free() in C-language.

Syntax :
new operator

```
        Data_type *var = new data_type; //for single memory
        allocation
        Data_type *var = new data_type[n] //for more than one
        memory allocation
```

delete operator

```
      delete var ; //for single memory cell
            delete [ ] var; // for an array
```

We can also initialize a variable during allocation.

```
            int *x =new int(5);
```

Example :

Wap to enter n number of elements into an array and display them.

```cpp
#include<iostream.h>
#include<iomanip.h>
void main()
 {
 int n;
 cout<<"Enter how many elements to be handle";
 cin>>n;
  int *p = new int[n];
  for(int i=0;i<n;i++)
    {
       cout<<"Enter  a number";
       cin>>*(p+i);
       }
       cout<<"THE ELEMENTS ARE";
  for(i=0;i<n;i++)
    cout<<setw(5)<<*(p+i);
    delete []p;
 }
```

Wap to enter N number of elements and display them with the help of class, constructor and destructor.

```cpp
#include<iostream.h>
#include<iomanip.h>
class dynamic
   {
     private:
        int *p,n;
     public:
        dynamic(int);
        ~dynamic();
        void show();
     };
dynamic :: dynamic (int a)
  {
  n=a;
    p = new int[n];
    if(p==NULL)
      cout<<"UNABLE TO ALLOCATE MEMORY";
      else
```

```
      cout<<"SUCESSFULLY ALLOCATED";
   }
dynamic :: ~dynamic()
   {
      delete [] p;
   }
void dynamic :: show()
 {
    for(int i=0;i<n;i++)
      {
        cout<<"Enter   a number";
        cin>>*(p+i);
        }
        cout<<"THE ELEMENTS ARE";
   for(i=0;i<n;i++)
     cout<<setw(5)<<*(p+i);
   }
void main()
 {
 int a;
 cout<<"Enter how many elements";
 cin>>a;
  dynamic obj(a);
  obj.show();
  }
```

4.13   This Pointer

This pointer is a special type of pointer which is used to know the address of the current object that means it always stores the address of current object. We can also handle the members of a class as

```
      this->member_name;
```

Example :

```
#include<iostream.h>
class even
  {
   private:
     int n;
   public:
     void input();
     void check();
   };
void even :: input()
   {
      cout<<"Enter a number";
```

```
       cin>>this->n;
    }
void even :: check()
   {
     cout<<"THE ADDRESS OF OBJECT IS "<<this;
     if(this->n %2==0)
        cout<<endl<<this->n<<"IS EVEN";
      else
        cout<<endl<<this->n<<"IS NOT EVEN";
   }
void main()
 {
    even obj;
    obj.input();
    obj.check();
 }
```

OUTPUT

Enter a number 5
THE ADDRESS OF OBJECT IS   0x8fa7fff4
5 IS NOT EVEN

4.14   Class Within Class

Like structure within structure we can also use a class as a member of another class which is known as the class with in class. It is also called as nested class.

Example

```
#include<iostream.h>
#include<iomanip.h>
class a
 {
   public:
     void input()
       {
       cout<<"HELLO";
       }
   };

class b
 {
   public :
      a obj;
      void print()
        {
```

```
    cout<<"INDIA";
    }
};

void main()
{
  b B;
  B.print();
  B.obj.input();
}
```

OR

```
#include<iostream.h>
class a
{
   private:
      int x;
   public :
      void check();
    class b
      {
       private:
          int y ;
       public:
          void print();
     };
  };
void a :: check()
 {
   cout<<"Enter the number";
   cin>>x;
     if(x>=0)
        cout<<endl<<"+VE";
     else
        cout<<endl<<"-VE";
 }
void a::b::print()
  {
    cout<<endl<<"Enter the number";
    cin>>y;
    if(y%2==0)
      cout<<endl<<"EVEN";
    else
      cout<<endl<<"ODD";
  }
void main()
 {
```

```
a obj;
a::b obj1;
obj.check();
obj1.print();      }
```

4.15   Questions

1. Define features of object-oriented paradigm.
2. What are the access specifiers used in class?
3. Differentiate between inline and macro.
4. What is the benefit of using friend function?
5. What are the types of constructors?
6. What is dynamic memory allocation?
7. What is the use of this pointer?
8. What are the types of manipulators in c++?
9. Discuss features of static data member and static member functions.
10. Differentiate between structure and class.

5.1 STACK

Stack is a linear data structure which follows the principle of LIFO (Last in First Out). In other words we can say that if the LIFO principle is implemented with the array than that will be called as the STACK.

5.2 Operations Performed With STACK

The most commonly implemented operations with the stack are PUSH, POP.

Besides these two more operations can also be implemented with the STACK such as PEEP and UPDATE.

The PUSH operation is known as the INSERT operation and the POP operation is known as DELETE operation. During the PUSH operation we have to check the condition for OVERFLOW and during the POP operation we have to check the condition for UNDERFLOW.

OVERFLOW

If one can try to insert an element with a filled stack then that situation will be called as the OVERFLOW.

In general if one can try to insert an element with a filled data structure then that will be called as OVERFLOW.

Condition for OVERFLOW

Top = size −1 (for the STACK starts with 0)
Top = size (for the STACK starts with 1)

Sachi Nandan Mohanty and Pabitra Kumar Tripathy. Data Structure and Algorithms Using C++: A Practical Implementation, (91–128) © 2021 Scrivener Publishing LLC

UNDERFLOW

If one can try to delete an element from an empty stack then that situation will be called as the UNDERFLOW.

In general if one can try to DELETE an element from an empty data structure then that will be called as OVERFLOW.

Condition for UNDERFLOW

Top = −1 (for the STACK starts with 0)
Top = 0 (for the STACK starts with 1)

EXAMPLES

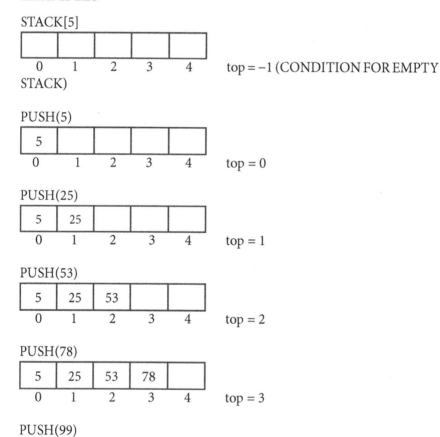

STACK[5]

0	1	2	3	4

top = −1 (CONDITION FOR EMPTY STACK)

PUSH(5)

5				
0	1	2	3	4

top = 0

PUSH(25)

5	25			
0	1	2	3	4

top = 1

PUSH(53)

5	25	53		
0	1	2	3	4

top = 2

PUSH(78)

5	25	53	78	
0	1	2	3	4

top = 3

PUSH(99)

5	25	53	78	99
0	1	2	3	4

top = 4

PUSH(145)
   "OVERFLOW"   (top = size − 1 Condition for OVERFLOW)

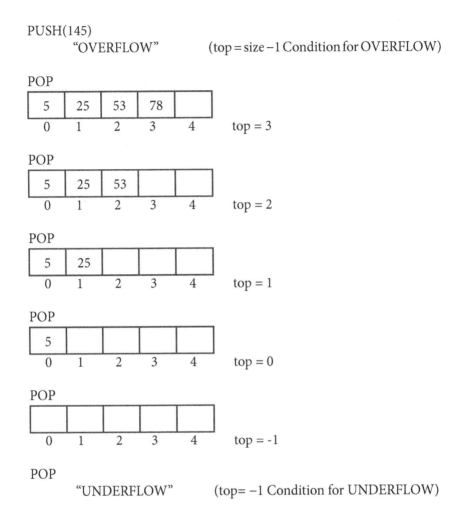

POP

5	25	53	78	
0	1	2	3	4

  top = 3

POP

5	25	53		
0	1	2	3	4

  top = 2

POP

5	25			
0	1	2	3	4

  top = 1

POP

5				
0	1	2	3	4

  top = 0

POP

0	1	2	3	4

  top = -1

POP
   "UNDERFLOW"   (top= −1 Condition for UNDERFLOW)

5.3   ALGORITHMS

ALGORITHM FOR PUSH OPERATION

PUSH(STACK[SIZE], NO, TOP)   [STACK[SIZE] is the Stack]
              [NO is the Number to Insert]
              [Top is the position of the stack]
STEP-1 : IF (TOP = SIZE - 1) THEN :
     WRITE : "OVERFLOW"
     RETURN
   [END OF IF]

STEP-2 : TOP : = TOP +1
                STACK[TOP] := NO
STEP-3 : RETURN

ALGORITHM FOR POP OPERATION

POP(STACK[SIZE], TOP)   [STACK[SIZE] is the Stack]
                                    [Top is the position of the stack]
STEP-1 : IF (TOP = - 1) THEN :
                WRITE : "UNDERFLOW"
                RETURN
            [END OF IF]
STEP-2 : WRITE : STACK[TOP]
                TOP := TOP -1
STEP-3 : RETURN

ALGORITHM FOR TRAVERSE OPERATION

TRAVERSE(STACK[SIZE], TOP)   [STACK[SIZE] is the Stack]
                                    [Top is the position of the stack]
STEP-1 : IF (TOP = - 1) THEN :
                WRITE : "STACK IS EMPTY"
                RETURN
                [END OF IF]
Step-2 : SET I : = 0
STEP-3 : REPEAT FOR I = TOP TO 0 BY -1
                WRITE : STACK[I]
                [END OF LOOP]
STEP-4 : RETURN

ALGORITHM FOR PEEP OPERATION

PEEP(STACK[SIZE], NO, TOP) [STACK[SIZE] is the Stack]
                                    [NO is the Number to Search]
                                    [Top is the position of the stack]
STEP-1 : IF (TOP = - 1) THEN :
                WRITE : "STACK IS EMPTY"
                RETURN
            [END OF IF]
STEP-2 : SET I: =0

STEP-3 : REPEAT FOR I = TOP TO 0 BY -1

    IF (NO = STACK[I]) THEN:

        WRITE : "NUMBER IS FOUND AT"

        WRITE : TOP-I+1

        WRITE : "POSITION"

      RETURN

      [END OF IF]

      IF I=0 THEN:

        WRITE : "NUMBER IS NOT FOUND"

      [END OF IF]

    [END OF LOOP]

STEP-4 : RETURN

OR

PEEP(STACK[SIZE], IN, TOP)   [STACK[SIZE] is the Stack]

                          [IN is the Index Number to Search]

                          [Top is the position of the stack]

STEP-1 : IF (TOP –IN +1 < 0) THEN :

    WRITE : "OUT OF BOUND"

    RETURN

    [END OF IF]

STEP-2 : WRITE : STACK[TOP-IN+1]

STEP-3 : RETURN

ALGORITHM FOR UPDATE OPERATION

UPDATE(STACK[SIZE], NO, TOP)   [STACK[SIZE] is the Stack]

                               [NO is the Number to Update]

                               [Top is the position of the stack]

STEP-1 : IF (TOP = - 1) THEN :

    WRITE : "STACK IS EMPTY"

    RETURN

    [END OF IF]

STEP-2 : SET I: =0

STEP-3 : REPEAT FOR I = TOP TO 0 BY -1

    IF (NO = STACK[I]) THEN:

      STACK[I] = NO

    RETURN

    [END OF IF]

IF I=0 THEN:
        WRITE : "UPDATE SUCCESSFULLY NOT COMPLETED"
  [END OF IF]
 [END OF LOOP]
STEP-4 : RETURN

5.4 Applications of STACK

- Checking of the parenthesis of an expression
- Reversing of a string
- In Recursion
- Evaluation of Expression

CHECKING OF PARENTHESIS OF AN EXPRESSION PROCESS

First scan the expression if an opening parenthesis is found then PUSH it and if a closing parenthesis is found then POP and this operation will continue up to all the elements of the expression are scanned.

Finally check the status of the TOP i.e/ if top == −1 then the expression is correct and if not then the expression is not correct.

Second if an closinging parenthesis is found but in the stack no parenthesis then also display that the expression is not correct.

PROGRAM

WAP to check the correctness of the PARENTHESIS of an expression by using STACK.

```
#include<stdio.h>
#include<stdlib.h>
#include<iostream>
using namespace std;
//declare the top
static int top = -1;
//declare the stack
char stack[25];
//defination for push()
void push(char no)
{
        //condition for overflow
if(top == 24)
cout<<endl<<"STACK OVERFLOW";
else
```

```
{   //insert the open grouping character into stack
top = top+1; //increase the value of top
stack[top] = no; //stare the character to stack
}
}
//defination of ppo()
void pop(char ch)
{
if(top == -1) //condition for underflow
{
cout<<"\n STACK UNDERFLOW";
cout<<"\n INVALID EXPRESSION";
exit(0);
}
//pop the character if proper closing charcter is found
if(ch==')' && stack[top]=='(' || ch==']' && stack[top]=='['
|| ch=='}' & stack[top]=='{')
--top; //decrease the valeu of top

}


int main()
{
 string str;
int i;
cout<<"\n ENTER THE EXPRESSION";
cin>>str;
for(i=0;str[i]!='\0';i++)
{
if(str[i]=='('||str[i]=='['||str[i]=='{')
push(str[i]);
if(str[i]== ')'|| str[i]==']' || str[i]=='}')
pop(str[i]);
}
if(top == -1)
cout<<"\n EQUATION IS CORRECT";
else
cout<<"\n INVALID EXPRESSION";
}
```

OUTPUT

```
ENTER THE EXPRESSION(a+b*[c-d])
EQUATION IS CORRECT
Process exited after 10.66 seconds with return value 0
Press any key to continue . . .


ENTER THE EXPRESSIONa*(b-c[+d)-e)
INVALID EXPRESSION
Process exited after 12.95 seconds with return value 0
Press any key to continue . . .
```

- **WAP TO REVERSE A STRING BY USING STACK.**

```cpp
#include<iostream>
#include<string.h>
using namespace std;

// A structure to represent a stack
class reverse
{
    public:
        int top;
        int size;
        char* stk;
};


reverse* BuildStack(unsigned size)
{
    reverse* stack = new reverse();
    stack->size = size;
    stack->top = -1;
    stack->stk = new char[(stack->size *
    sizeof(char))];
    return stack;
}

// Stack is full when top is equal to the last index
int Filled(reverse* stack)
{ return stack->top == stack->size - 1; }
```

```
// Stack is empty when top is equal to -1
int Empty(reverse* stack)
{ return stack->top == -1; }

// Function to add an item to stack.
// It increases top by 1
void push(reverse* stack, char item)
{
    if (Filled(stack))
        return;
    stack->stk[++stack->top] = item;
}

// Function to remove an item from stack.
// It decreases top by 1
char pop(reverse* stack)
{
    if (Empty(stack))
        return -1;
    return stack->stk[stack->top--];
}

// A stack based function to reverse a string
void Reverse(char str[])
{
    // Create a stack of capacity
    //equal to length of string
    int n = strlen(str)   ;
    reverse* stack = BuildStack(n);

    // Push all characters of string to stack
    int i;
    for (i = 0; i < n; i++)
        push(stack, str[i]);

    // Pop all characters of string and
    // put them back to str
    for (i = 0; i < n; i++)
        str[i] = pop(stack);
}

// Driver code
int main()
{
    char str[50];
    cout<<endl<<"Enter a string";
    gets(str);
```

```
Reverse(str);
cout << "Reversed string is " << str;

return 0;
}
```

Output

In recursive methods the stack is used to store the values in each calling of the function

• EXPRESSION CONVERSIONS

In general the expressions are represented in the form of INFIX notations that is the operators are used in between the operands. But during the evaluation process the given expression is converted to POSTFIX or PREFIX according to the requirements.

INFIX : The operator is used in between the operands.
    EX : A+B

POSTFIX : The operator is used after the operands. It is also known as POLISH notation.
    EX : AB+

PREFIX : The operator is used before the operands. It is also known as REVERSE POLISH notation.
    EX: +AB

During conversion we have to concentrate on the precedence of the operators such as

PRECEDENCE
    FIRST   : ( ), [ ], { }
    SECOND   : ^ , $, arrow mark
    THIRD   : * , / [Left to Right]
    FOURTH   : + , - (Left to Right)

CONVERSION OF INFIX TO POSTFIX(reverse polish) ALGORITHM

STEP 1 : First Insert a opening parenthesis at the beginning and closing parenthesis at the end of the expression.

STEP 2 : Arrange the expression in the ARRAY.

STEP 3 : Scan every element from the array and if operand than store it in the POSTFIX and if operator than PUSH it into the STACK followed by STEP-4 and STEP-5

STEP 4 : If the scanned operator having Less or Equal precedence than the existing operator than pop out the operators from the stack till a less precedence operator or opening parenthesis is found.

STEP 5 : If the scanned operator is a closing parenthesis than pop the operators from the STACK up to the Opening Parenthesis and omit them and poped operators will store in the POSTFIX.

STEP 6 : Repeat step-3, step-4, step-5 till all the elements are scanned from the array.

STEP 7 : Print the POSTFIX as the result.

CONVERSION OF INFIX TO PREFIX(POLISH) ALGORITHM

STEP 1 : First Insert an opening parenthesis at the beginning and closing parenthesis at the end of the expression.

STEP 2 : Arrange the expression in reverse order in the ARRAY by swapping the parenthesis.(i.e/ for open use close and vice_versa)

STEP 3 : Scan every element from the array and if operand than store it in the PREFIX and if operator than PUSH it into the STACK followed by STEP-4 and STEP-5

STEP 4 : If the scanned operator having Less precedence than the existing operator than pop out the operators from the stack till a less precedence or Equal precedence operator or opening parenthesis is found.

STEP 5 : If the scanned operator is a closing parenthesis than pop the operators from the STACK up to the Opening Parenthesis and omit them and poped operators will store in the PREFIX.

STEP 6 : Repeat step-3, step-4, step-5 till all the elements are scanned from the array.

STEP 7 : Print the PREFIX in reverse order as the result.

EXAMPLE :

Convert   A + B – (C * D – E + F ^ G) + (H + I * J) into POSTFIX by using STACK.

ARRAY	STACK	POSTFIX
(	(	
A	(	A
+	(+	A
B	(+	AB
-	(-	AB +
(	(-(	AB+
C	(-(	AB+C
*	(-(*	AB+C
D	(-(*	AB+CD
-	(-(-	AB+CD*
E	(-(-	AB+CD*E
+	(-(+	AB+CD*E-
F	(-(+	AB+CD*E-F
^	(-(+^	AB+CD*E-F
G	(-(+^	AB+CD*E-FG
)	(-	AB+CD*E-FG^+
+	(+	AB+CD*E-FG^+-
(	(+(	AB+CD*E-FG^+-
H	(+(	AB+CD*E-FG^+-H
+	(+(+	AB+CD*E-FG^+-H
I	(+(+	AB+CD*E-FG^+-HI
*	(+(+*	AB+CD*E-FG^+-HI

ARRAY	STACK	POSTFIX
J	(+(+*	AB+CD*E-FG^+-HIJ
)	(+	AB+CD*E-FG^+-HIJ*+
)		AB+CD*E-FG^+-HIJ*++

Convert   A + B − (C * D − E + F ^ G) + (H + I * J) into PREFIX by using STACK.

ARRAY	STACK	PREFIX
(	(	
(	((	
J	((	J
*	((*	J
I	((*	JI
+	((+	JI*
H	((+	JI*H
)	(	JI*H+
+	(+	JI*H+
(	(+(	JI*H+
G	(+(	JI*H+G
^	(+(^	JI*H+G
F	(+(^	JI*H+GF
+	(+(+	JI*H+GF^
E	(+(+	JI*H+GF^E
-	(+(+-	JI*H+GF^E
D	(+(+-	JI*H+GF^ED
*	(+(+-*	JI*H+GF^ED

ARRAY	STACK	PREFIX
C	(+(+-*	JI*H+GF^EDC
)	(+	JI*H+GF^EDC*-+
-	(+-	JI*H+GF^EDC*-+
B	(+-	JI*H+GF^EDC*-+B
+	(+-+	JI*H+GF^EDC*-+B
A	(+-+	JI*H+GF^EDC*-+BA
)		JI*H+GF^EDC*-+BA+-+

FINAL RESULT I.E/ PREFIX IS   +-+AB+-*CDE^FG+H*IJ

❖ **CONVERSION OF POSTFIX TO INFIX**
   ALGORITHM

   STEP-1 : Arrange the given postfix in an array
   STEP-2 : Scan each element from the array and push it into the
   STACK
   STEP-3 : If an operator is found than process it (convert it to infix)
   by considering the conjugative two operands and put
   then in a pair of parenthesis.
   STEP-4 : Finally display the result.

   EXAMPLE :
   Convert ABC*D-E^F/+ to INFIX

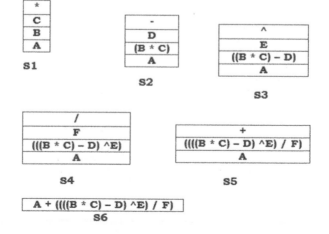

❖ CONVERSION OF PREFIX TO INFIX
ALGORITHM

STEP-1 : Arrange the given prefix in an array in reverse order.

STEP-2 : Scan each element from the array and push it into the STACK

STEP-3 : If an operator is found than process it (convert it to infix) by considering the conjugative two operands and put then in a pair of parenthesis.

STEP-4 : Finally display the result in reverse order.

EXAMPLE :

Convert   +A/^ - *BCDEF   to INFIX

First REVERSE it as FEDCB * - ^ /A +

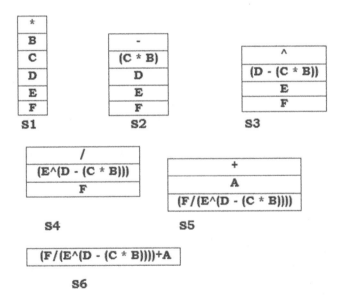

Finally Reverse it as A + ((((B*C) – D) ^ E) / F)

Evaluation of Expression by using STACK.
Evaluate 12, 5, 2, *, 4, -, 2, ^, 6, /, +

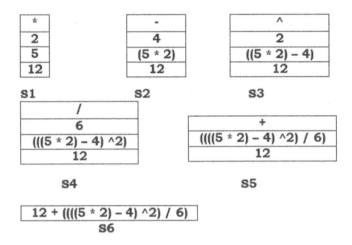

RESULT : 18

5.5 Programming Implementations of STACK

- **Wap to perform the PUSH,POP, and TRAVERSE operation with the STACK.**

```cpp
#include<iostream>
#include<stdlib.h>
using namespace std;
static int *s,size,top=-1;
//method to push an integer into stack
void push(int no)
    {
if(top == size-1)
    cout<<"\n STACK OVERFLOW";
else
  {
    top = top+1;
    *(s+top) = no;
  }
    }
    //method to pop an element from stack
void pop()
  {
if(top == -1)
    cout<<"\n STACK UNDERFLOW";
```

```
    else
      {
    cout<<*(s+top)<< " IS DELETED";
     --top;
      }
     }
    //method to display the elements of the stack
void traverse()
    {
int i;
if(top == -1)
     cout<<"\n STACK IS EMPTY";
else
    for(i = top; i>=0;i--)
       cout<<*(s+i)<<" ";
   }
   //driver program
int main()
 {
 int opt;
cout<<"\n Enter the size of the stack";
cin>>size; //ask user about the size of stack
s= (int *)malloc(size * sizeof(int)); //dynamically
allocate memory for stack
//infinite loop to handle the operations of stack
while(1)
    {
cout<<"\n Enter the choice";
cout<<"\n 1.PUSH  2. POP  3. DISPLAY 0. EXIT";
cin>>opt;
    if(opt==1)
         {
   cout<<"\n Enter the number to insert";
   cin>>opt;
      push(opt);
         }
else
    if(opt==2)
        pop();
    else
      if(opt==3)
        traverse();
      else
        if(opt==0)
           exit(0);
          else
            cout<<"\n INVALID CHOICE";
    }
}
```

OUTPUT

```
Enter the size of the stack5

Enter the choice
1.PUSH  2. POP  3. DISPLAY 0. EXIT2

STACK UNDERFLOW
Enter the choice
1.PUSH  2. POP  3. DISPLAY 0. EXIT1

Enter the number to insert25

Enter the choice
1.PUSH  2. POP  3. DISPLAY 0. EXIT1

Enter the number to insert63

Enter the choice
1.PUSH  2. POP  3. DISPLAY 0. EXIT1

Enter the number to insert85

Enter the choice
1.PUSH  2. POP  3. DISPLAY 0. EXIT1

Enter the number to insert95

Enter the choice
1.PUSH  2. POP  3. DISPLAY 0. EXIT1

Enter the number to insert85

Enter the choice
1.PUSH  2. POP  3. DISPLAY 0. EXIT1

Enter the number to insert54

STACK OVERFLOW
Enter the choice
1.PUSH  2. POP  3. DISPLAY 0. EXIT3
85 95 85 63 25
Enter the choice
1.PUSH  2. POP  3. DISPLAY 0. EXIT2
85 IS DELETED
Enter the choice
1.PUSH  2. POP  3. DISPLAY 0. EXIT2
95 IS DELETED
Enter the choice
1.PUSH  2. POP  3. DISPLAY 0. EXIT3
85 63 25
Enter the choice
1.PUSH  2. POP  3. DISPLAY 0. EXIT0

----------------------------------------
Process exited after 48 seconds with return value 0
Press any key to continue . . .
```

STACK OPERATIONS USING STL

```cpp
#include <iostream>
#include <stack>
using namespace std;

int main ()
{
    stack <int> myStack;
    int n,opt;
```

```
while(1)
 {
   cout<<endl<<"1. PUSH   2. POP  3. SIZE OF STACK   4.
   TOP OF STACK   5. QUIT";
   cin>>opt;
   if(opt==1)
     {
         cout<<endl<<"Enter a number to push";
         cin>>n;
         myStack.push(n);
          }
           else
           if(opt==2)
             {
                if(myStack.empty())
                   cout<<endl<<"Underflow";
                 else
                   {
                       myStack.pop();
                       cout<<endl<<"Pop operation
                       completed successfully";
                          }
               }
    else
    if(opt==3)
     {
         cout<<endl<<myStack.size()<<" elements are in
         stack";
          }
           else
           if(opt==4)
           {
                if(myStack.empty())
                   cout<<endl<<"NO ELEMENTS ARE IN
                   STACK";
               else
                       cout<<endl<<"The top value is :
                       "<<myStack.top();
           }

                 else
                 if(opt==5)
                 exit(0);

               else
               cout<<endl<<"Invalid choice";
     }

   return 0;

}
```

OUTPUT

```
1. PUSH   2. POP  3. SIZE OF STACK  4. TOP OF STACK  5. QUIT1
Enter a number to push23
1. PUSH   2. POP  3. SIZE OF STACK  4. TOP OF STACK  5. QUIT1
Enter a number to push45
1. PUSH   2. POP  3. SIZE OF STACK  4. TOP OF STACK  5. QUIT1
Enter a number to push66
1. PUSH   2. POP  3. SIZE OF STACK  4. TOP OF STACK  5. QUIT2
Pop operation completed successfully
1. PUSH   2. POP  3. SIZE OF STACK  4. TOP OF STACK  5. QUIT3
2 elements are in stack
1. PUSH   2. POP  3. SIZE OF STACK  4. TOP OF STACK  5. QUIT4
The top value is : 45
1. PUSH   2. POP  3. SIZE OF STACK  4. TOP OF STACK  5. QUIT5
_____
Process exited after 24.29 seconds with return value 0
Press any key to continue . . .
```

POSTFIX EVALUATION

```cpp
#include<iostream>
using namespace std;
int stack[1000];//declare a stack of size 1000
static int top = -1;//set the value of top to -1 for empty
stack
 //push method to push the characters of expression
void push(int x)
{
        stack[++top] = x;
}
 //pop method will delete the top element of stack
int pop()
{
        return stack[top--];
}
//method to check the validity of expression
int isValid(char str[])
 {
      int i,cd=0,co=0;
      for(i=0;i<str[i]!='\0';i++)
       {
              if(str[i]>='0' && str[i]<='9')
                cd++;  //count number of digits
                else
                co++;//count number of operators
       }
```

```
            if(cd-co==1)   //for a valid expression number of
            digit - number of operator must be 1
            return 1;//return 1 for valid expressison
            else
            return 0; //return 0 for invalid expression
    }
   //driver program
int main()
{
            char postfix[1000];//declare the postfix as string
            to store the expression
            int a,b,c,val;
            //read the postfix expression
            cout<<"Enter the expression :";
            cin>>postfix;
            if(!isValid(postfix))
            {
                  cout<<endl<<"Invalid expression";
                  exit(0);
                        }

            //loop to scan each character of the expression
            for(int i=0;postfix[i]!='\0';i++)
            {

                  if(postfix[i]>='0' && postfix[i]<='9')//
                  check for digit
                  {
                        val = postfix[i] - 48;//convert to
                        numeric format
                        push(val);//push it to stack
                  }
                  else
                  {
                        a = pop(); //pop an element
                        b = pop(); //again pop another
                        element for operation
                        switch(postfix[i]) //switch case is
                        use to check the type of operator
                        {
                                case '+': //condition for +
                                {
                                        c = a + b; //add two
                                        numbers
                                          break;
                                }
                                case '-': //condition for -
                                {
                                        c = b - a; //subtract
                                          break;
```

```
                                      }
                                      case '*':
                                      {
                                              c = a * b;//multiply
                                               break;
                                      }
                                      case '/':
                                      {
                                              c = b / a;//divide
                                               break;
                                      }
                             }
                             push(c);//push the result into stack
                     }

        }
        //prin tthe result
        cout<<"\nThe Value of expression "<<postfix<<" is
        "<<pop();
        return 0;

}
```

OUTPUT

```
Enter the expression : 512+4*+3-
The Value of expression 512+4*+3- is 14
Process exited after 10.63 seconds with return value 0
Press any key to continue . . .
```

PROGRAM TO CONVERT INFIX TO POSTFIX (ONLY +,-,*,/)

```
#include<iostream>
#include<string.h>
using namespace std;

char str[100];   //declare a string variable to store the
operators as stack
int top=-1;   //initially set -1 to top as empty stack
//push method
void push(char s)
{
 top=top+1;    //increase the value of top
 str[top]=s;//assign the operator into stack
}
```

```cpp
//pop method
char pop()
{
char i;
 if(top==-1)   //condition for empty stack
   {
    cout<<endl<<"Stack is empty";
    return 0;
   }
   else
    {
    i=str[top];   //store the popped operator
    top=top-1;
   }
 return i;//return the popped operator
}
//method precedence
int preced(char c)
{
if(c=='/'||c=='*')
 return 3;   //return 3 for * and /
if(c=='+'||c=='-')
return 2; //return 2 for + and -
return 1;//return 1 for other operator if any
}
//method to convert the infix to postfix
void infx2pofx(char in[])
    {
    int l;
    static  int i=0,px=0;
    char s,t;
    char pofx[80];
    l=strlen(in);//find the length of infix expression
    while(i<l)
     {
      s=in[i];//extract one by one characer from infix

        switch(s) //check for operator precedence
          {
          case '(' : push(s);break;
          case ')' :
              t=pop();   //pop from the stack when close
              parenthesis is found
            while(t != '(')
              {
              pofx[px]=t;
              px=px+1;
              t=pop();
              }
            break;
```

```
        case '+' :
        case '-' :
        case '*' :
        case '/' :
            while(preced(str[top])>=preced(s))
             {
             t=pop();
             pofx[px]=t;
             px++;
             }
            push(s);
               break;

            default : pofx[px++]=s;
             break;
           }
       i=i+1;
       }


while(top>-1)
        {
        t=pop();
        pofx[px++]=t;
        }
        pofx[px++]='\0';
        puts(pofx);

        return;
        }
//driver program
int main(void)
 {
 char ifx[50];

 cout<<endl<<"Enter the infix expression";
 //read the infix expression
 gets(ifx);
 infx2pofx(ifx); //call to the method

 return 0;
 }
```

OUTPUT

```
Enter the infix expressionA+B-(C*D/E)+F-G
AB+CD*E/-F+G-
_____
Process exited after 11.17 seconds with return value 0
Press any key to continue . . .
```

PROGRAM TO CONVERT POSTFIX TO INFIX (ONLY +,-,*,/)

```cpp
#include <bits/stdc++.h>
using namespace std;
  //method to return true if operand otherwise return false
bool checkOperand(char x)
{
   if((x >= 'a' && x <= 'z') || (x >= 'A' && x <= 'Z'))
                                  return true;
                                  else
                                  return false;
}

//method to convert the postfix to infix
string Infix2Postfix(string post)
{
    stack<string> infix;

    for (int i=0; post[i]!='\0'; i++)
    {
        // Push operands
        if (checkOperand(post[i]))
        {
            string op(1, post[i]);
            infix.push(op);
        }

        // We assume that input is
        // a valid postfix and expect
        // an operator.
        else
        {
            string op1 = infix.top();
            infix.pop();
            string op2 = infix.top();
            infix.pop();
            infix.push("(" + op2 + post[i] + op1 + ")"); //
            reform the expression
        }
    }
```

```
    return infix.top(); //return the expression
}

//main() method
int main()
{
    string post;
                    cout<<endl<<"Enter the postfix
                    expression";
                    getline(cin,post) ;
    cout << Infix2Postfix(post);
    return 0;
}
```

OUTPUT

```
Enter the postfix expressionAB+CD*E/-F+G-
((((A+B)-((C*D)/E))+F)-G)

Process exited after 14.49 seconds with return value 0
Press any key to continue . . .
```

PROGRAM FOR INFIX EVALUATION

```cpp
#include <bits/stdc++.h>
using namespace std;
//method declarations
int priority(char)   ;
int operate(int,char,int);
int solve(string);

//driver program
int main()
{
string infix;//declare a string to store the infix
expression
cout<<endl<<"Enter an Infix expression(Provide a space
between operator and operands)";
getline(cin,infix);//read the expression
cout<<endl<<infix<<" = "<<solve(infix);//print the result
    return 0;
}


//returns the precedence of the operator
int priority(char op){
    if(op == '+'||op == '-')
    return 1;
```

```
    if(op == '*'||op == '/')
    return 2;
    return 0;
}

//perform the operation according to the operator given
int operate(int x, char ch, int y)
   {

   if(ch=='+')
     return x + y;
     else
     if(ch=='-')
         return x - y;
         else
         if(ch=='*')
             return x * y;
             else
             if(ch=='/')
                 return x / y;
}

//method to return the result of the expression
int solve(string expression)
{
    int i,x,y,n,res;
    char ch;

    //numArr is used to store the numbers
    stack <int> numArr;

    // opList is sued to store the operators
    stack <char> opList;

    for(i = 0; i < expression.length(); i++){

       //condition for space then no action is needed
       if(expression[i] == ' ')
           continue;

       //if the scanned character is an opening bracket then
       push it into the opList stack
        else if(expression[i] == '('){
            opList.push(expression[i]);
        }

       //if scanned digit is a number then  push it into the
       stack
         else if(isdigit(expression[i]))
```

```cpp
    {
    n = 0;

    //form the number by accumulating the sequence of
    digits till operator or space is found
    //it is used for the numbers having more than 1
    digits
    while(i < expression.length() &&
                isdigit(expression[i]))
    {
        n = (n*10) + (expression[i]-'0'); //form the
        number
        i++;
    }

    numArr.push(n); //push the number into the stack
    }

//scanned charcater is a closing bracket then perform
operation till open bracket
    else if(expression[i] == ')')
    {
        while(!opList.empty() && opList.top() != '(') //
        condition for open bracket and till stack is
        empty
        {
            y = numArr.top(); //extract the top element
            into y
            numArr.pop();  //pop the stack

            x = numArr.top(); //extract the top element
            into x
            numArr.pop();  //pop the stack

            ch = opList.top(); //extract the operator in
            top o the stack
            opList.pop(); //pop the stack

              res = operate(x,ch, y);//perform the
              operation
            numArr.push(res); //push the result into the
            stack
        }

        //pop the opening bracket
        if(!opList.empty())
            opList.pop();
    }
```

```
    //if the scanned character is operator
    else
    {


            //perform the operation if the operator in
opList having equal or higher priority to the scanned
character, then perform the operation
            while(!opList.empty() && priority(opList.top()
                              >= priority(expression[i]))
                                                {
            y = numArr.top(); //extract the top element
            into y
            numArr.pop();  //pop the stack

            x = numArr.top(); //extract the top element
            into x
            numArr.pop();  //pop the stack

            ch = opList.top(); //extract the operator in
            top o the stack
            opList.pop(); //pop the stack

              res = operate(x,ch, y);//perform the
              operation
            numArr.push(res); //push the result into the
            stack
        }
            opList.push(expression[i]);
    }
}


    while(!opList.empty())
      {
      y = numArr.top(); //extract the top element into y
            numArr.pop();  //pop the stack

              x = numArr.top(); //extract the top element
              into x
              numArr.pop();  //pop the stack

              ch = opList.top(); //extract the operator in
              top o the stack
              opList.pop(); //pop the stack

              res = operate(x,ch, y);//perform the operation
              numArr.push(res); //push the result into the
              stack
      }
    }
```

```
    // Top of 'values' contains result, return it.
    return numArr.top();
}
```

OUTPUT

```
Enter an Infix expression(Provide a space between operator and operands)
10 * 12 + ( 120 + 10 ) - 3 * 2 + 1

10 * 12 + ( 120 + 10 ) - 3 * 2 + 1 = 245

Process exited after 23.71 seconds with return value 0
Press any key to continue . . .
```

```c
/* peep operation of the stack using arrays */
# include<stdio.h>
# include<ctype.h>
int top = -1,n;
int *s;
/* Definition of the push function */
void push(int d)
{
        if(top ==(n-1))
                printf("\n OVERFLOW");
        else
        {
                ++top;
                *(s+top) = d;
        }
}
/* Definition of the peep function */
void peep()
{
int i;
        int p;
        printf("\nENTER THE INDEX TO PEEP");
        scanf("%d",&i);

        if((top-i+1) <0)
        {
                Printf("\n OUT OF BOUND");
        }
        else
        {
                Printf("THE PEEPED ELEMENT IS %d",
*(s+(top-i+1)));
        }
}
```

```
/* Definition of the display function */

void display()
{
        int i;
        if(top == -1)
        {
                printf("\n Stack is empty");
        }
        else
        {
                for(i = top; i >= 0; --i)
                        printf("\n %d", *(s+i) );
        }
}
void main()                     /* Function main */
{       int  no;
        clrscr();
printf("\nEnter the boundary of the stack");
scanf("%d",&n);
        stack = (int *)malloc(n * 2);
        while(1)
            {
        printf("WHICH OPERATION DO YOU WANT TO PERFORM:\n");
                printf(" \n 1. Push  2. PEEP 0. EXIT");
                scanf("%d",&no);
                if(no==1)
                {
                        printf("\n Input the element to push:");
                        scanf("%d", &no);
                        push(no);
                          printf("\n After inserting ");
                                display();
                }
                   else
                     if(no==2)
                       {
                       peep();
                                display();
                       }
                    Else
                      if(no == 0)
                              exit(0);
                  else
                        printf("\n INVALID OPTION");
                }
```

/* update operation of the stack using arrays */

```
# include<stdio.h>
# include<ctype.h>
int top = -1,n;
int flag = 0;
int *stack;
void push(int *, int);
int update(int *);
void display(int *);
/* Definition of the push function */



void push(int *s, int d)
{
        if(top ==n-1)
                flag = 0;
        else
        {
                flag = 1;
                ++top;
                *(s+top) = d;
        }
}
/* Definition of the update function */
int update(int *s)
{
int i;
        int u;
        printf("\nEnter the index");
        scanf("%d",&i);
        if((top-i+1) <0)
        {
                u = 0;
                flag = 0;
        }
        else
        {
                flag = 1;
                u=*(s+(top-i+1));
                printf("\nENTER THE NUMBER TO UPDATE");
                scanf("%d",s+(top-i+1));
        }
        return (u);
        }
/* Definition of the display function */
void display(int *s)
{
```

```
        int i;
        if(top == -1)
        {
                printf("\n Stack is empty");
        }
        else
        {
                for(i = top; i >= 0; --i)
                        printf("\n %d", *(s+i) );
        }
}

void main()
{
        int   no,q=0;
        char ch;
        int top= -1;
printf("\nEnter the boundary of the stack");
scanf("%d",&n);
        stack = (int *)malloc(n * 2);
        up:
        printf("WHICH OPERATION DO YOU WANT TO PERFORM:\n");
                printf(" \n Push->i\n update->p");
                printf("\nInput the choice : ");
                fflush(stdin);
                scanf("%c",&ch);
                printf("Your choice is: %c",ch);
                if(tolower(ch)=='i')
                {
                        printf("\n Input the element to push:");
                        scanf("%d", &no);
                        push(stack, no);
                        if(flag)
                        {
                                printf("\n After inserting ");
                                display(stack);
                                if(top == (n-1))
                                        printf("\n Stack is
full");
                        }
                        else
                                printf("\n Stack overflow after
pushing");
                }
                 else
                   if(tolower(ch)=='p')
                   {
                     no = update(stack);
                     if(flag)
```

```
                {
                        printf("\n The No %d is updated",
                        no);
                printf("\n Rest data in stack is as
                follows:\n");

                        display(stack);
                }
                else
                        printf("\n Stack underflow" );
                        }
        opt:
printf("\nDO YOU WANT TO OPERATE MORE");
fflush(stdin);
scanf("%c",&ch);
  if(toupper(ch)=='Y')
     goto up;
        else
            if(tolower(ch)=='n')
               exit();
                  else
                     {
                     printf("\nINVALID CHARACTER...Try
                     Again");
                      goto opt;
                     }
}
```

- Wap to convert the Infix to Prefix notation

```
#include<stdio.h>
#include<conio.h>
#include<string.h>
char str[100];
int top=-1;
void push(char s)
{
 top=top+1; str[top]=s;
}

char pop()
{
char i;
 if(top==-1)
  {
   printf("\n The stack is Empty");
   getch();
   return 0;
  }
```

```
    else
      {
      i=str[top];
      top=top-1;
      }
    return i;
}

int preced(char c)
{
if(c=='$'||c=='^')
   return 4;
if(c=='/'||c=='*')
 return 3;
if(c=='+'||c=='-')
return 2;
return 1;
}

void infx2prefx(char in[])
    {
    int l;
  static   int i=0,px=0;
    char s,t;
    char pofx[80];
    l=strlen(in);
    while(i<l)
      {
        s=in[i];

        switch(s)
          {
          case ')' : push(s);break;
          case '(' : t=pop();

  while(t != ')')
              {
              pofx[px]=t;
              px=px+1;
              t=pop();
              }
            break;
          case '+' :
          case '-' :
          case '*' :
          case '/' :
          case '^' :
```

```
                    while(preced(str[top])>preced(s))
                      {
                      t=pop();
                      pofx[px]=t;
                      px++;
                      }
                    push(s);
                       break;

                    default : pofx[px++]=s;
                       break;
                    }
          i=i+1;
         }
       while(top>-1)
         {
         t=pop();
         pofx[px++]=t;
         }
         pofx[px++]='\0';
         strrev(pofx);
         puts(pofx);

         return;
         }
int main(void)
  {
  char ifx[50];
  printf("\n Enter the infix expression ::");
  gets(ifx);
  strrev(ifx);
//scanf("%s",ifx);
  infx2prefx(ifx);

  return 0;
  }
```

5.6   Questions

1. In which principle does STACK work?
2. Write some implementations of stack.
3. What is polish and reverse polish notation?
4. Write a recursive program to check the validity of an expression in terms of parenthesis ().{},[].

5. Write a recursive program to reverse a string using stack.
6. Explain structurally how stack is used in recursion with a suitable example.
7. Convert (a+b*c) –(d/e^g) into equivalent prefix and postfix expression.
8. What are overflow and underflow conditions in STACK?
9. Evaluate: 5,3,2,*,+,4,- using stack.
10. Write a recursive method to find the factorial of a number.

Queue

6.1 Queue

Queue is a linear data structure which follows the principle of FIFO. In other words we can say that if the FIFO principle is implemented with the array than that will be called as the QUEUE.

The most commonly implemented operations with the stack are INSERT, DELETE.

Besides these two more operations can also be implemented with the QUEUE such as PEEP and UPDATE.

During the INSERT operation we have to check the condition for OVERFLOW and during the DELETE operation we have to check the condition for UNDERFLOW.

The end at which the insertion operation is performed that will be called as the REAR end and the end at which the delete operation is performed is known as FRONT end.

6.2 Types of Queue

- Linear Queue
- Circular Queue
- D - Queue (Double ended queue)
- Priority Queue.

6.3 Linear Queue

OVERFLOW

If one can try to insert an element with an filled QUEUE than that situation will be called as the OVERFLOW.

Sachi Nandan Mohanty and Pabitra Kumar Tripathy. Data Structure and Algorithms Using C++: A Practical Implementation, (129–166) © 2021 Scrivener Publishing LLC

Condition for OVERFLOW
Rear = size -1 (for the QUEUE starts with 0)
Rear = size (for the QUEUE starts with 1)

UNDERFLOW
If one can try to delete an element from an empty QUEUE than that situation will be called as the UNDERFLOW.

Condition for UNDERFLOW
Front = -1 (for the QUEUE starts with 0)
front = 0 (for the QUEUE starts with 1)

CONDITION FOR EMPTY QUEUE
Front = -1 and Rear = -1 [for the QUEUE starts with 0]
Front = 0 and Rear = 0 [for the QUEUE starts with 1]

EXAMPLES

QUEUE[5]

  0   1   2   3   4   front = -1 , rear = -1

INSERT(5)

5				

  0   1   2   3   4   front = 0, rear = 0

INSERT(25)

5	25			

  0   1   2   3   4   front = 0, rear = 1

INSERT(53)

5	25	53		

  0   1   2   3   4   front = 0, rear = 2

INSERT(78)

5	25	53	78	

  0   1   2   3   4   front = 0, rear = 3

INSERT(99)

5	25	53	78	99
0	1	2	3	4

front = 0, rear = 4

INSERT(145)

"OVERFLOW"   (rear = size - 1 Condition for OVERFLOW)

DELETE

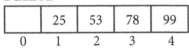

	25	53	78	99
0	1	2	3	4

front = 1, rear = 4

DELETE

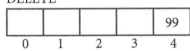

		53	78	99
0	1	2	3	4

front = 2, rear = 4

DELETE

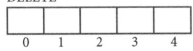

			78	99
0	1	2	3	4

front = 3, rear = 4

DELETE

				99
0	1	2	3	4

front = 4, rear = 4

DELETE

0	1	2	3	4

front = -1, rear = -1

DELETE

"UNDERFLOW"   (front = -1 Condition for UNDERFLOW

ALGORITHM FOR INSERT OPERATION

INSERT(QUEUE[SIZE], FRONT, REAR, NO)

STEP 1 : IF (REAR = SIZE – 1) THEN :
        WRITE : "OVERFLOW"
        RETURN
    [END OF IF]

STEP 2 : IF (REAR = -1) THEN :
                FRONT := 0
                REAR :=0
     ELSE :
                REAR :=REAR+1
     [END OF IF]
STEP 3: QUEUE[REAR] :=NO
STEP 4: RETURN

ALGORITHM FOR DELETE OPERATION

DELET(QUEUE[SIZE], FRONT, REAR)

STEP 1 : IF (FRONT = -1) THEN :
                WRITE : "UNDERFLOW"
                RETURN
     [END OF IF]
STEP 2 : WRITE: QUEUE[FRONT]
STEP 3 : IF (FRONT ==REAR) THEN :
                FRONT := -1
                REAR :=-1
     ELSE :
                FRONT := FRONT +1
     [END OF IF]
STEP 4: RETURN

ALGORITHM FOR TRAVERSE OPERATION

TRAVERSE(QUEUE[SIZE], FRONT, REAR)

STEP 1 : IF (FRONT = -1) THEN :
                WRITE : " QUEUE IS EMPTY "
                RETURN
     [END OF IF]
STEP 2 : SET I:=0
STEP 3 : REPEAT FOR I = FRONT TO REAR
                WRITE : QUEUE[I]
     [END OF LOOP]
STEP 4: RETURN

ALGORITHM FOR PEEP OPERATION

PEEP(QUEUE[SIZE], NO, FRONT, REAR)

[QUEUE[SIZE] is the Stack]
[NO is the Number to Search]
[Front & Rear are the positions
of the stack]

STEP-1 : IF (REAR = - 1) THEN :
WRITE : "STACK IS EMPTY"
RETURN
[END OF IF]
STEP-2 : SET I: =0
STEP-3 : REPEAT FOR I = FRONT TO REAR
IF (NO = QUEUE[I]) THEN:
WRITE : "NUMBER IS FOUND AT"
WRITE : I+1
WRITE : "POSITION"
RETURN
[END OF IF]
IF I= REAR THEN:
WRITE : "NUMBER IS NOT FOUND"
[END OF IF]
[END OF LOOP]
STEP-4 : RETURN

ALGORITHM FOR UPDATE OPERATION

UPDATE(QUEUE[SIZE], NO, FRONT, REAR)

[QUEUE[SIZE] is the QUEUE]
[NO is the Number to Update]
[FRONT & REAR is the position
of the stack]

STEP-1 : IF (REAR = - 1) THEN :
WRITE : "STACK IS EMPTY"
RETURN
[END OF IF]
STEP-2 : SET I: =0
STEP-3 : REPEAT FOR I = FRONT TO REAR
IF (NO = QUEUE[I]) THEN:
QUEUE[I] = NO

```
                RETURN
                [END OF IF]
                IF I=REAR THEN:
                        WRITE   : "UPDATE  SUCCESSFULLY  NOT
                        COMPLETED"
                [END OF IF]
            [END OF LOOP]
STEP-4 : RETURN
```

6.4   Circular Queue

In circular queue the rear and front end of the queue are inter connected, i.e/ after reaching to the rear end if the front end is not at zero than rear will again set to zero , and same also implemented with the front end also.

OVERFLOW

If one can try to insert an element with an filled QUEUE than that situation will be called as the OVERFLOW.

Condition for OVERFLOW

rear = size -1 and front = 0 OR FRONT = REAR +1(for the QUEUE starts with 0)

Rear = size and front = 1 OR FRONT = REAR +1(for the QUEUE starts with 1)

UNDERFLOW

If one can try to delete an element from an empty QUEUE than that situation will be called as the UNDERFLOW.

Condition for UNDERFLOW

Front = -1 (for the QUEUE starts with 0)

front = 0 (for the QUEUE starts with 1)

CONDITION FOR EMPTY QUEUE

Front = -1 and Rear = -1 [for the QUEUE starts with 0]

Front = 0 and Rear = 0 [for the QUEUE starts with 1]

EXAMPLES

C_QUEUE[5]

0	1	2	3	4

front = -1 , rear = -1

INSERT(5)

5				
0	1	2	3	4

front = 0, rear = 0

INSERT(25)

5	25			
0	1	2	3	4

front = 0, rear = 1

INSERT(53)

5	25	53		
0	1	2	3	4

front = 0, rear = 2

INSERT(78)

5	25	53	78	
0	1	2	3	4

front = 0, rear = 3

INSERT(99)

5	25	53	78	99
0	1	2	3	4

front = 0, rear = 4

INSERT(145)
    "OVERFLOW"   (rear = size - 1 Condition for OVERFLOW)

DELETE

	25	53	78	99
0	1	2	3	4

front = 1, rear = 4

DELETE

		53	78	99
0	1	2	3	4

front = 2, rear = 4

DELETE

			78	99
0	1	2	3	4

front = 3, rear = 4

INSERT(87)

87			78	99
0	1	2	3	4

front = 3, rear = 0

INSERT(65)

87	65		78	99
0	1	2	3	4

front = 3, rear = 1

INSERT(5)

87	65	5	78	99
0	1	2	3	4

front = 3, rear = 2

INSERT(89)
      "OVER FLOW"

DELETE

87	65	5		99
0	1	2	3	4

front = 4, rear = 2

DELETE

87	65	5		
0	1	2	3	4

front = 0, rear = 2

DELETE

	65	5		
0	1	2	3	4

front = 1, rear = 2

DELETE

		5		
0	1	2	3	4

front = 2, rear = 2

DELETE

| 0 | 1 | 2 | 3 | 4 |

front = -1, rear = -1

DELETE
    "UNDERFLOW"   (front = -1 Condition for UNDERFLOW

ALGORITHM FOR INSERT OPERATION

INSERT(C_QUEUE[SIZE], FRONT, REAR, NO)

STEP 1 : IF (REAR = SIZE -1 AND FRONT = 0 OR FRONT = REAR +1)
        THEN :
                WRITE : "OVERFLOW"
                RETURN
        [END OF IF]
STEP 2 : IF (REAR = SIZE - 1) THEN :
                REAR :=0
        ELSE :
          IF(REAR = -1) THEN:
                    FRONT :=0
                    REAR := 0
        ELSE
                REAR :=REAR+1
        [END OF IF]
STEP 3: C_QUEUE[REAR] :=NO
STEP 4: RETURN

ALGORITHM FOR DELETE OPERATION

DELET(C_QUEUE[SIZE], FRONT, REAR)

STEP 1 : IF (FRONT = -1) THEN :
                WRITE : "UNDERFLOW"
                RETURN
        [END OF IF]
STEP 2 : WRITE: C_QUEUE[FRONT]
STEP 3 :IF (FRONT ==REAR) THEN :
                FRONT := -1
                REAR :=-1
        ELSE :

```
            IF(FRONT = SIZE-1) THEN:
                  FRONT = 0
      ELSE:
                  FRONT := FRONT +1
      [END OF IF]
STEP 4:  RETURN
```

ALGORITHM FOR TRAVERSE OPERATION

TRAVERSE(C_QUEUE[SIZE], FRONT, REAR)

```
STEP 1 : IF (FRONT = -1) THEN :
                  WRITE : " QUEUE IS EMPTY "
                  RETURN
         [END OF IF]
STEP 2 : SET I:=0
STEP 3 :  IF (FRONT > REAR ) THEN:
                  REPEAT FOR I =  FRONT TO SIZE-1
                        WRITE : C_QUEUE[I]
                  [END OF LOOP]
                  REPEAT FOR I = 0 TO REAR
                        WRITE : C_QUEUE[I]
                  [END OF LOOP]

      ELSE:
                  REPEAT FOR I = FRONT TO REAR
                        WRITE : C_QUEUE[I]
                  [END OF LOOP]
STEP 4:  RETURN
```

6.5   Double Ended Queue

The Double ended queue is also called as D-QUEUE or DE-QUEUE or DEQUE which allows to perform the insertion and deletion operation at both the ends. Depending upon the operations this can be categorized into two types as
- Input Restricted DEQUE
- Output Restricted DEQUE

INPUT RESTRICTED DEQUE

In this type of queue the insertion operation is restricted i.e/ it allows the insertion operation at one end but the deletion operation is at both the ends. One can perform the insertion operation at the rear end only but the insertion and deletion operation can be performed at front end.

OUTPUT RESTRICTED DEQUE

In this type of queue the Deletion operation is restricted i.e/ it allows the deletion operation at one end but the insertion operation is at both the ends. One can perform the deletion operation at the front end only but the insertion and deletion operation can be performed at rear end.

6.6   Priority Queue

Priority queues are a kind of queue in which the elements are dequeued in priority order.

- They are a mutable data abstraction: enqueues and dequeues are destructive.
- Each element has a **priority**, an element of a totally ordered set (usually a number)
- More important things come out *first*, even if they were added later
- Our convention: smaller number = higher priority
- There is no (fast) operation to find out whether an arbitrary element is in the queue
- Useful for event-based simulators (with priority = simulated time), real-time games, searching, routing, compression via Huffman coding

Depending on the heaps the priority queue are also of two types such as
    Min Priority Queue
    Max Priority Queue

The Set of operations for Max Priority Queue are

- Insert(A,N) : Inserts an element N into A
- Maximum(A,X) : Finds the X from A where X is the Maximum

- Extract_Max(A) : Remove and returns the element of S with largest Key
- Increase_Key(A,x,k) : Increases the value of element x's to the new value k which is assumed to be at least as large as x's current key value.

The Set of operations for Min Priority Queue are

- Insert
- Minimum
- Extract_Min
- Decrease_Key

The most important application of Max Priority Queue is to schedule jobs on a shared computer. The Max Priority queue keeps track of the jobs to be performed and their relative priorities. When a job is finished or interrupted the highest priority job is selected from those pending using Extract-Max, A new job can be added to the queue at any time by using Insert.

EXTRACT_MAX operation returns the largest element. So to find the largest element from an unordered list takes $\theta(n)$ times. An alternative is to use an ordered linear list . The elements are in non decreasing order if a sequential representation is used.

The Extract-Max operation takes $\theta(1)$ and the Insert time is O(n). When Max heap is used both Extract-max and insert can be performed in O(logn) time.

ALGORITHM MAXIMUM(A,X)

1. return A[1]

ALGORITHM EXTRACT-MAX(A)

1. If heapsize[A]<1
2. then Write : "Heap Underflow"
3. Max ←A[1]
4. A[1] ←A[heapsize[A]]
5. heapsize[A] ←heapsize[A]-1
6. Max_Heap(A,1)
7. retrun Max

ALGORITHM INCREASE-KEY(A,i,key))

1. if key <A[i]
2. then write "key is smaller than the current key"
3. A[i] ← key
4. while i > 1 and A[PARENT(i)]< A[i]
5. do exchange A[i] ↔A[PARENT(i)]
6. i ← Parent(i)

ALGORITHM INSERT(A,key)

1. heapsize[A] ← heapsize[A] + 1
2. A[heapsize[A]] ← -∞
3. INCREASE-KEY(A, heapsize[A],key)

The running time of INSERT on an n-element heap is O(lgn)
A heap can support any priority-queue operation on a set of size
  n in O(lgn) time.

OPERATIONS FOR MIN PRIORITY QUEUE

ALGORITHM MINIMUM(A,X)

2. return A[1]

ALGORITHM EXTRACT-MIN(A)

8. If heapsize[A]<1
9. then Write : "Heap Underflow"
10. Max ←A[1]
11. A[1] ←A[heapsize[A]]
12. heapsize[A] ←heapsize[A]-1
13. Max_Heap(A,1)
14. retrun Min

ALGORITHM DECREASE-KEY(A,i,key))

7. if key >A[i]
8. then write "key is greater than the current key"
9. A[i] ← key
10. while i > 1 and A[PARENT(i)]> A[i]

11. do exchange A[i] ↔A[PARENT(i)]
12. i ← Parent(i)

ALGORITHM INSERT(A,key)

4. heapsize[A] ← heapsize[A] + 1
5. A[heapsize[A]] ← -∞
6. DECREASE-KEY(A, heapsize[A],key)

6.7   Programs

1.   /* INSERTION AND DELETION IN A QUEUE ARRAY
IMPLEMENTATION */

```cpp
# include<iostream>
#include<stdlib.h>
using namespace std;
int *q,size,front=-1,rear=-1;
void  insert(int n)
{
      if(rear ==size-1)
            cout<<"\n QUEUE OVERFLOW";
   else
      {
      rear ++;
            *(q+rear) = n ;
            if(front == -1)
                  front = 0;
      }
}
/* Function to delete an element from queue */
void Delete()
{
      if (front == -1)
      {
            cout<<"\n Underflow";
            return ;
      }
      cout<<"\n Element deleted : "<<*(q+front);
      if(front == rear)
      {
            front = -1;
            rear = -1;
      }
      else
```

```
                        front = front + 1;
}
void display()
{
        int i;
        if (front == -1)
                cout<<"\n EMPTY QUEUE";
         else
            {
cout<<"\nTHE QUEUE ELEMENTS ARE";
         for(i = front ; i <= rear; i++)
         cout<<"\t"<<*(q+i);
            }
}
int main()
{
        int opt;
cout<<"\n Enter the size of the QUEUE";
cin>>size;
q= (int *)malloc(size * sizeof(int));
while(1)
    {
cout<<"\n Enter the choice";
cout<<"\n 1.INSERT  2. DELETE  3. DISPLAY 0. EXIT";
cin>>opt;
    if(opt==1)
            {
  cout<<"\n Enter the number to insert";
  cin>>opt;
        insert(opt);
            }
else
    if(opt==2)
        Delete();
    else
      if(opt==3)
        display();
      else
        if(opt==0)
           exit(0);
          else
            cout<<"\n INVALID CHOICE";
    }
  }
```

Output

```
Enter the size of the QUEUE4

Enter the choice
1.INSERT  2. DELETE  3. DISPLAY  0. EXIT1

Enter the number to insert23

Enter the choice
1.INSERT  2. DELETE  3. DISPLAY  0. EXIT1

Enter the number to insert43

Enter the choice
1.INSERT  2. DELETE  3. DISPLAY  0. EXIT1

Enter the number to insert65

Enter the choice
1.INSERT  2. DELETE  3. DISPLAY  0. EXIT1

Enter the number to insert77

Enter the choice
1.INSERT  2. DELETE  3. DISPLAY  0. EXIT1

Enter the number to insert88

QUEUE OVERFLOW
Enter the choice
1.INSERT  2. DELETE  3. DISPLAY  0. EXIT3

THE QUEUE ELEMENTS ARE  23      43      65      77
Enter the choice
1.INSERT  2. DELETE  3. DISPLAY  0. EXIT2

Element deleted : 23
Enter the choice
1.INSERT  2. DELETE  3. DISPLAY  0. EXIT2

Element deleted : 43
Enter the choice
1.INSERT  2. DELETE  3. DISPLAY  0. EXIT2

Element deleted : 65
Enter the choice
1.INSERT  2. DELETE  3. DISPLAY  0. EXIT2

Element deleted : 77
Enter the choice
1.INSERT  2. DELETE  3. DISPLAY  0. EXIT2

Underflow
Enter the choice
1.INSERT  2. DELETE  3. DISPLAY  0. EXIT0
--------------------------------------------------
Process exited after 22.92 seconds with return value 0
Press any key to continue . . .
```

2. CIRCULAR QUEUE OPERTIONS

```cpp
#include<iostream>
#include<iomanip>
using namespace std;
//body of class
class CircularQueue
{
        private :  //declare data members
                int front,rear,size,*cq;
        public:
                CircularQueue(int);   //constructor
                //method declarations
                void Enqueue(int);
                void Dequeue();
                void Print();
                bool isEmpty();
                bool isFull();
                void Clear();
                int getFront();
                int getRear();
  };
//body of constructor
CircularQueue :: CircularQueue(int n)
 {
        size= n;
        front=-1; //initialize front
        rear=-1;  //initialize rear
        cq = new int[size]; //allocate memory for
        circular queue
 }
 //method will return the value of rear
int CircularQueue :: getRear()
 {
        return rear;
 }
 //method will return the value of front
 int CircularQueue :: getFront()
  {
        return front;
  }
  //method will clear the elements of queue
  void CircularQueue :: Clear()
   {
        front=-1;  //set front to -1
        rear=-1;  //set rear to -1
   }
```

```cpp
//method will return true if circular queue is
full
bool CircularQueue :: isFull()
 {   //condition for circular queue is full
   if(front==0 && rear == size-1 || front ==
   rear+1)
   return true;
   .else
   return false;
   }
   //method will return true if the circular
   queue is empty
   bool CircularQueue :: isEmpty()
    {
            if(front==-1) //condition for empty
            return true;
            else
            return false;
    }
   //method will print the elements of circular
   queue
   void CircularQueue :: Print()
        {
int i;
if (isEmpty())  //check for empty queue
       printf("\n CIRCULAR QUEUE IS EMPTY");
   else
if (front > rear)  //print the elements when
front > rear
{
       for(i = front; i <= size-1; i++)
             cout<<cq[i]<<setw(5);
       for(i = 0; i <= rear; i++)
             cout<<cq[i]<<setw(5);
}
else   //print the elements from front to rear
       for(i = front; i <= rear; i++)
             cout<<cq[i]<<setw(5);

        }
//method will insert an element into circular queue
void CircularQueue :: Enqueue(int n)
{

       if (isFull())  //condition for overflow
       {
            printf("\n Overflow");
            return;
```

```
        }

        if (rear == -1) /* Insert first element */
              {
                   front = 0;
                   rear = 0;
              }
        else
                   if (rear == size-1)  //if rear is
                   at last then assign it to first
                   rear = 0;
                 else
                           rear++;  //increment the
                           value of rear
        //assign the number into circular queue
        cq[rear]= n ;
}
//method to delete the elements from queue
void CircularQueue :: Dequeue()
{
        int ch;
        if (isEmpty()) //condition for underflow
        {
              printf("\nUnderflow");
              return ;
        }
        //print the element which is to be delete
        cout<<endl<<cq[front]<<" deleted from circular
        queue";

        if(front ==rear) //condition for queue having
        single element
        {
              Clear();
        }
        else
if ( front == size-1)
              front = 0;
else
              front++;
        }

        //driver program
int main()
  {
int opt,n;
char ch;
cout<<endl<<"Enter the size of circular queue";
```

```
cin>>n; //ask user about the size of circular queue
CircularQueue obj(n); //declare an object

//infinite loop to control the program
while(1)
    {
cout<<endl<<"******* M E N U ********";
cout<<endl<<"e. ENQUEUE\nd. Dequeue\nm. isEmpty\nu.
isFull\nc.Clear\nf. Get Front\nr. Get Rear\np. Print\
nq. Quit";
cout<<endl<<"Enter Choice   : ";
cin>>ch;

//condition for enqueue()
if(ch=='e' || ch=='E')
    {
  cout<<endl<<"Enter the number to insert";
  cin>>opt;

      obj.Enqueue(opt);
        }
else  //condition for dequeue()
    if(ch=='d' || ch=='D')
      {
        obj.Dequeue();
      }
      else  //condition for call to isEmpty()
      if(ch=='m' || ch=='M')
          {
            if(obj.isEmpty())
              cout<<endl<<"Circular Queue is EMPTY";
            else
                      cout<<endl<<"Circular
                      Queue is not empty" ;
            }
            else  //condition to call isFull()
            if(ch=='u' || ch=='U')
              {
                if(obj.isFull())
              cout<<endl<<"Circular Queue is FULL";
              else
                      cout<<endl<<"Circular
                      Queue is not Full" ;
                }
            else //condition to call clear()
                  if(ch=='c' || ch=='C')
                    obj.Clear();
                  else
```

```
   if(ch=='f' || ch=='F')   //condition to call
getFront()
     cout<<endl<<"Front = "<<obj.getFront();
     else
   if(ch=='r' || ch=='R')   //condition to call
getRear()
     cout<<endl<<"Rear = "<<obj.getRear();
     else //condition to call Print()
     if(ch=='p' || ch=='P')
     obj.Print();
     else  //condition to terminate the program
     if(ch=='q' || ch=='Q')
        exit(0);
   else
     cout<<endl<<"Invalid Choice";
}
}
```

OUTPUT

```
Enter the size of circular queue3

******* M E N U *******
e. ENQUEUE
d. Dequeue
m. isEmpty
u. isFull
c.Clear
f. Get Front
r. Get Rear
p. Print
q. Quit
Enter Choice   : P

 CIRCULAR QUEUE IS EMPTY
******* M E N U *******
e. ENQUEUE
d. Dequeue
m. isEmpty
u. isFull
c.Clear
f. Get Front
r. Get Rear
p. Print
q. Quit
Enter Choice   : R

Rear = -1
******* M E N U *******
e. ENQUEUE
d. Dequeue
m. isEmpty
u. isFull
c.Clear
f. Get Front
r. Get Rear
p. Print
q. Quit
Enter Choice   : F

Front = -1
******* M E N U *******
e. ENQUEUE
d. Dequeue
m. isEmpty
u. isFull
c.Clear
f. Get Front
r. Get Rear
p. Print
q. Quit
Enter Choice   : U

Circular Queue is not Full
******* M E N U *******
e. ENQUEUE
d. Dequeue
m. isEmpty
u. isFull
c.Clear
f. Get Front
r. Get Rear
p. Print
q. Quit
Enter Choice   : M
```

```
Circular Queue is EMPTY
******* M E N U ********
e. ENQUEUE
d. Dequeue
m. isEmpty
u. isFull
c.Clear
f. Get Front
r. Get Rear
p. Print
q. Quit
Enter Choice   : E

Enter the number to insert12

******* M E N U ********
e. ENQUEUE
d. Dequeue
m. isEmpty
u. isFull
c.Clear
f. Get Front
r. Get Rear
p. Print
q. Quit
Enter Choice   : E

Enter the number to insert34

******* M E N U ********
e. ENQUEUE
d. Dequeue
m. isEmpty
u. isFull
c.Clear
f. Get Front
r. Get Rear
p. Print
q. Quit
Enter Choice   : E

Enter the number to insert56

******* M E N U ********
e. ENQUEUE
d. Dequeue
m. isEmpty
u. isFull
c.Clear
f. Get Front
r. Get Rear
p. Print
q. Quit
Enter Choice   : E

Enter the number to insert2

 Overflow
```

```
******** M E N U ********
e. ENQUEUE
d. Dequeue
m. isEmpty
u. isFull
c.Clear
f. Get Front
r. Get Rear
p. Print
q. Quit
Enter Choice   : P
12   34   56
******** M E N U ********
e. ENQUEUE
d. Dequeue
m. isEmpty
u. isFull
c.Clear
f. Get Front
r. Get Rear
p. Print
q. Quit
Enter Choice   : D

12 deleted from circular queue
******** M E N U ********
e. ENQUEUE
d. Dequeue
m. isEmpty
u. isFull
c.Clear
f. Get Front
r. Get Rear
p. Print
q. Quit
Enter Choice   : D

34 deleted from circular queue
******** M E N U ********
e. ENQUEUE
d. Dequeue
m. isEmpty
u. isFull
c.Clear
f. Get Front
r. Get Rear
p. Print
q. Quit
Enter Choice   : P
56
```

```
******* M E N U ********
e. ENQUEUE
d. Dequeue
m. isEmpty
u. isFull
c.Clear
f. Get Front
r. Get Rear
p. Print
q. Quit
Enter Choice   : U

Circular Queue is not Full
******* M E N U ********
e. ENQUEUE
d. Dequeue
m. isEmpty
u. isFull
c.Clear
f. Get Front
r. Get Rear
p. Print
q. Quit
Enter Choice   : M

Circular Queue is not empty
******* M E N U ********
e. ENQUEUE
d. Dequeue
m. isEmpty
u. isFull
c.Clear
f. Get Front
r. Get Rear
p. Print
q. Quit
Enter Choice   : E

Enter the number to insert34

******* M E N U ********
e. ENQUEUE
d. Dequeue
m. isEmpty
u. isFull
c.Clear
f. Get Front
r. Get Rear
p. Print
q. Quit
Enter Choice   : E

Enter the number to insert77

******* M E N U ********
e. ENQUEUE
d. Dequeue
m. isEmpty
u. isFull
c.Clear
f. Get Front
r. Get Rear
p. Print
q. Quit
Enter Choice   : P
56   34   77
```

```
******* M E N U ********
e. ENQUEUE
d. Dequeue
m. isEmpty
u. isFull
c.Clear
f. Get Front
r. Get Rear
p. Print
q. Quit
Enter Choice   : C

******* M E N U ********
e. ENQUEUE
d. Dequeue
m. isEmpty
u. isFull
c.Clear
f. Get Front
r. Get Rear
p. Print
q. Quit
Enter Choice   : D

Underflow
******* M E N U ********
e. ENQUEUE
d. Dequeue
m. isEmpty
u. isFull
c.Clear
f. Get Front
r. Get Rear
p. Print
q. Quit
Enter Choice   : Q

--------------------------------------
Process exited after 203.3 seconds with return value 0
Press any key to continue . . .
```

3. CIRCULAR QUEUE PROGRAM FOR INSERT,DELETE,SERCH AND TRAVERSE OPERATIONS

```cpp
#include<iostream>
using namespace std;
//structure of class cqueue
class cqueue
{
    private:
        int front,rear,cnt,queue[10];
    public:
        cqueue(); //constructor
        void enqueue(); //prototype of enqueue()
        void dequeue(); //prototype of dequeue()
        int count(); //count the number of
        elements in queue
        void traverse(); //traverse the queue elements
        bool search(int); //search an element in
        circular queue
};
```

```
cqueue :: cqueue()
  {
      front=-1;   //assign -1 to front and rear for empty
      queue
        rear=-1;
        cnt=0;//set 0 to count
  }
  //method to insert an element into the queue
  void cqueue :: enqueue()
   {
      //condition for overflow
      if(front == 0 && rear==9 || front == rear+1)
        {
              cout<<endl<<"OVERFLOW";
        }
        else
          {
              if(rear==-1)  //condition for queue does not
              having any element
                    {
                        front=0;   //set the front and rear to
                        0
                        rear=0;
                    }
                    else
                    if(rear==9 && front!=0)  //condition
                    for rear is at last but queue having
                    empty space
                        {
                          rear=0;
                          }
                          else
                          {  //increase the rear for
                          insertion
                                rear++;
                          }
                          //insert an element into the
                          queue
              cout<<endl<<"Enter an element to insert into
              queue";
              cin>>queue[rear];
          }

        }
  //method to delete an element from queue
  void cqueue :: dequeue()
   {
      if(front==-1)  //condition for underflow
      {
```

```cpp
            cout<<endl<<"UNDERFLOW";
        }
        else
        {   //print the element to delete
            cout<<endl<<queue[front]<<" deleted from queue";
            //set the front
            if(front==rear)   //queue having single
            element
                {
                    front=-1;
                    rear=-1;
                }
                else
            if(front==9)    //condition for front is
            at last
            front=0;
            else
            front=front+1;   //increase the front
        }
    }
    //method to traverse the queue
    void cqueue :: traverse()
    {
        int i;
        if(front==-1) //condition for empty queue
        {
            cout<<endl<<"EMPTY QUEUE";
        }
        else
        if(front >rear)   //condition for front
        is greater to rear
        {
            for(i=front;i<=9;i++)   //print
            the elements from front to last
            cout<<queue[i]<<"   ";
            for(i=0;i<=rear;i++) //print the
            elements from 0 to rear
             cout<<queue[i]<<"   ";
        }
        else
        for(i=front;i<=rear;i++) //print the
        elements from front to rear
        cout<<queue[i]<<"   ";
    }
    //method to count the number of elements in queue
    int cqueue :: count()
    {
        int i;
        cnt=0;
```

```
        if(rear==-1)  //condition for queue does
        not having element
          return cnt;//return cnt as 0
            else
        if(front >rear)  //condition having
        front greater to rear
          {
                for(i=front;i<=9;i++)  //count number
                of elements from front to last
                cnt++;
                for(i=0;i<=rear;i++) //count the
                elements from 0 to rear
                 cnt++;
          }
          else
          for(i=front;i<=rear;i++) //count the
          elements from front to rear
          cnt++;

        return cnt; //return count
  }
//method to search an element in queue
bool cqueue :: search(int n)
  {
        int i;
        if(rear==-1) //if queue does not having
        any element then return false
        return false;

        if(front >rear)  //condition having
        front greater to rear
          {
                for(i=front;i<=9;i++)//search number
                of elements from front to last
                    if(n==queue[i])
                    return true;
                for(i=0;i<=rear;i++)//search the
                elements from 0 to rear
                 if(n==queue[i])
                    return true;
          }
          else
          for(i=front;i<=rear;i++)//search the
          elements from front to rear
          if(n==queue[i])
                    return true;
        return false;
  }
//driver program
```

```cpp
int main()
{
    int opt,n;
    cqueue obj;
    cout<<endl<<"***********************\n";
    cout<<endl<<"CIRCULAR QUEUE OPERATIONS";
    cout<<endl<<"****************\n";
    //loop to operate the operations with queue
    till user wants
        while(1)
        {
    //display the menu
    cout<<endl<<"1. INSERT 2. DELETE 3. COUNT 4.
    SEARCH 5. TRAVERSE 0.EXIT";
    cout<<endl<<"Enter your choice";
    cin>>opt; //read the choice
    if(opt==1) //condition for insert operation
    obj.enqueue();
    else
    if(opt==2) //condition for delete operation
    obj.dequeue();
    else
    if(opt==3) //condition for count operation
    cout<<endl<<"Circular queue having "<<obj.
    count()<<" number of elements";
    else
    if(opt==4) //condition for search operation
    {
        cout<<endl<<"Enter an element to
        search";
        cin>>n;
        if(obj.search(n))
        cout<<endl<<n<<" is inside the queue";
        else
        cout<<endl<<n<<" is not inside the
        queue";
    }
    else
    if(opt==5) //condition for traverse
    operation
    obj.traverse();
    else
    if(opt==0) //condition for terminate the
    loop
    break;
    else  //invalid option
    cout<<endl<<"Invalid choice";
        }
}
```

OUTPUT

```
*******************************
CIRCULAR QUEUE OPERATIONS
*******************************

1. INSERT 2. DELETE 3. COUNT 4. SEARCH 5. TRAVERSE 0.EXIT
Enter your choice1

Enter an element to insert into queue23

1. INSERT 2. DELETE 3. COUNT 4. SEARCH 5. TRAVERSE 0.EXIT
Enter your choice1

Enter an element to insert into queue34

1. INSERT 2. DELETE 3. COUNT 4. SEARCH 5. TRAVERSE 0.EXIT
Enter your choice1

Enter an element to insert into queue5

1. INSERT 2. DELETE 3. COUNT 4. SEARCH 5. TRAVERSE 0.EXIT
Enter your choice1

Enter an element to insert into queue65

1. INSERT 2. DELETE 3. COUNT 4. SEARCH 5. TRAVERSE 0.EXIT
Enter your choice1

Enter an element to insert into queue76

1. INSERT 2. DELETE 3. COUNT 4. SEARCH 5. TRAVERSE 0.EXIT
Enter your choice1

Enter an element to insert into queue87

1. INSERT 2. DELETE 3. COUNT 4. SEARCH 5. TRAVERSE 0.EXIT
Enter your choice1

Enter an element to insert into queue5

1. INSERT 2. DELETE 3. COUNT 4. SEARCH 5. TRAVERSE 0.EXIT
Enter your choice1

Enter an element to insert into queue3

1. INSERT 2. DELETE 3. COUNT 4. SEARCH 5. TRAVERSE 0.EXIT
Enter your choice1

Enter an element to insert into queue76

1. INSERT 2. DELETE 3. COUNT 4. SEARCH 5. TRAVERSE 0.EXIT
Enter your choice1

Enter an element to insert into queue43

1. INSERT 2. DELETE 3. COUNT 4. SEARCH 5. TRAVERSE 0.EXIT
Enter your choice1

OVERFLOW
1. INSERT 2. DELETE 3. COUNT 4. SEARCH 5. TRAVERSE 0.EXIT
Enter your choice5
23   34   5   65   76   87   5   3   76   43
```

```
1. INSERT 2. DELETE 3. COUNT 4. SEARCH 5. TRAVERSE 0.EXIT
Enter your choice2

23 deleted from queue
1. INSERT 2. DELETE 3. COUNT 4. SEARCH 5. TRAVERSE 0.EXIT
Enter your choice2

34 deleted from queue
1. INSERT 2. DELETE 3. COUNT 4. SEARCH 5. TRAVERSE 0.EXIT
Enter your choice2

5 deleted from queue
1. INSERT 2. DELETE 3. COUNT 4. SEARCH 5. TRAVERSE 0.EXIT
Enter your choice1

Enter an element to insert into queue33

1. INSERT 2. DELETE 3. COUNT 4. SEARCH 5. TRAVERSE 0.EXIT
Enter your choice1

Enter an element to insert into queue44

1. INSERT 2. DELETE 3. COUNT 4. SEARCH 5. TRAVERSE 0.EXIT
Enter your choice3

Circular queue having 9 number of elements
1. INSERT 2. DELETE 3. COUNT 4. SEARCH 5. TRAVERSE 0.EXIT
Enter your choice1

Enter an element to insert into queue56

1. INSERT 2. DELETE 3. COUNT 4. SEARCH 5. TRAVERSE 0.EXIT
Enter your choice1

OVERFLOW
1. INSERT 2. DELETE 3. COUNT 4. SEARCH 5. TRAVERSE 0.EXIT
Enter your choice3

Circular queue having 10 number of elements
1. INSERT 2. DELETE 3. COUNT 4. SEARCH 5. TRAVERSE 0.EXIT
Enter your choice5
65  76  87  5  3  76  43  33  44  56
1. INSERT 2. DELETE 3. COUNT 4. SEARCH 5. TRAVERSE 0.EXIT
Enter your choice3

Circular queue having 10 number of elements
1. INSERT 2. DELETE 3. COUNT 4. SEARCH 5. TRAVERSE 0.EXIT
Enter your choice33

Invalid choice
1. INSERT 2. DELETE 3. COUNT 4. SEARCH 5. TRAVERSE 0.EXIT
Enter your choice4

Enter an element to search33

33 is inside the queue
1. INSERT 2. DELETE 3. COUNT 4. SEARCH 5. TRAVERSE 0.EXIT
Enter your choice4

Enter an element to search1

1 is not inside the queue
1. INSERT 2. DELETE 3. COUNT 4. SEARCH 5. TRAVERSE 0.EXIT
Enter your choice5
65  76  87  5  3  76  43  33  44  56
```

```
1. INSERT 2. DELETE 3. COUNT 4. SEARCH 5. TRAVERSE 0.EXIT
Enter your choice2

65 deleted from queue
1. INSERT 2. DELETE 3. COUNT 4. SEARCH 5. TRAVERSE 0.EXIT
Enter your choice2

76 deleted from queue
1. INSERT 2. DELETE 3. COUNT 4. SEARCH 5. TRAVERSE 0.EXIT
Enter your choice2

87 deleted from queue
1. INSERT 2. DELETE 3. COUNT 4. SEARCH 5. TRAVERSE 0.EXIT
Enter your choice2

5 deleted from queue
1. INSERT 2. DELETE 3. COUNT 4. SEARCH 5. TRAVERSE 0.EXIT
Enter your choice2

3 deleted from queue
1. INSERT 2. DELETE 3. COUNT 4. SEARCH 5. TRAVERSE 0.EXIT
Enter your choice2

76 deleted from queue
1. INSERT 2. DELETE 3. COUNT 4. SEARCH 5. TRAVERSE 0.EXIT
Enter your choice2

43 deleted from queue
1. INSERT 2. DELETE 3. COUNT 4. SEARCH 5. TRAVERSE 0.EXIT
Enter your choice5
33  44  56
1. INSERT 2. DELETE 3. COUNT 4. SEARCH 5. TRAVERSE 0.EXIT
Enter your choice3

Circular queue having 3 number of elements
1. INSERT 2. DELETE 3. COUNT 4. SEARCH 5. TRAVERSE 0.EXIT
Enter your choice2

33 deleted from queue
1. INSERT 2. DELETE 3. COUNT 4. SEARCH 5. TRAVERSE 0.EXIT
Enter your choice2

44 deleted from queue
1. INSERT 2. DELETE 3. COUNT 4. SEARCH 5. TRAVERSE 0.EXIT
Enter your choice1

Enter an element to insert into queue56

1. INSERT 2. DELETE 3. COUNT 4. SEARCH 5. TRAVERSE 0.EXIT
Enter your choice5
56  56
1. INSERT 2. DELETE 3. COUNT 4. SEARCH 5. TRAVERSE 0.EXIT
Enter your choice2

56 deleted from queue
1. INSERT 2. DELETE 3. COUNT 4. SEARCH 5. TRAVERSE 0.EXIT
Enter your choice2

56 deleted from queue
1. INSERT 2. DELETE 3. COUNT 4. SEARCH 5. TRAVERSE 0.EXIT
Enter your choice2
UNDERFLOW
```

```
1. INSERT 2. DELETE 3. COUNT 4. SEARCH 5. TRAUERSE 0.EXIT
Enter your choice3

Circular queue having 0 number of elements
1. INSERT 2. DELETE 3. COUNT 4. SEARCH 5. TRAUERSE 0.EXIT
Enter your choice4

Enter an element to search56

56 is not inside the queue
1. INSERT 2. DELETE 3. COUNT 4. SEARCH 5. TRAUERSE 0.EXIT
Enter your choice0
_____
Process exited after 100.8 seconds with return value 0
Press any key to continue . . .
```

4. PROGRAM FOR DE-QUEUE INSERTION AND DELETION

```cpp
#include<iostream>
using namespace std;
#define SIZE 50
class dequeue {
    int a[50],f,r;
    public:
        dequeue();
        void insert_at_beg(int);
        void insert_at_end(int);
        void delete_fr_front();
        void delete_fr_rear();
        void show();
};
dequeue::dequeue() {
    f=-1;
    r=-1;
}
void dequeue::insert_at_end(int i) {
    if(r>=SIZE-1) {
        cout<<"\n insertion is not possible, overflow!!!!";
    } else {
        if(f==-1) {
            f++;
            r++;
        } else {
            r=r+1;
        }
        a[r]=i;
        cout<<"\nInserted item is"<<a[r];
    }
}
void dequeue::insert_at_beg(int i) {
```

```
    if(f==-1) {
       f=0;
       a[++r]=i;
       cout<<"\n inserted element is:"<<i;
    } else if(f!=0) {
       a[--f]=i;
       cout<<"\n inserted element is:"<<i;
    } else {
       cout<<"\n insertion is not possible, overflow!!!";
    }
}
void dequeue::delete_fr_front() {
    if(f==-1) {
       cout<<"deletion is not possible::dequeue is empty";
       return;
    }
    else {
       cout<<"the deleted element is:"<<a[f];
       if(f==r) {
          f=r=-1;
          return;
       } else
          f=f+1;
    }
}
    void dequeue::delete_fr_rear() {
       if(f==-1) {
          cout<<"deletion is not possible::dequeue is empty";
          return;
       }
       else {
          cout<<"the deleted element is:"<<a[r];
          if(f==r) {
             f=r=-1;
          } else
             r=r-1;
       }
    }
    void dequeue::show() {
       if(f==-1) {
          cout<<"Dequeue is empty";
       } else {
          for(int i=f;i<=r;i++) {
             cout<<a[i]<<" ";
          }
       }
    }
```

```cpp
int main() {
    int c,i;
    dequeue d;
    do //perform switch opeartion
        {
        cout<<"\n 1.insert at beginning";
        cout<<"\n 2.insert at end";
        cout<<"\n 3.show";
        cout<<"\n 4.deletion from front";
        cout<<"\n 5.deletion from rear";
        cout<<"\n 6.exit";
        cout<<"\n enter your choice:";
        cin>>c;
        switch(c) {
            case 1:
                cout<<"enter the element to be inserted";
                cin>>i;
                d.insert_at_beg(i);
            break;
            case 2:
                cout<<"enter the element to be inserted";
                cin>>i;
                d.insert_at_end(i);
            break;
            case 3:
                d.show();
            break;
            case 4:
                d.delete_fr_front();
            break;
            case 5:
                d.delete_fr_rear();
            break;
            case 6:
                exit(1);
            break;
            default:
                cout<<"invalid choice";
            break;
        }
    } while(c!=7);
}
```

6.8   Questions

1. What is queue data structure?
2. What is the benefit of circular queue over linear queue?
3. What is double-ended queue?
4. What are the operations performed with priority queue?
5. Write a few applications of priority queue.
6. Mention the overflow and underflow condition of circular queue.
7. Write a program to show the implementation of double ended queue.

Linked List

The linked list is the way of representing the data structure that may be linear or nonlinear. The elements in the linked list will be allocated randomly inside the memory with a relation in between them. The elements in the linked list is known as the NODES.

The link list quite better than the array due to the proper usage of memory.

7.1 Why Use Linked List?

The array always requires the memory that are in sequential order but the linked list requires a single memory allocation which is sufficient enough to store the data. In case of array the memory may not be allotted even if the memory space is greater than the required space because that may not be in sequential order.

7.2 Types of Link List

The link list are of Four types such as

- Single Link List
- Double Link List
- Circular Link List
- Header Link List

Sachi Nandan Mohanty and Pabitra Kumar Tripathy. Data Structure and Algorithms Using C++: A Practical Implementation, (167–248) © 2021 Scrivener Publishing LLC

7.3   Single Link List

STRUCTURE OF THE NODE OF A LINKED LIST

The node of a link list having the capacity to store the data as well as the address of its next node and the data may varies depending on the users requirement so it will be better to choose the data type of the node as STRUCTURE which will have the ability to store different types of elements. The general format of the node is

```
Struct tagname
      {
Data type member1;
Data type member2;
...................... .
......................
...................... . .
Data type membern;
Struct tagname *var;
      };
```

Example:

```
struct link
      {
  int info;
struct link *next;
      };
```

This structure is also called as self referential structure.

CONCEPT OF CREATION OF A LINKED LIST

```
int *p,q=5;
p=&q;
*p = *p + 5
```
After this the value of q is being changed to 10.

The main observation here is that if a pointer variable points to another variable then what ever the changes made with the pointer that will directly affect to the variable whose address is stored inside the pointer and concept is used to design/create the linked list.

LOGIC FOR CREATION

```
struct link
    {
  int info;
  struct link *next;
    };
```
struct link start, *node;

LOGIC

NODE = &START
Node->next = (struct link *)malloc(sizeof(struct link))
Node = node->next
Node->next = NULL
Input node->info

ALGORITHM FOR CREATION OF SINGLE LINK LIST

```
struct link
  {
  int info;
struct link *next;
  };
```
CREATE(START,NODE)   [START IS THE STRUCTURE TYPE
                                OF VARIABLE]
                                [NODE IS THE STRUCTURE TYPE
                                OF POINTER]

STEP-1 : NEXT[START]: = NULL
STEP-2 : NODE := ADDRESS OF START
STEP-3 : ALLOCATE A MEMORY TO NEXT[NODE]
        NODE :=NEXT[NODE]
        INPUT : INFO[NODE]
        NEXT[NODE] : = NULL
STEP-4 : REPEAT STEP-3 TO CREATE MORE NODES
STEP-5 : RETURN

ALGORITHM FOR TRAVERSING OF SINGLE LINK LIST

```
struct link
  {
  int info;
struct link *next;
  };
```
TRAVERSE(START,NODE)   [START IS THE STRUCTURE TYPE
                OF VARIABLE]
                [NODE IS THE STRUCTURE TYPE
                OF POINTER]
STEP-1 : NODE := NEXT[START]
STEP-2 : REPEAT WHILE (NEXT[NODE] #NULL)
        WRITE : INFO[NODE]
Node:=NODE[NEXT]
        END OF LOOP
STEP-3 : RETURN

INSERTION

The insertion process with link list can be discussed in four different ways such as

- Insertion at Beginning
- Insertion at End
- Insertion when node number is known
- Insertion when information is known

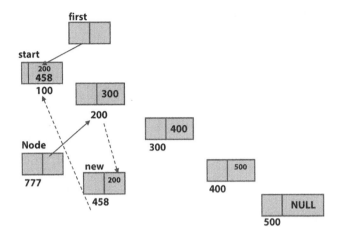

LOGIC

First = &start
Node = start.next
Allocate a memory to NEW
Input NEW->info
First->next = NEW
NEW->next = node.

ALGORITHM FOR INSERTION AT BEGINNING

```
struct link
  {
  int info;
struct link *next;
   };
INSBEG(START,FIRST,NODE) [START IS THE STRUCTURE TYPE
                          OF VARIABLE]
                         [NODE and FIRST IS THE STRUCTURE
                          TYPE OF POINTER VARIABLE]
STEP-1 : FIRST := ADDRESS OF START
         NODE := NEXT[START]
STEP-2 : ALLOCATE A MEMORY TO NEW
         INPUT : INFO[NEW]
         NEXT[FIRST] :=  NEW
         [NEXT]NEW := NODE
STEP-3 : RETURN
```

ALGORITHM FOR INSERTION AT LAST

```
struct link
 {
 int info;
struct link *next;
   };
```
INSLAST(START,FIRST,NODE)   [START IS THE STRUCTURE
                               TYPE OF VARIABLE]
                               [NODE and FIRST IS THE STRUCTURE
                               TYPE OF POINTER VARIABLE]
STEP-1 : FIRST := ADDRESS OF START
         NODE := NEXT[START]
STEP-2 : REPEAT WHILE(NODE != NULL)
              NODE := NEXT[NODE]
              FIRST := NEXT[FIRST]
         [END OF LOOP]
STEP-3 : ALLOCATE A MEMORY TO NEW
         INPUT : INFO[NEW]
         NEXT[FIRST]:= NEW
         [NEXT]NEW := NODE
STEP-4 : RETURN

ALGORITHM FOR INSERTION OF NODE WHEN NODE NUMBER IS KNOWN

```
struct link
 {
 int info;
struct link *next;
   };
```
INSNODE(START,FIRST,NODE,NO) [START IS THE STRUCTURE
                              TYPE OF VARIABLE]
                             [NODE and FIRST IS THE STRUCTURE
                             TYPE OF POINTER VARIABLE]
                             [NO IS THE NODE NUMBER]
STEP-1 : FIRST := ADDRESS OF START
         NODE := NEXT[START]
             COUNT :=1

```
STEP-2 :  REPEAT WHILE(NODE != NULL)
              IF(COUNT = NO) THEN:
                  ALLOCATE A MEMORY TO NEW
                  INPUT : INFO[NEW]
                  NEXT[FIRST]:= NEW
                  [NEXT]NEW := NODE
                  RETURN
              ELSE :
                  NODE := NEXT[NODE]
                  FIRST := NEXT[FIRST]
                  COUNT:=COUNT+1
                  [END OF IF]
              [END OF LOOP]
STEP-5 : RETURN
```

ALGORITHM FOR INSERTION OF NODE WHEN INFORMATION IS KNOWN

```
struct link
 {
  int info;
struct link *next;
    };
INSNODE(START,FIRST,NODE,NO) [START IS THE STRUCTURE
                    TYPE OF VARIABLE]
                    [NODE and FIRST IS THE STRUCTURE
                    TYPE OF POINTER VARIABLE]
                    [NO IS THE INFORMATION TO INSERT]
STEP-1 : FIRST := ADDRESS OF START
            NODE := NEXT[START]
STEP-2 : REPEAT WHILE(NODE != NULL)
              IF(INFO[NODE] >= NO) THEN:
                  ALLOCATE A MEMORY TO NEW
                  INPUT : INFO[NEW]
                  NEXT[FIRST]:= NEW
                  [NEXT]NEW := NODE
                  RETURN
```

```
            ELSE :
                 NODE := NEXT[NODE]
                 FIRST := NEXT[FIRST]
            [END OF IF]
            [END OF LOOP]
STEP-5 : RETURN
```

ALGORITHM FOR DELETION FROM BEGINNING

```
struct link
  {
  int info;
struct link *next;
  };
DELBEG(START,FIRST,NODE)[START IS THE STRUCTURE TYPE
                         OF VARIABLE]
                        [NODE and FIRST IS THE STRUCTURE
                         TYPE OF POINTER VARIABLE]
STEP-1 : FIRST := ADDRESS OF START
         NODE := NEXT[START]
STEP-2 : WRITE : INFO[NODE]
         NEXT[FIRST] := NEXT[NODE]
              FREE(NODE):
STEP-3 : RETURN
```

ALGORITHM FOR DELETION THE LAST NODE

```
struct link
  {
  int info;
struct link *next;
  };
DELLAST(START,FIRST,NODE)      [START IS THE STRUCTURE
                         TYPE OF VARIABLE]
                        [NODE and FIRST IS THE STRUCTURE
                         TYPE OF POINTER VARIABLE]
STEP-1 : FIRST := ADDRESS OF START
         NODE := NEXT[START]
```

```
                COUNT :=1
STEP-2 :  REPEAT WHILE(NODE != NULL)
                NODE := NEXT[NODE]
                COUNT:=COUNT+1
                [END OF LOOP]
STEP-3 : NODE := NEXT[START]
STEP-4 : REPEAT WHILE(COUNT !=1)
                NODE := NEXT[NODE]
                FIRST := NEXT[FIRST]
                COUNT := COUNT-1
                [END OF LOOP]
STEP-3 :  WRITE : INFO[NODE]
                NEXT[FIRST] := NEXT[NODE]
                FREE(NODE)
STEP-4 : RETURN
```

ALGORITHM FOR DELETION OF NODE WHEN NODE NUMBER IS KNOWN

```
struct link
 {
 int info;
 struct link *next;
  };
DELNODE(START,FIRST,NODE,NO) [START IS THE STRUCTURE
                TYPE OF VARIABLE]
                [NODE and FIRST IS THE STRUCTURE
                TYPE OF POINTER VARIABLE]
                [NO IS THE NODE NUMBER]

STEP-1 : FIRST := ADDRESS OF START
            NODE := NEXT[START]
                COUNT :=1
STEP-2 :  REPEAT WHILE(NODE != NULL)
            IF(COUNT = NO) THEN:
                WRITE : INFO[NODE]
                NEXT[FIRST]:=NEXT[NODE]
                FREE(NODE)
                RETURN
```

```
        ELSE :
            NODE := NEXT[NODE]
            FIRST := NEXT[FIRST]
            COUNT:=COUNT+1
            [END OF IF]
        [END OF LOOP]
STEP-5 : RETURN
```

ALGORITHM FOR DELETION OF NODE WHEN INFORMATION IS KNOWN

```
struct link
  {
  int info;
struct link *next;
  };
DELINFO(START,FIRST,NODE,NO) [START IS THE STRUCTURE
                    TYPE OF VARIABLE]
                    [NODE and FIRST IS THE STRUCTURE
                    TYPE OF POINTER VARIABLE]
                    [NO IS THE INFORMATION TO INSERT]

STEP-1 : FIRST := ADDRESS OF START
        NODE := NEXT[START]
STEP-2 : REPEAT WHILE(NODE != NULL)
        IF(INFO[NODE] = NO) THEN:
            WRITE : INFO[NODE]
            NEXT[FIRST]:=NEXT[NODE]
            FREE(NODE)
          RETURN
        ELSE :
            NODE := NEXT[NODE]
            FIRST := NEXT[FIRST]
        [END OF IF]
        [END OF LOOP]
STEP-5 : RETURN
```

7.4   Programs Related to Single Linked List

7.4.1   /* Creation of a Linked List */

```cpp
#include<iostream>
#include<iomanip>
#include<stdlib.h>
using namespace std;
struct link
{
      int info;
      struct link *next;
};
struct link start;
/* Function main */
void create(struct link *);
void display (struct link *);
int main()
{
      struct link *node;
      create(node);
      display(node);
}


void create(struct link *node) /*LOGIC TO CREATE A LINK
LIST*/
{
      char ch='y';
      start.next = NULL;
      node = &start;      /* Point to the start of the list */
      while(ch =='y' || ch=='Y')
      {
            node->next = (struct link* ) malloc(sizeof(struct link));
            node = node->next;
            cout<<"\n ENTER A NUMBER : ";
            cin>>node->info;
            node->next = NULL;
            cout<<"\n DO YOU WANT TO CRTEATE MORE NODES: ";
            cin>>ch;
      }
}
```

```
void display(struct link *node)
{                               /*DISPLAY THE LINKED
LIST*/
        node = start.next;
        cout<<"\n After Inserting a node list is as
        follows:\n";
        while (node)
        {
                cout<<setw(5)<<node->info;
                node = node->next;
        }
}
```

Output

```
ENTER A NUMBER : 5

DO YOU WANT TO CRTEATE MORE NODES: y

ENTER A NUMBER : 32

DO YOU WANT TO CRTEATE MORE NODES: y

ENTER A NUMBER : 58y

DO YOU WANT TO CRTEATE MORE NODES:
ENTER A NUMBER : 98

DO YOU WANT TO CRTEATE MORE NODES: y

ENTER A NUMBER : 5

DO YOU WANT TO CRTEATE MORE NODES: n

After Inserting a node list is as follows:
    5   32   58   98    5

Process exited after 12.23 seconds with return value 0
Press any key to continue . . .
```

7.4.2   /* Insert a Node Into a Simple Linked List at the Beginning */

```
#include<iostream>
#include<iomanip>
#include<stdlib.h>
using namespace std;
struct list
{
        int info;
        struct list *next;
};
```

```
struct list start, *first, *New;
/* Function main */
void create(struct list *);
void display (struct list  *);
void insert(struct list *);

int main()
{
       struct list *node;
create(node);
       insert(node);
       display(node);
}


void create(struct list *node) /*LOGIC TO CREATE A LINK LIST*/
{
       char ch='y';
       start.next = NULL;
       node = &start;       /* Point to the start of the list */
       while(ch =='y' || ch=='Y')
       {
              node->next = (struct list* ) malloc(sizeof(struct
list));
              node = node->next;
              cout<<"\n ENTER A NUMBER : ";
              cin>>node->info;
              node->next = NULL;
              cout<<"\n DO YOU WANT TO CRTEATE MORE NODES: ";
              cin>>ch;
       }
}


void display(struct list *node)
{                                 /*DISPLAY THE LINKED LIST*/
       node = start.next;
       cout<<"\n After Inserting a node list is as
       follows:\n";
       while (node)
       {
              cout<<setw(5)<<node->info;
              node = node->next;
       }
}

void insert(struct list *node)
{                                 /*INSERT AN ELEMENT AT THE
FIRST NODE*/
       node = start.next;
```

```
        first = &start;
        New = (struct list* ) malloc(sizeof(struct list));
        New->next = node ;
        first->next = New;
        cout<<"\n Input the fisrt node value: ";
        cin>>New->info;
}
```

Output

```
ENTER A NUMBER : 3

DO YOU WANT TO CRTEATE MORE NODES: y

ENTER A NUMBER : 8

DO YOU WANT TO CRTEATE MORE NODES: y

ENTER A NUMBER : 9

DO YOU WANT TO CRTEATE MORE NODES: n

Input the fisrt node value: 34

After Inserting a node list is as follows:
    34    3    8    9

Process exited after 10.15 seconds with return value 0
Press any key to continue . . .
```

7.4.3   /* Insert a Node Into a Simple Linked List at the End of the List */

```cpp
#include<iostream>
#include<iomanip>
#include<stdlib.h>
using namespace std;
struct list
{
        int info;
        struct list *next;
};
struct list start, *first, *New,*last;
/* Function main */
void create(struct list *);
void display (struct list  *);
void insert(struct list *);

int main()
{
        struct list *node;
create(node);
```

```
        insert(node);
        display(node);
}

void create(struct list *node) /*LOGIC TO CREATE A LINK
LIST*/
{
        char ch='y';
        start.next = NULL;
        node = &start;         /* Point to the start of the list */
        while(ch =='y' || ch=='Y')
        {
                node->next = (struct list* )
                malloc(sizeof(struct list));
                node = node->next;
                cout<<"\n ENTER A NUMBER : ";
                cin>>node->info;
                node->next = NULL;
                cout<<"\n DO YOU WANT TO CRTEATE MORE NODES: ";
                cin>>ch;
        }
}


void display(struct list *node)
{                                   /*DISPLAY THE LINKED LIST*/
        node = start.next;
        cout<<"\n After Inserting a node list is as follows:\n";
        while (node)
        {
                cout<<setw(5)<<node->info;
                node = node->next;
        }
}

void insert(struct list *node)
{                                   /* LOGIC OF INSERTION(LAST NODE) */
        node = start.next;
        last = &start;
        while(node)
        {
                node = node->next;
                last= last->next;
        }
        if(node == NULL)
        {
                New = (struct list* ) malloc(sizeof(struct list));
                New->next = node ;
                last->next = New;
```

```
            cout<<"\n ENTER THE VALUE OF LAST NODE: ";
            cin>>New->info;
    }
}
```

Output

```
ENTER A NUMBER : 12

DO YOU WANT TO CRTEATE MORE NODES: y

ENTER A NUMBER : 65

DO YOU WANT TO CRTEATE MORE NODES: y

ENTER A NUMBER : 98

DO YOU WANT TO CRTEATE MORE NODES: y

ENTER A NUMBER : 22

DO YOU WANT TO CRTEATE MORE NODES: n

ENTER THE VALUE OF LAST NODE: 3

After Inserting a node list is as follows:
    12    65    98    22    3

Process exited after 8.413 seconds with return value 0
Press any key to continue . . .
```

7.4.4   /* Insert a Node Into a Simple Linked List When the Node Is Known */

```
#include<iostream>
#include<iomanip>
#include<stdlib.h>
using namespace std;
struct link
{
        int info;
        struct link *next;
};
struct link start, *first, *New,*previous;
/* Function main */
void create(struct link *);
void display (struct link  *);
void insert(struct link *);

int main()
{
        struct link *node;
create(node);
```

```
        insert(node);
        display(node);
}


void create(struct link *node) /*LOGIC TO CREATE A LINK
LIST*/
{
        char ch='y';
        start.next = NULL;
        node = &start;       /* Point to the start of the list */
        while(ch =='y' || ch=='Y')
        {
                node->next = (struct link* )
                malloc(sizeof(struct link));
                node = node->next;
                cout<<"\n ENTER A NUMBER : ";
                cin>>node->info;
                node->next = NULL;
                cout<<"\n DO YOU WANT TO CRTEATE MORE NODES: ";
                cin>>ch;
        }
}


void display(struct link *node)
{                                    /*DISPLAY THE LINKED LIST*/
        node = start.next;
        cout<<"\n After Inserting a node list is as
        follows:\n";
        while (node)
        {
                cout<<setw(5)<<node->info;
                node = node->next;
        }
}

void insert(struct link *node)
{                           /* Inserting a node */
        int non = 0;
        int pos;
        node = start.next;
        previous = &start;
        cout<<"\n ENTER THE POSITION TO INSERT:";
        cin>>pos;
        while(node)
        {
                if((non+1) == pos)
                {
```

```
                    New = (struct link* ) malloc(sizeof(struct
link));

                    New->next = node ;
                    previous->next = New;
                    cout<<endl<<"\n Input the node value: ";
                    cin>>New->info;
                    break ;
            }
            else
            {
                    node = node->next;
                    previous= previous->next;
            }
            non++;
        }
}
```

OUTPUT

7.4.5   /* Insert a Node Into a Simple Linked List Information Is Known and Put After Some Specified Node */

```
#include<iostream>
#include<iomanip>
#include<stdlib.h>
using namespace std;
struct link
{
```

```
        int info;
        struct link *next;
};
struct link start, *first, *New,*before;
/* Function main */
void create(struct link *);
void display (struct link  *);
void insert(struct link *);

int main()
{
        struct link *node;
create(node);
        insert(node);
        display(node);
}


void create(struct link *node) /*LOGIC TO CREATE A LINK
LIST*/
{
        char ch='y';
        start.next = NULL;
        node = &start;       /* Point to the start of the list */
        while(ch =='y' || ch=='Y')
        {
                node->next = (struct link* )
                malloc(sizeof(struct link));
                node = node->next;
                cout<<"\n ENTER A NUMBER : ";
                cin>>node->info;
                node->next = NULL;
                cout<<"\n DO YOU WANT TO CRTEATE MORE NODES: ";
                cin>>ch;
        }
}


void display(struct link *node)
{                                   /*DISPLAY THE LINKED LIST*/
        node = start.next;
        cout<<"\n After Inserting a node list is as
        follows:\n";
        while (node)
        {
                cout<<setw(5)<<node->info;
                node = node->next;
        }
}
```

```
void insert(struct link *node)
{
        int no= 0;
        int ins;
        node = start.next;
        before = &start;
        cout<<"\n Input value node the node you want to
        insert:";
        fflush(stdin);
        cin>>ins;
        while(node)
        {
                if(node->info <= ins)
                {
                        New = (struct link* ) malloc(sizeof(struct
link));
                        New->next = node;
                        before->next = New;
                        New->info = ins;
                        break ;
                }
                else
                {
                        node = node->next;
                        before= before->next;
                }
                no++;
        }
}
```

Output

```
ENTER A NUMBER : 12

DO YOU WANT TO CRTEATE MORE NODES: y

ENTER A NUMBER : 32

DO YOU WANT TO CRTEATE MORE NODES: y

ENTER A NUMBER : 85

DO YOU WANT TO CRTEATE MORE NODES: y

ENTER A NUMBER : 95

DO YOU WANT TO CRTEATE MORE NODES: y

ENTER A NUMBER : 4

DO YOU WANT TO CRTEATE MORE NODES: n

Input value node the node you want to insert:95

After Inserting a node list is as follows:
    95    12    32    85    95    4

Process exited after 12.81 seconds with return value 0
Press any key to continue . . .
```

7.4.6   /* Deleting the First Node From a Simple Linked List */

```cpp
#include<iostream>
#include<iomanip>
#include<stdlib.h>
using namespace std;
struct link
{
      int info;
      struct link *next;
};
struct link start, *previous,*node;
/* Function main */
void create(struct link *);
void display (struct link  *);
void delet(struct link *);

int main()
{
create(node);
printf("\n THE CREATED LINKED LIST IS :\n");
      display(node);
      delet(node);
```

```cpp
printf("\n AFTER DELETING THE FIRST NODE THE LINKED LIST IS ");
        display(node);
}


void create(struct link *node) /*LOGIC TO CREATE A LINK LIST*/
{
        char ch='y';
        start.next = NULL;
        node = &start;        /* Point to the start of the list */
        while(ch =='y' || ch=='Y')
        {
                node->next = (struct link* ) malloc(sizeof(struct
link));
                node = node->next;
                cout<<"\n ENTER A NUMBER : ";
                cin>>node->info;
                node->next = NULL;
                cout<<"\n DO YOU WANT TO CRTEATE MORE NODES: ";
                cin>>ch;
        }
}


void display(struct link *node)
{                                       /*DISPLAY THE LINKED LIST*/
        node = start.next;

        while (node)
        {
                cout<<setw(5)<<node->info;
                node = node->next;
        }
}

void delet(struct link *node)
{
        node = start.next;
        previous = &start;
        if (node == NULL)
                cout<<"\n Under flow";
        else
        {
                previous->next = node->next;
                free(node);
        }
}
```

Output

```
ENTER A NUMBER : 12

DO YOU WANT TO CRIEATE MORE NODES: Y

ENTER A NUMBER : 34

DO YOU WANT TO CRIEATE MORE NODES: Y

ENTER A NUMBER : 65

DO YOU WANT TO CRIEATE MORE NODES: Y

ENTER A NUMBER : 32

DO YOU WANT TO CRIEATE MORE NODES: N

THE CREATED LINKED LIST IS :
   12   34   65   32
AFTER DELETING THE FIRST NODE THE LINKED LIST IS    34   65   32

Process exited after 62.4 seconds with return value 0
Press any key to continue . . .
```

7.4.7 /* Deleting the Last Node From a Simple Linked List */

```cpp
#include<iostream>
#include<iomanip>
#include<stdlib.h>
using namespace std;
struct link
{
        int info;
        struct link *next;
};
struct link start, *previous,*node;
/* Function main */
void create(struct link *);
void display (struct link  *);
void delet(struct link *);

int main()
{
create(node);
printf("\n THE CREATED LINKED LIST IS :\n");
        display(node);
        delet(node);
printf("\n AFTER DELETING THE LAST NODE THE LINKED LIST IS ");
        display(node);

}


void create(struct link *node) /*LOGIC TO CREATE A LINK LIST*/
{
```

```cpp
    char ch='y';
    start.next = NULL;
    node = &start;     /* Point to the start of the list */
    while(ch =='y' || ch=='Y')
    {
    node->next = (struct link* ) malloc(sizeof(struct link));
        node = node->next;
        cout<<"\n ENTER A NUMBER : ";
        cin>>node->info;
        node->next = NULL;
        cout<<"\n DO YOU WANT TO CRTEATE MORE NODES: ";
        cin>>ch;
    }
}


void display(struct link *node)
{                                   /*DISPLAY THE LINKED LIST*/
    node = start.next;

    while (node)
    {
        cout<<setw(5)<<node->info;
        node = node->next;
    }
}

void delet(struct link *node)
{
    int n = 0;
    node = start.next;
    previous = &start;
    if (node == NULL)
                cout<<"\n Underflow";
            else
            while(node)
            {
                node = node->next;
                previous = previous->next;
                n++;
            }

    node = start.next;
    previous = &start;
    while(n != 1)
    {
        node = node->next;
        previous = previous->next;
        n --;
```

```
        }

                previous->next = node->next;
                free(node);
        }
```

Output

7.4.8 /* Deleting a Node From a Simple Linked List When Node Number Is Known */

```
#include<iostream>
#include<iomanip>
#include<stdlib.h>
using namespace std;
struct link
{
        int info;
        struct link *next;
};
struct link start, *previous,*node;
/* Function main */
void create(struct link *);
void display (struct link  *);
void delet(struct link *);

int main()
{
```

```
create(node);
printf("\n THE CREATED LINKED LIST IS :\n");
        display(node);
        delet(node);
printf("\n AFTER DELETION THE INKED LIST IS ");
        display(node);

}


void create(struct link *node) /*LOGIC TO CREATE A LINK
LIST*/
{
        char ch='y';
        start.next = NULL;
        node = &start;      /* Point to the start of the list */
        while(ch =='y' || ch=='Y')
        {
                node->next = (struct link* ) malloc(sizeof(struct
link));
                node = node->next;
                cout<<"\n ENTER A NUMBER : ";
                cin>>node->info;
                node->next = NULL;
                cout<<"\n DO YOU WANT TO CRTEATE MORE NODES: ";
                cin>>ch;
        }
}


void display(struct link *node)
{                                    /*DISPLAY THE LINKED LIST*/
        node = start.next;

        while (node)
        {
                cout<<setw(5)<<node->info;
                node = node->next;
        }
}

void delet(struct link *node)
{
        int n = 1;
        int pos;
        node = start.next;
        previous = &start;
        printf("\n Input node number you want to delete:");
        scanf(" %d", &pos);
```

```
    while(node)
    {
        if(n == pos)
        {
            previous->next = node->next;
            free(node);
            break ;
        }
        else
        {
            node = node->next;
            previous = previous->next;
        }
        n++;
    }
}
```

OUTPUT

```
ENTER A NUMBER : 45

DO YOU WANT TO CRTEATE MORE NODES: Y

ENTER A NUMBER : 32

DO YOU WANT TO CRTEATE MORE NODES: Y

ENTER A NUMBER : 95

DO YOU WANT TO CRTEATE MORE NODES: Y

ENTER A NUMBER : 25

DO YOU WANT TO CRTEATE MORE NODES: N

THE CREATED LINKED LIST IS :
   45   32   95   25
Input node number you want to delete:3

AFTER DELETION THE INKED LIST IS     45   32   25

Process exited after 14.11 seconds with return value 0
Press any key to continue . . .
```

7.4.9   Deleting a Node From a Simple Linked List When Information of a Node Is Given

```
#include<iostream>
#include<iomanip>
#include<stdlib.h>
using namespace std;
struct link
```

```
{
        int info;
        struct link *next;
};
struct link start, *previous,*node;
/* Function main */
void create(struct link *);
void display (struct link  *);
void delet(struct link *);

int main()
{
create(node);
printf("\n THE CREATED LINKED LIST IS :\n");
        display(node);
        delet(node);
printf("\n AFTER DELETION THE INKED LIST IS ");
        display(node);

}


void create(struct link *node) /*LOGIC TO CREATE A LINK LIST*/
{
        char ch='y';
        start.next = NULL;
        node = &start;       /* Point to the start of the list */
        while(ch =='y' || ch=='Y')
        {
                node->next = (struct link* ) malloc(sizeof(struct
                link));
                node = node->next;
                cout<<"\n ENTER A NUMBER : ";
                cin>>node->info;
                node->next = NULL;
                cout<<"\n DO YOU WANT TO CRTEATE MORE NODES: ";
                cin>>ch;
        }
}


void display(struct link *node)
{                                  /*DISPLAY THE LINKED LIST*/
        node = start.next;

        while (node)
        {
                cout<<setw(5)<<node->info;
                node = node->next;
        }
```

```
}

void delet(struct link *node)
{
        int non= 1;
        int dnode;
        node = start.next;
        previous = &start;
        printf("\n Input information of a node you want to
        delete: ");
        scanf("%d", &dnode);
        while(node)
        {
if(node->info == dnode)
        {
printf("\n Position of the information in the list is : %d",
non);
                        previous->next = node->next;

                        free(node);
                        break ;
                }
                else
                {
                        node = node->next;
                        previous = previous->next;
                }
                non++;
        }
}
```

OUTPUT

```
ENTER A NUMBER : 25

DO YOU WANT TO CRTEATE MORE NODES: Y

ENTER A NUMBER : 54

DO YOU WANT TO CRTEATE MORE NODES: Y

ENTER A NUMBER : 76

DO YOU WANT TO CRTEATE MORE NODES: Y

ENTER A NUMBER : 89

DO YOU WANT TO CRTEATE MORE NODES: Y

ENTER A NUMBER : 32

DO YOU WANT TO CRTEATE MORE NODES: N

THE CREATED LINKED LIST IS :
   25    54    76    89    32
Input information of a node you want to delete: 54

Position of the information in the list is : 2
AFTER DELETION THE INKED LIST IS    25    76    89    32

Process exited after 15.22 seconds with return value 0
Press any key to continue . . .
```

ALGORITHM FOR SEARCHING

```
struct link
 {
 int info;
struct link *next;
 };
```

SEARCH(START,NODE,NO) [START IS THE STRUCTURE TYPE
                OF VARIABLE]
                [NODE IS THE STRUCTURE TYPE OF
                POINTER VARIABLE]
                [NO IS THE INFORMATION TO SEARCH]

STEP-1 : NODE := NEXT[START]

STEP-2 : SET COUNT :=1
    SET OPT := 0

STEP-3 : REPEAT WHILE(NODE != NULL)
        IF(COUNT = NO) THEN:
        WRITE : INFO[NODE]

```
                    WRITE : "IS FOUND AT "
                    WRITE : COUNT
                    WRITE : "POSITION"
                    OPT:=1
                    RETURN
              ELSE :
                    NODE := NEXT[NODE]
                    FIRST := NEXT[FIRST]
                    COUNT:=COUNT+1
                    [END OF IF]
              [END OF LOOP]
STEP-4 : IF (OPT != 1)
              WRITE : "THE NUMBER IS NOT FOUND"
          [END OF IF]
STEP-5 : RETURN
```

7.4.10   /* SEARCH A NODE INTO A SIMPLE LINKED LIST WITH INFORMATION IS KNOWN */

```cpp
#include<iostream>
#include<iomanip>
#include<stdlib.h>
using namespace std;
struct link
{
        int info;
        struct link *next;
};
struct link start, *new1,*node;
/* Function main */
void create(struct link *);
void display (struct link  *);
void search(struct link *);

int main()
{
create(node);
printf("\n THE CREATED LINKED LIST IS :\n");
        display(node);

        search (node);

}
```

```
void create(struct link *node) /*LOGIC TO CREATE A LINK LIST*/
{
        char ch='y';
        start.next = NULL;
        node = &start;        /* Point to the start of the list */
        while(ch =='y' || ch=='Y')
        {
                node->next = (struct link* )
                malloc(sizeof(struct link));
                node = node->next;
                cout<<"\n ENTER A NUMBER : ";
                cin>>node->info;
                node->next = NULL;
                cout<<"\n DO YOU WANT TO CRTEATE MORE NODES: ";
                cin>>ch;
        }
}


void display(struct link *node)
{                                    /*DISPLAY THE LINKED LIST*/
        node = start.next;

        while (node)
        {
                cout<<setw(5)<<node->info;
                node = node->next;
        }
}

void search(struct link *node)
{
        int val;
        int flag = 0,n=0;
        node = &start ;
        cout<<"\n ENTER THE NUMBER TO SEARCH";
        cin>>val;
        if (node == NULL)
        {
                cout<<"\n List is empty";
        }
        while(node)
        {
                if( val == node->info )
                {
        cout<<"\n THE NUMBER "<<val<<" IS AT "<<n<<" POSITION
IN THE LIST";
                        node = node->next;
                        flag = 1;
```

```
                        break;
                }
                else
                {
                        node = node->next;
                }
                n++;
        }
        if(!flag)
        {
                cout<<"\n THE NUMBER %d IS NOT FOUND IN THE
LIST"<<val;
        }
}
```

OUTPUT

```
ENTER A NUMBER : 25
DO YOU WANT TO CRTEATE MORE NODES: y
ENTER A NUMBER : 3
DO YOU WANT TO CRTEATE MORE NODES: y
ENTER A NUMBER : 85
DO YOU WANT TO CRTEATE MORE NODES: y
ENTER A NUMBER : 95
DO YOU WANT TO CRTEATE MORE NODES: y
ENTER A NUMBER : 24
DO YOU WANT TO CRTEATE MORE NODES: n
THE CREATED LINKED LIST IS :
    25     3    85    95    24
ENTER THE NUMBER TO SEARCH24

THE NUMBER 24 IS AT 5 POSITION IN THE LIST
Process exited after 14.51 seconds with return value 0
Press any key to continue . . .
```

7.4.11   /* Sorting a Linked List in Ascending Order */

```
#include<iostream>
#include<iomanip>
#include<stdlib.h>
using namespace std;
struct link
{
        int info;
        struct link *next;
};
```

```
struct link start, *New,*node,*temp;
/* Function main */
void create(struct link *);
void display (struct link  *);
void sort(struct link *);

int main()
{
create(node);
cout<<"\n THE CREATED LINKED LIST IS :\n";
        display(node);

        sort(node);
        cout<<"\n AFTER SORT THE LINKED LIST IS :\n";
        display(node);


}


void create(struct link *node) /*LOGIC TO CREATE A LINK LIST*/
{
        char ch='y';
        start.next = NULL;
        node = &start;        /* Point to the start of the list */
        while(ch =='y' || ch=='Y')
        {
                node->next = (struct link* ) malloc(sizeof(struct
                link));
                node = node->next;
                cout<<"\n ENTER A NUMBER : ";
                cin>>node->info;
                node->next = NULL;
                cout<<"\n DO YOU WANT TO CRTEATE MORE NODES: ";
                cin>>ch;
        }
}


void display(struct link *node)
{                                        /*DISPLAY THE LINKED LIST*/
        node = start.next;

        while (node)
        {
```

```
              cout<<setw(5)<<node->info;
              node = node->next;
       }
}

void sort(struct link *node)
{
       for(New = start.next; New->next != NULL; New =
New->next)
              {
              for(temp = New->next; temp != NULL; temp =
temp->next)
                   {
                   if(New->info > temp->info)
                     {
                        int t = New->info;
                        New->info = temp->info;
                        temp->info = t;
                     }
                   }
              }
   }
```

OUTPUT

```
ENTER A NUMBER : 58

DO YOU WANT TO CRTEATE MORE NODES: y

ENTER A NUMBER : 7

DO YOU WANT TO CRTEATE MORE NODES: y

ENTER A NUMBER : 65

DO YOU WANT TO CRTEATE MORE NODES: y

ENTER A NUMBER : 3

DO YOU WANT TO CRTEATE MORE NODES: y

ENTER A NUMBER : 11

DO YOU WANT TO CRTEATE MORE NODES: n

THE CREATED LINKED LIST IS :
   58    7   65    3   11
AFTER SORT THE LINKED LIST IS :
    3    7   11   58   65
_____
Process exited after 9.188 seconds with return value 0
Press any key to continue . . .
```

7.4.12   /* Reversing a Linked List */

```
#include <stdio.h>
#include <alloc.h>
struct link
{
        int info;
        struct link *next;
};
int i, no;
struct link *start, *node, *previous, *current, *counter;
void display(struct link *);
void create(struct link *);
struct link * reverse(struct link *);
void main()
{
        struct link *node;
        struct link *p;
        node = (struct link *) malloc(sizeof(struct link));
        create(node);
        printf("\n Original List is as follows:\n");
        display(node);
        p = ( struct link *)malloc(sizeof(struct link));
        p = reverse(node);
        printf("\n After reverse operation list is as
follows:\n");
        display(p);
}
struct link * reverse(struct link *start)
{
        current = start;
        previous = NULL ;

        while( current != NULL )
        {
                counter = (struct link *)malloc(sizeof(struct link));
                counter = current->next ;
                current->next = previous ;
                previous = current ;
                current = counter;
        }
        start = previous;
        return(start);
}
void  display(struct link *node)
{
        while (node != NULL)
        {
```

```
                    printf(" %d", node->info);
                    node = node->next;
            }
}
void create(struct link *node)
{
        int i;
        int no;
        printf("\n Input the number of nodes you want to
        create:");
        scanf("%d", &no);
        for (i = 0; i < no ; i++)
        {
                printf("\nEnter the number");
                scanf("%d", &node->info);
                node->next = (struct link* ) malloc(sizeof(struct
                link));
                if( i == no - 1)
                        node->next = NULL;
                else
                        node = node->next;
        }
        node->next = NULL;
}
```

7.4.13   Program for Student Data Using Linked List

```
# include<iostream>
#include<fstream>
#include<stdlib.h>
#include<iomanip>
using namespace std;
struct student
 {
        string fname,lname;
        int yob,mob,dob;
        char sex;
        float mark;
        struct student *next;
 };
struct student start,*last,*New;
//method declarations
void insert(struct student *);
void create(struct student *);
void display(struct student *);
void average(struct student *);
void maximum(struct student *);
void search(struct student *);
```

```cpp
//driver program
int main()
{                        /* FUNCTION MAIN */
     struct student *node;
     create(node);   //create the link list
     int opt;
     //infinite loop
     while(1)
       {//display the menu
             cout<<endl<<"1. Add Friend \n2. Display
friends\n 8. Print Average age of friends\n 9. Print Male
Friends\N0. Exit\n";
             cout<<endl<<"Enter choice";
             cin>>opt; //read the choice
             //call to the corresponding methods according
to the users input
             if(opt==1)
               insert(node);
             else
               if(opt==2)
                 display(node);
                 else
                 if(opt==8)
                   average(node);
                   else
                 if(opt==9)
                   printmale(node);
                   else
                 if(opt==0)
                   exit(0);
                   else
                 cout<<endl<<"Invalid choice";
         }

}
//create method read the data from file and stores it into
link list
void create(struct student *node)
{
     int n;
     char ch;
     string name;
     start.next = NULL;  /* Empty list */
     node = &start;      /* Point to the start of the list */

     while(1)
      {

             //allocate memory for a node of list
```

```
            node->next = (struct student* ) malloc(sizeof
            (struct student));
            node = node->next; //shift the node to next node
            cout<<endl<<"Enter the first name";
            cin>>name;
            node->fname=name;
            cout<<endl<<"Enter the last name";
            cin>>name;
            node->lname=name;
            cout<<endl<<"Enter the year of birth";
            cin>>n;
            node->yob=n;
            cout<<endl<<"Enter the month of birth";
            cin>>n;
            node->mob=n;
            cout<<endl<<"Enter the day of birth";
            cin>>n;
            node->dob=n;
            cout<<endl<<"Enter the sex[m/f]";
            cin>>ch;
            node->sex=ch;

node->next = NULL;//assign NULL to end
cout<<endl<<"Do you want to create more nodes[y/n]";
cin>>ch;
if(ch=='n'|| ch=='N')
break;
        }
 }


//insert a new node
void insert(struct student *node)
{
string name;
int n;
char ch;
        node = start.next;
        last = &start;
        while(node)//loop will continue till end
        {
                node = node->next;
                last= last->next;
        }
        if(node == NULL)
        {
                //allocate new memory for new node
                New = (struct student* ) malloc(sizeof(struct
                student));
                //logic for insertion
```

```
                    New->next = node ;
                    last->next = New;
                    //ask data to user
                    cout<<endl<<"Enter the first name";
                    cin>>name;
                    New->fname=name;
                    cout<<endl<<"Enter the last name";
                    cin>>name;
                    New->lname=name;
                    cout<<endl<<"Enter the year of birth";
                    cin>>n;
                    New->yob=n;
                    cout<<endl<<"Enter the month of birth";
                    cin>>n;
                    New->mob=n;
                    cout<<endl<<"Enter the day of birth";
                    cin>>n;
                    New->dob=n;
                    cout<<endl<<"Enter the sex[m/f]";
                    cin>>ch;
                    New->sex=ch;
          }
}
//method to diaply the data
void display(struct student *node)
{
          node = start.next;//points to first node oflist
          while (node)//loop will continue till end of list
          {//print the data
cout<<endl<<node->fname<<"\t"<<node->lname<<"\t"<<node-
>yob<<"\t"<<node->mob<<"\t"<<node->dob<<"\t"<<node->sex;
node = node->next;//shift the pointer to next node
          }
 }


 void printmale(struct stiudent *node)
  {
          node = start.next;//points to first node oflist
          while (node)//loop will continue till end of list
          {
                    if(node->sex=='m'||node->sex=='M')
          //print the data
cout<<endl<<node->fname<<"\t"<<node->lname<<"\t"<<node-
>yob<<"\t"<<node->mob<<"\t"<<node->dob<<"\t"<<node->sex;
node = node->next;//shift the pointer to next node
          }
  }

  void average(struct stiudent *node)
  {
```

```
        float avg;
        int sum=0,c=0;
        node = start.next;//points to first node oflist
        while (node)//loop will continue till end of list
        {
                c++;
                sum=sum+ node->age;

node = node->next;//shift the pointer to next node
        }
        avg=(float)sum/c;
    }

  void youngest(struct stiudent *node)
    {
        int minyear,minmon,minday,c=0;
        string name1,name2;
        node = start.next;//points to first node oflist
        minyear=node->yob;
        minmon=node->mob;
        minday=node->dob;

        while (node)//loop will continue till end of list
        {
                if(minyear>node->yob)
                    {
                        name1=node->fname;
                        name2=node->lname;
                    }
                if(minyear == node->yob && minmom > node->mob)
                    {
                        name1=node->fname;
                        name2=node->lname;
                        }
        if(minyear == node->yob && minmom == node->mob &&
minday >node->dob)
                    {
                        name1=node->fname;
                        name2=node->lname;
                        }
node = node->next;//shift the pointer to next node
        }
        cout<<endl<<"Youngest Friend is "<<name1<<"\t"<<name2;
    }

  void oldest(struct stiudent *node)
    {
        int minyear,minmon,minday,c=0;
```

```
      string name1,name2;
      node = start.next;//points to first node oflist
      minyear=node->yob;
      minmon=node->mob;
      minday=node->dob;

      while (node)//loop will continue till end of list
      {
            if(minyear < node->yob)
               {
                  name1=node->fname;
                  name2=node->lname;
                  }
            if(minyear == node->yob && minmom < node->mob)
               {
                  name1=node->fname;
                  name2=node->lname;
                  }
      if(minyear == node->yob && minmom == node->mob &&
minday < node->dob)
               {
                  name1=node->fname;
                  name2=node->lname;
                  }
node = node->next;//shift the pointer to next node
      }
   cout<<endl<<"Oldest Friend is "<<name1<<"\t"<<name2;
 }
```

OUTPUT

```
1. Display Student Details
2. Claculate average of all student marks
3. Search for a particular student's mark
4. Find Maximum
5. Add a new student
6. Quit program
Enter choice1

John      101561724        78
Andy      101453421        67
Bahara    101452731        54
Sam       202673489        23
Peter     101345782        98
Mathew    101672431        90
Adam      101872354        80
Sandra    101892312        75
Samy      101673423        34
Amanda    101782314        65
1. Display Student Details
2. Claculate average of all student marks
3. Search for a particular student's mark
4. Find Maximum
5. Add a new student
6. Quit program
Enter choice2

Average mark is : 66.40
1. Display Student Details
2. Claculate average of all student marks
3. Search for a particular student's mark
4. Find Maximum
5. Add a new student
6. Quit program
Enter choice3

Enter the id of student to know the mark101872354

The mark of student with ID 101872354 is 80.00
1. Display Student Details
2. Claculate average of all student marks
3. Search for a particular student's mark
4. Find Maximum
5. Add a new student
6. Quit program
Enter choice4

Peter with ID 101345782 secures highest mark as 98.00
```

```
1. Display Student Details
2. Claculate average of all student marks
3. Search for a particular student's mark
4. Find Maximum
5. Add a new student
6. Quit program
Enter choice5

Enter the nameSonu

Enter the ID101782876

Enter the mark95

1. Display Student Details
2. Claculate average of all student marks
3. Search for a particular student's mark
4. Find Maximum
5. Add a new student
6. Quit program
Enter choice1

John      101561724        78.00
Andy      101453421        67.00
Babara    101452731        54.00
Sam       202673489        23.00
Peter     101345782        98.00
Mathew    101672431        90.00
Adam      101872354        80.00
Sandra    101892312        75.00
Samy      101673423        34.00
Amanda    101782314        65.00
Sonu      101782876        95.00
1. Display Student Details
2. Claculate average of all student marks
3. Search for a particular student's mark
4. Find Maximum
5. Add a new student
6. Quit program
Enter choice2

Average mark is : 69.00
1. Display Student Details
2. Claculate average of all student marks
3. Search for a particular student's mark
4. Find Maximum
5. Add a new student
6. Quit program
Enter choice6

_____
Process exited after 98.42 seconds with return value 0
Press any key to continue . . .
```

7.5   Double Link List

The double link list is designed in such a way that each node of the list can able to store two address parts one is its next and other is its previous node.
   The general format of the node of a double link list is

```
Struct tagname
  {
Data type member1;
```

```
Data type member2;
..............................
..............................
..............................
Data type membern;
Struct link *var1,*var2;
    };
```

Ex:

```
Struct Dlink
   {
   int info;
   struct Dlink *next,*prev ;
     };
```

Graphically

START

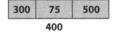

```
NULL        200
     100
```

```
     100   59   300
           200
```

```
          200   75   400
                300
```

```
               300   75   500
                     400
```

```
                    400         NULL
```

LOGIC FOR CREATION

```
Struct link
   {
        int info;
          struct link *next,*prev;
     };

Struct link   start,*node;
Node=&start;
Allocate a memory to node->next
Node->next ->prev = node
Node = node->next
Node->next = NULL
```

ALGORITHM FOR CREATION OF A DOUBLE LINK LIST

CREATE(START,NODE)
STEP-1 : NEXT[START]:=NULL
        PREV[START] :=NULL
STEP-2 : ALLOCATE A MEMORY TO NEXT[NODE]
        PREV[NEXT][NODE] := NODE
        NODE := NEXT[NODE]
        NEXT[NODE] := NULL
STEP-3 INPUT : INFO[NODE]
STEP-4 : REPEAT STEP-2 AND STEP-3 TO CREATE MORE NODES
STEP-5 : RETURN

ALGORITHM FOR TRAVERSE OF A DOUBLE LINK LIST

TRAVERSE(START,NODE)
STEP-1 : NODE : = NEXT[START]
STEP-2 : WRITE : "FORWARD TRAVERSE"
STEP-3 : REPEAT WHILE (NEXT[NODE] != NULL)
        WRITE : INFO[NODE]
        NODE := NEXT[NODE]
        [END OF LOOP]
STEP-4 : WRITE : "REVERSE TRAVERSE"
STEP-5 : REPEAT WHILE (PREV[NODE]!=NULL)
        WRITE : INFO[NODE]
         NODE : = PREV[NODE]
        [END OF LOOP]
STEP-6 : RETURN

ALGORITHM FOR INSERTION OF A NODE AT BEGIN

INSBEG(START,NODE)
STEP-1 : NODE : = NEXT[START]
STEP-2 : ALLOCATE A MEMORY TO NEW
STEP-3 : PREV[NEW] := PREV[NODE]
        NEXT[NEW] := NODE
        NEXT[PREV[NODE]] := NEW
        PREV[NODE] :=NEW
STEP-4 : INPUT : INFO[NEW]
STEP-5 : RETURN

ALGORITHM FOR INSERTION OF A NODE AT END

INSLAST(START,NODE)
STEP-1 : NODE : = NEXT[START]
STEP-2 : REPEAT WHILE (NEXT[NODE]!=NULL)
         NODE : = NEXT[NODE]
         [END OF LOOP]
STEP-3 : ALLOCATE A MEMORY TO NEW
STEP-4 : PREV[NEW] := PREV[NODE]
         NEXT[NEW] := NODE
         NEXT[PREV[NODE]] := NEW
         PREV[NODE] :=NEW
STEP-4 : INPUT : INFO[NEW]
STEP-5 : RETURN

ALGORITHM FOR INSERTION OF A NODE WHEN NODE NUMBER IS KNOWN

INSNODE(START,NODE,NO)
STEP-1 : NODE : = NEXT[START]
STEP-2 : COUNT :=1
STEP-3 : REPEAT WHILE (NEXT[NODE]!=NULL)
         IF(COUNT = NO) THEN:
             ALLOCATE A MEMORY TO NEW
                 PREV[NEW] := PREV[NODE]
                 NEXT[NEW] := NODE
                 NEXT[PREV[NODE]] := NEW
                 PREV[NODE] :=NEW
         ELSE:
             NODE : = NEXT[NODE]
             COUNT := COUNT+1
         [END OF IF]
         [END OF LOOP]
STEP-4 : INPUT : INFO[NEW]
STEP-5 : RETURN

ALGORITHM FOR INSERTION OF A NODE WHEN INFORMATION IS KNOWN

INSINFO(START,NODE,VAL)
STEP-1 : NODE : = NEXT[START]
STEP-2 : REPEAT WHILE (NEXT[NODE]!=NULL)
          IF(INFOR[NODE] <=VAL) THEN:
                  ALLOCATE A MEMORY TO NEW
                  PREV[NEW] := PREV[NODE]
                  NEXT[NEW] := NODE
                  NEXT[PREV[NODE]] := NEW
                  PREV[NODE] :=NEW
          ELSE:
             NODE : = NEXT[NODE]
          [END OF IF]
          [END OF LOOP]
STEP-3 : INFO[NEW] :=VAL
STEP-4 : RETURN

DELETION

ALGORITHM FOR DELETION OF A NODE AT BEGIN

DELBEG(START,NODE)
STEP-1 : NODE : = NEXT[START]
STEP-2 : WRITE : INFO[NODE]
STEP-3 : NEXT[PREV[NODE]] := NEXT[NODE]
          PREV[NEXT[NODE]] := PREV[NODE]
STEP-4 : FREE(NODE)
STEP-5 : RETURN

ALGORITHM FOR DELETION OF A NODE AT END

DELLAST(START,NODE)
STEP-1 : NODE : = NEXT[START]
STEP-2 : COUNT : = 1
STEP-3 : REPEAT WHILE (NEXT[NODE]!=NULL)
          NODE : = NEXT[NODE]
          COUNT : = COUNT+1
          [END OF LOOP]

STEP-4 : NODE : NEXT[START]
STEP-5 : REPEAT WHILE (COUNT != 1)
       NODE : = NEXT[NODE]
       COUNT : = COUNT-1
    [END OF LOOP]

STEP-6 : WRITE : INFO[NODE]
STEP-7 : NEXT[PREV[NODE]] := NEXT[NODE]
       PREV[NEXT[NODE]] := PREV[NODE]
STEP-8 : FREE(NODE) **STEP-9** : RETURN

OR

DELLAST(START,NODE)
STEP-1 : NODE : = NEXT[START]
STEP-2 : REPEAT WHILE (NEXT[NODE]!=NULL)
       NODE : = NEXT[NODE]
       COUNT : = COUNT+1
    [END OF LOOP]
STEP-3 : NODE : PREV[NODE]
STEP-4 : WRITE : INFO[NODE]
STEP-5 : NEXT[PREV[NODE]] := NEXT[NODE]
       PREV[NEXT[NODE]] := PREV[NODE]
STEP-6 : FREE(NODE)
STEP-7 : RETURN

ALGORITHM FOR DELETION OF A NODE WHEN NODE NUMBER IS KNOWN

INSNODE(START,NODE,NO)
STEP-1 : NODE : = NEXT[START]
STEP-2 : COUNT :=1
STEP-3 : REPEAT WHILE (NEXT[NODE]!=NULL)
    IF(COUNT = NO) THEN:
       WRITE : INFO[NODE]
       NEXT[PREV[NODE]] := NEXT[NODE]
        PREV[NEXT[NODE]] := PREV[NODE]
      FREE(NODE)

```
        ELSE:
              NODE : = NEXT[NODE]
              COUNT := COUNT+1
        [END OF IF]
        [END OF LOOP]
STEP-4 : RETURN
```

ALGORITHM FOR INSERTION OF A NODE WHEN INFORMATION IS KNOWN

```
INSINFO(START,NODE,VAL)
STEP-1 : NODE : = NEXT[START]
STEP-2 : REPEAT WHILE (NEXT[NODE]!=NULL)
        IF(INFOR[NODE] =VAL) THEN:
              WRITE : INFO[NODE]
              NEXT[PREV[NODE]] := NEXT[NODE]
                PREV[NEXT[NODE]] := PREV[NODE]
            FREE(NODE)

        ELSE:
              NODE : = NEXT[NODE]
        [END OF IF]
        [END OF LOOP]
STEP-3 : RETURN
```

7.6 Programs on Double Linked List

7.6.1 /* Creation of Double Linked List */

```cpp
#include <iostream>
#include<iomanip>
# include <stdlib.h>
using namespace std;
struct link
{
      int info;
      struct link *next;
      struct link *previous;
};
struct link start;
void create (struct link *);
void display (struct link *);
```

```
void create(struct link *node)
{
      char ch='y';
      start.next = NULL;   /* Empty list */
      start.previous = NULL;
      node = &start;       /* Point to the start of the list */
      while( ch == 'y' || ch=='Y')
      {
            node->next = (struct link *)
            malloc(sizeof(struct link));
            node->next->previous = node;
            node = node->next;
            cout<<"\n ENTER THE NUMBER";
            fflush(stdin);
            cin>>node->info;
            node->next = NULL;
            fflush(stdin);
            cout<<"\nDO YOU WANT TO CREATE MORE NODES[Y/N] ";
            fflush(stdin);
            cin>>ch;
      }
}

void display (struct link *node)
{
      node = start.next;
      cout<<endl<<"Link list elements printing in Forward
Direction\n";
      while(node->next)
      {
      cout<<setw(5)<<node->info;
            node = node->next;
      }
            cout<<setw(5)<<node->info;
      cout<<endl<<"Link list elements printing in Backward
Direction\n";
      do {
            cout<<setw(5)<<node->info;
            node = node->previous;
      } while (node->previous);
}
int main()
{
      struct link *node;
      create(node);
      cout<<"\n AFTER CREATING THE LINKED LIST IS \n";
      display(node);
}
```

Output

```
ENTER THE NUMBER25

DO YOU WANT TO CREATE MORE NODES[Y/N] y

ENTER THE NUMBER32

DO YOU WANT TO CREATE MORE NODES[Y/N] y

ENTER THE NUMBER95

DO YOU WANT TO CREATE MORE NODES[Y/N] y

ENTER THE NUMBER54

DO YOU WANT TO CREATE MORE NODES[Y/N] n

AFTER CREATING THE LINKED LIST IS

Link list elements printing in Forward Direction
    25    32    95    54
Link list elements printing in Backward Direction
    54    95    32    25

Process exited after 8.334 seconds with return value 0
Press any key to continue . . .
```

7.6.2   /* Inserting First Node in the Doubly Linked List */

```cpp
# include <iostream>
#include<iomanip>
# include <stdlib.h>
using namespace std;
struct link
{
       int info;
       struct link *next;
       struct link *previous;
};
struct link start,*New;
void create (struct link *);
void display (struct link *);
void insert(struct link *);


void create(struct link *node)
{
       char ch='y';
       start.next = NULL;   /* Empty list */
       start.previous = NULL;
       node = &start;       /* Point to the start of the list */
       while( ch == 'y' || ch=='Y')
```

```
        {
                node->next = (struct link *)
                malloc(sizeof(struct link));
                node->next->previous = node;
                node = node->next;
                cout<<"\n ENTER THE NUMBER";
                fflush(stdin);
                cin>>node->info;
                node->next = NULL;
                fflush(stdin);
                cout<<"\nDO YOU WANT TO CREATE MORE NODES[Y/N] ";
                fflush(stdin);
                cin>>ch;
        }
}

void display (struct link *node)
{
        node = start.next;
        cout<<endl<<"Link list elements printing in Forward
        Direction\n";
        while(node->next)
        {
        cout<<setw(5)<<node->info;
                node = node->next;
        }
                cout<<setw(5)<<node->info;
        cout<<endl<<"Link list elements printing in Backward
        Direction\n";
        do {
                cout<<setw(5)<<node->info;
                node = node->previous;
        } while (node->previous);
}

void insert(struct link *node)
{
        node = start.next;
        New = (struct link *) malloc(sizeof(struct link ));
        fflush(stdin);
        cout<<"\n Input the first node  value: ";
        cin>>New->info;
        New->next = node;
        New->previous = node->previous;
        node->previous->next = New;
        node->previous = New;
}
```

```
int main()
{
        struct link *node;
        create(node);
        cout<<"\n AFTER CREATING THE LINKED LIST IS \n";
        display(node);
        insert(node);
        cout<<"\n List after insertion of first node \n";
        display (node);
}
```

OUTPUT

```
ENTER THE NUMBER25
DO YOU WANT TO CREATE MORE NODES[Y/N] y
 ENTER THE NUMBER32
DO YOU WANT TO CREATE MORE NODES[Y/N] y
 ENTER THE NUMBER95
DO YOU WANT TO CREATE MORE NODES[Y/N] y
 ENTER THE NUMBER88
DO YOU WANT TO CREATE MORE NODES[Y/N] n
 AFTER CREATING THE LINKED LIST IS

Link list elements printing in Forward Direction
   25    32    95    88
Link list elements printing in Backward Direction
   88    95    32    25
 Input the first node  value: 33

 List after insertion of first node

Link list elements printing in Forward Direction
   33    25    32    95    88
Link list elements printing in Backward Direction
   88    95    32    25    33
_____
Process exited after 24.19 seconds with return value 0
Press any key to continue . . .
```

7.6.3   /*Inserting a Node in the Doubly Linked List When Node Number Is Known*/

```
# include <iostream>
#include<iomanip>
# include <stdlib.h>
using namespace std;
struct link
```

```
{
        int info;
        struct link *next;
        struct link *previous;
};
struct link start,*New;
void create (struct link *);
void display (struct link *);
void insert(struct link *);


void create(struct link *node)
{
        char ch='y';
        start.next = NULL;   /* Empty list */
        start.previous = NULL;
        node = &start;       /* Point to the start of the list */
        while( ch == 'y' || ch=='Y')
        {
                node->next = (struct link *)
                malloc(sizeof(struct link));
                node->next->previous = node;
                node = node->next;
                cout<<"\n ENTER THE NUMBER";
                fflush(stdin);
                cin>>node->info;
                node->next = NULL;
                fflush(stdin);
                cout<<"\nDO YOU WANT TO CREATE MORE NODES[Y/N] ";
                fflush(stdin);
                cin>>ch;
        }
}

void display (struct link *node)
{
        node = start.next;
        cout<<endl<<"Link list elements printing in Forward
        Direction\n";
        while(node->next)
        {
        cout<<setw(5)<<node->info;
                node = node->next;
        }
                cout<<setw(5)<<node->info;
        cout<<endl<<"Link list elements printing in Backward
        Direction\n";
        do {
                cout<<setw(5)<<node->info;
```

```
                node = node->previous;
        } while (node->previous);
}

void insert(struct link *node)
{
        int n,i;
cout<<"\nENTER THE NODE NUMBER TO INSERT";
cin>>n;
i=1;
        node = start.next;
        New = (struct link *)malloc(sizeof(struct link ));
        fflush(stdin);
        cout<<"\n ENTER THE VALUE TO INSERT ";
        cin>>New->info;
        while(node)
         {
         if(i==n)
          {
        New->next = node;
        New->previous = node->previous;
        node->previous->next = New;
        node->previous = New;
        break;
         }

else
           {
           node=node->next;
           i++;
           }
          }
}


int main()
{
        struct link *node;
        create(node);
        cout<<"\n AFTER CREATING THE LINKED LIST IS \n";
        display(node);
        insert(node);
        cout<<"\n List after insertion of first node \n";
        display (node);

}
```

OUTPUT

```
ENTER THE NUMBER25
DO YOU WANT TO CREATE MORE NODES[Y/N] y
 ENTER THE NUMBER78
DO YOU WANT TO CREATE MORE NODES[Y/N] y
 ENTER THE NUMBER6
DO YOU WANT TO CREATE MORE NODES[Y/N] y
 ENTER THE NUMBER32
DO YOU WANT TO CREATE MORE NODES[Y/N] y
 ENTER THE NUMBER12
DO YOU WANT TO CREATE MORE NODES[Y/N] n
 AFTER CREATING THE LINKED LIST IS
Link list elements printing in Forward Direction
    25    78     6    32    12
Link list elements printing in Backward Direction
    12    32     6    78    25
ENTER THE NODE NUMBER TO INSERT2
 ENTER THE VALUE TO INSERT 100
 List after insertion of first node
Link list elements printing in Forward Direction
    25   100    78     6    32    12
Link list elements printing in Backward Direction
    12    32     6    78   100    25
Process exited after 16.89 seconds with return value 0
Press any key to continue . . .
```

7.6.4   /*Inserting a Node in the Doubly Linked List When Information Is Known*/

```cpp
# include <iostream>
#include<iomanip>
# include <stdlib.h>
using namespace std;
struct link
{
      int info;
      struct link *next;
      struct link *previous;
};
struct link start,*New;
void create (struct link *);
void display (struct link *);
void insert(struct link *);
```

```
void create(struct link *node)
{
        char ch='y';
        start.next = NULL;    /* Empty list */
        start.previous = NULL;
        node = &start;        /* Point to the start of the list */
        while( ch == 'y' || ch=='Y')
        {
                node->next = (struct link *)
                malloc(sizeof(struct link));
                node->next->previous = node;
                node = node->next;
                cout<<"\n ENTER THE NUMBER";
                fflush(stdin);
                cin>>node->info;
                node->next = NULL;
                fflush(stdin);
                cout<<"\nDO YOU WANT TO CREATE MORE NODES[Y/N] ";
                fflush(stdin);
                cin>>ch;
        }
}

void display (struct link *node)
{
        node = start.next;
        cout<<endl<<"Link list elements printing in Forward
        Direction\n";
        while(node->next)
        {
        cout<<setw(5)<<node->info;
                node = node->next;
        }
                cout<<setw(5)<<node->info;
        cout<<endl<<"Link list elements printing in Backward
        Direction\n";
        do {
                cout<<setw(5)<<node->info;
                node = node->previous;
        } while (node->previous);
}
```

```cpp
void insert(struct link *node)
{
        int n;
cout<<"\nENTER THE INFORMATION VALUE TO INSERT";
cin>>n;
        node = start.next;
        while(node)
         {
         if(node->info >= n)
         {
         New=(struct link *)malloc(sizeof(struct link));
         New->info = n;
        New->next = node;
        New->previous = node->previous;
        node->previous->next = New;
node->previous = New;
        break;
        }
        else

  {

            node=node->next;
              }
            }
}


int main()
{
        struct link *node;
        create(node);
        cout<<"\n AFTER CREATING THE LINKED LIST IS \n";
        display(node);
        insert(node);
        cout<<"\n List after insertion of first node \n";
        display (node);


}
```

OUTPUT

```
ENTER THE NUMBER25
DO YOU WANT TO CREATE MORE NODES[Y/N] Y
ENTER THE NUMBER95
DO YOU WANT TO CREATE MORE NODES[Y/N] Y
ENTER THE NUMBER35
DO YOU WANT TO CREATE MORE NODES[Y/N] Y
ENTER THE NUMBER
21
DO YOU WANT TO CREATE MORE NODES[Y/N] N
AFTER CREATING THE LINKED LIST IS
Link list elements printing in Forward Direction
   25   95   35   21
Link list elements printing in Backward Direction
   21   35   95   25
ENTER THE INFORMATION VALUE TO INSERT50

List after insertion of first node

Link list elements printing in Forward Direction
   25   50   95   35   21
Link list elements printing in Backward Direction
   21   35   95   50   25
_____
Process exited after 21.42 seconds with return value 0
Press any key to continue . . .
```

7.6.5   /* Delete First Node From a Double Linked List */

```cpp
# include <iostream>
#include<iomanip>
# include <stdlib.h>
using namespace std;
struct link
{
     int info;
     struct link *next;
     struct link *previous;
};
struct link start,*New;
void create (struct link *);
void display (struct link *);
void Delete(struct link *);
```

```
void create(struct link *node)
{
        char ch='y';
        start.next = NULL;   /* Empty list */
        start.previous = NULL;
        node = &start;       /* Point to the start of the list */
        while( ch == 'y' || ch=='Y')
        {
                node->next = (struct link *) malloc(sizeof(struct
link));
                node->next->previous = node;
                node = node->next;
                cout<<"\n ENTER THE NUMBER";
                fflush(stdin);
                cin>>node->info;
                node->next = NULL;
                fflush(stdin);
                cout<<"\nDO YOU WANT TO CREATE MORE NODES[Y/N] ";
                fflush(stdin);
                cin>>ch;
        }
}

void display (struct link *node)
{
        node = start.next;
        cout<<endl<<"Link list elements printing in Forward
        Direction\n";
        while(node->next)
        {
        cout<<setw(5)<<node->info;
                node = node->next;
        }
                cout<<setw(5)<<node->info;
        cout<<endl<<"Link list elements printing in Backward
        Direction\n";
        do {
                cout<<setw(5)<<node->info;
                node = node->previous;
        } while (node->previous);
}

void Delete(struct link *node)
{
        node = start.next;
        if( node == NULL)
        {
                printf("\n Underflow");
```

```
        }
        else
        {
                node->previous->next = node->next ;
                node->next->previous = node->previous ;
                free(node);
        }
}


int main()
{
        struct link *node;
        create(node);
        cout<<"\n AFTER CREATING THE LINKED LIST IS \n";
        display(node);
        Delete(node);
        cout<<"\n List Deletion of first node \n";
        display (node);


}
```

OUTPUT

```
 ENTER THE NUMBER25
DO YOU WANT TO CREATE MORE NODES [Y/N] Y
 ENTER THE NUMBER36
DO YOU WANT TO CREATE MORE NODES [Y/N] Y
 ENTER THE NUMBER85
DO YOU WANT TO CREATE MORE NODES [Y/N] Y
 ENTER THE NUMBER9P5
DO YOU WANT TO CREATE MORE NODES [Y/N] Y
 ENTER THE NUMBER12
DO YOU WANT TO CREATE MORE NODES [Y/N] N
 AFTER CREATING THE LINKED LIST IS
Link list elements printing in Forward Direction
    25    36    85    9    12
Link list elements printing in Backward Direction
    12    9    85    36    25
 List Deletion of first node
```

```
Link list elements printing in Forward Direction
    36   85    9   12
Link list elements printing in Backward Direction
    12    9   85   36
----------------------------------------------------
Process exited after 11.9 seconds with return value 0
Press any key to continue . . .
```

7.6.6 /*Delete the Last Node From the Double Linked List*/

```cpp
# include <iostream>
#include<iomanip>
# include <stdlib.h>
using namespace std;
struct link
{
      int info;
      struct link *next;
      struct link *previous;
};
struct link start,*New;
void create (struct link *);
void display (struct link *);
void Delete(struct link *);


void create(struct link *node)
{
      char ch='y';
      start.next = NULL;  /* Empty list */
      start.previous = NULL;
      node = &start;      /* Point to the start of the list */
      while( ch == 'y' || ch=='Y')
      {
            node->next = (struct link *) malloc(sizeof(struct
link));
            node->next->previous = node;
            node = node->next;
            cout<<"\n ENTER THE NUMBER";
            fflush(stdin);
            cin>>node->info;
            node->next = NULL;
            fflush(stdin);
            cout<<"\nDO YOU WANT TO CREATE MORE NODES[Y/N] ";
            fflush(stdin);
            cin>>ch;
```

```cpp
        }
}

void display (struct link *node)
{
        node = start.next;
        cout<<endl<<"Link list elements \n";
        while(node->next)
        {
        cout<<setw(5)<<node->info;
                node = node->next;
        }
                cout<<setw(5)<<node->info;

}

void Delete(struct link *node)
{
        int n=0;

        node = start.next;
        if( node == NULL)
        {
                cout<<"\n Underflow";
        }
        else
                while(node->next)
                {
                        node = node->next;
                        n++;
                }
node = start.next;
        while(n != 1)
        {
                node = node->next;
                n--;
        }
        node=node->next;


        node->previous->next = NULL;
        free(node);
}
```

```
int main()
{
        struct link *node;
        int n;
        create(node);
        cout<<"\n AFTER CREATING THE LINKED LIST IS \n";
        display(node);
        Delete(node);
        cout<<"\n List Deletion of Last node \n";
        display (node);



}
```

OUTPUT

```
ENTER THE NUMBER12
DO YOU WANT TO CREATE MORE NODES[Y/N] y
 ENTER THE NUMBER54
DO YOU WANT TO CREATE MORE NODES[Y/N] y
 ENTER THE NUMBER67
DO YOU WANT TO CREATE MORE NODES[Y/N] y
 ENTER THE NUMBER8
DO YOU WANT TO CREATE MORE NODES[Y/N] n
 AFTER CREATING THE LINKED LIST IS

Link list elements
    12   54   67    8
 List Deletion of Last node

Link list elements
    12   54   67
_____
Process exited after 29.63 seconds with return value 0
Press any key to continue . . .
```

7.7   Header Linked List

The header link list is a special type of linked list in which a special node will be usd as header node. The purpose of this node is to store the total number of elements present in the linked list. On necessity we can easily access the elements of the linked list.

Types of Header Linked List

Basically two types of header linked list are used as

Grounded Header Linked List and Circular Header Linked list.

1. **Grounded Header Linked List**

   In this type of linked list the last node will have the NULL pointer.. In the header linked list the **start** pointer always points to the header node. **start -> next = NULL** indicates that the grounded header linked list is *empty*. Like single linked list and double linked list we can also perform all type of operations with this type of header linked list.

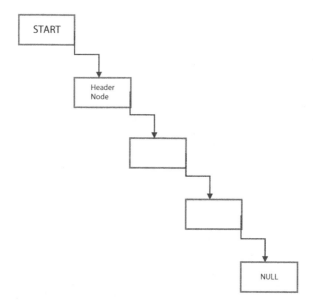

2. **Circular Header Linked List**

   In this type of linked list the last node will point or connected to header node. Because in circular linked list the last node will connect to the first node of linked list. So formally we can say that the list does not indicate first or last nodes. In this case, external pointers provide a frame of reference because last node of a circular linked list doesnot contain the **NULL** pointer. Like single linked list and double linked list we can also perform all type of operations with this type of header linked list.

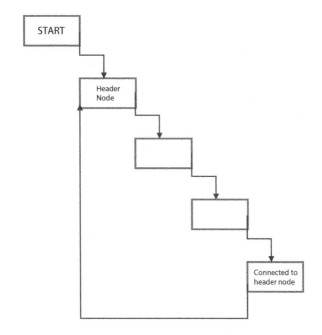

7.7.1 /* Inserting a Node Into a Header Linked List */

```c
# include <stdio.h>
# include <alloc.h>
struct link
{
        int info;
        struct link *next;
};
int i;
int number;
struct link *start, *new;
void insert(struct link *);
void create(struct link *);
void display(struct link *);
void create(struct link *node)
{
        char ch='y';

        start->next = NULL;  /* Empty list */

        node = start;       /* Point to the header node of the
list */
```

```
        node->next = (struct link* ) malloc(sizeof(struct
link)); /* Create header node */
        i = 0;
        while(ch == 'y' || ch=='Y')
        {
                node->next = (struct link* )
malloc(sizeof(struct link));
                node = node->next;
                printf("\nENTER THE NUMBER");
                scanf("%d", &node->info);
                node->next = NULL;
                fflush(stdin);
                printf("\nDO YOU WANT TO CREATE MORE NODES[Y/N]");
                scanf("%c",&ch);
                i++;
        }
        printf("\n NUMBER OF NODES = %d", i);
        node = start;
        node->info = i; /*ASSIGN TOTAL NUMBER OF NODES INTO
THE HEADER LIST*/
}

void insert(struct link *node)
    {
        int n = 1;
        int no,count;
        node=start;
        count = node->info;
        node = node->next;
        printf("\nENTER THE NODE NUMBER TO INSERT");
        fflush(stdin);
scanf("%d", &no);
        while(count)
        {
                if(n == no)
                {
                        new = (struct link* )
malloc(sizeof(struct link));
                        new->next = node->next ;
                        node->next = new;
                        printf("\nENTER THE VALUE");
                        fflush(stdin);
                        scanf("%d", &new->info);
                        node = node->next;
                }
                else
                {
```

```
                        node = node->next;
                        count--;
                }
                n++;
        }
        node = start;
        node->info = node->info+1;
}
void display(struct link *node)
    {
int count;
node=start;
        count = node->info;
        node = node->next;
        printf("\n THE LINKED LIST IS \n");
        while (count)
        {
                printf(" %d", node->info);
                node = node->next;
                count --;
        }
    }
void main()
{
        struct link *node;
        clrscr();
        create(node);
        display(node);
        insert (node);
        display(node);
}
```

7.8   Circular Linked List

As the name specifies this type of linked lists forms a circle. That means the last node of the list will be connected to the beginning of the linked list. This can be of

Single Circular linked list
Double circular linked list
Example

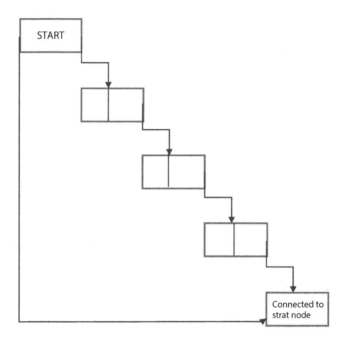

Advantages of Circular Linked Lists:

1) Any node can be a starting point. We can traverse the whole list by starting from any point. We just need to stop when the first visited node is visited again.

2) Useful for implementation of queue. Unlike this implementation, we do not need to maintain two pointers for front and rear if we use circular linked list. We can maintain a pointer to the last inserted node and front can always be obtained as next of last.

3) Circular lists are useful in applications to repeatedly go around the list. For example, when multiple applications are running on a PC, it is common for the operating system to put the running applications on a list and then to cycle through them, giving each of them a slice of time to execute, and then making them wait while the CPU is given to another application. It is convenient for the operating system to use a circular list so that when it reaches the end of the list it can cycle around to the front of the list.

4) Circular Doubly Linked Lists are used for implementation of advanced data structures like Fibonacci Heap.

• CREATING CIRCULAR HEADER LINKED LIST */

```c
# include <stdio.h>
# include <stdlib.h>
#include<conio.h>
struct link
{
        int info;
        struct link *next;
};

int i; /* Represents number of nodes in the list */
int number=0;
struct link start,*node, *new1;
void create()
{
        char ch;
        node = &start;          /* Point to the header node in
the list */
        i = 0;
        do
        {
                node->next = (struct link* ) malloc(sizeof(
struct link));
                node = node->next;
                printf("\n Input the node: %d:", (i+1));
                scanf("%d", &node->info);
                fflush(stdin);
                printf("\n DO YOU WANT TO CREATE MORE[Y/N] ");
                ch = getchar();
                i++;
        }while(ch=='y' || ch=='Y');
                node->next = &start;

        start.info = i; /* Assign total number of nodes to
the header node */
}
void insertion()
{
struct link *first;
first=&start;
node=start.next;
        int opt;
        int count = node->info;
        int node_number = 1;
        int insert_node;
        node = node->next;
        printf("\n Input node number you want to insert: ");
        printf("\n Value should be less are equal to the");
        printf("\n number of nodes in the list: ");
```

```
        scanf("%d", &insert_node);
while(count--)
        {
                if(node_number == insert_node)
                {
                        new1 = (struct link* )
malloc(sizeof(struct link));
                        first->next=new1;
                        new1->next = node;
                        printf("\n Input the node value: ");
                        scanf("%d", &new1->info);
                        opt=1;
                        break;
                }
                else
                {
                        node = node->next;
                        first=first->next;
                }
                node_number ++;
        }
        if (opt==1)
        {
                node = &start;   /* Points to header node */
                node->info = node->info+1;
        }
}
/* Display the list */
void display()
{
node=&start;
        int count = node->info;
        do
        {
                printf(" \n%5d ", node->info);
                node = node->next;
        }while(count--);
}
int main()
{

        create();
        printf("\n Before inserting a node list is as
follows:\n");
        display();
        insertion();
        printf("\n After inserting a node list is as
follows:\n");
        display();
}
```

7.9   Application of Linked List

1. Representation of different data structures link stacks and queues,sparse matrix,tree,graph, etc…
2. Implementation of graphs: Adjacency list representation of graphs is most popular which is uses linked list to store adjacent vertices.
3. Dynamic memory allocation: We use linked list of free blocks.
4. Maintaining directory of names
5. Performing arithmetic operations on long integers
6. Manipulation of polynomials by storing constants in the node of linked list

7.9.1   Addition of Two Polynomial

```
Struct poly
{
  int coef,exp;
   struct poly *next;
};
SUM(P1,P2,P3)
STEP-1 : REPEAT WHILE (P1 != NULL AND P2 != NULL)
       IF (DEGREE[P1] > DEGREE(P2)) THEN :
          ADD(P3, DEGREE[P1], COEF[P1])
           P1 := NEXT[P1]
       ELSE :
               IF(DEGREE[P1] < DEGREE(P2)) THEN :
          ADD(P3, DEGREE[P2], COEF[P2])
           P2 := NEXT[P2]
        ELSE :
          ADD(P3, DEGREE(P1),(COEF(P1) + COEF(P2))
               P1 := NEXT[P1]
                       P2 := NEXT[P2]
       [END OF IF]
       [END OF LOOP]
STEP-2 : IF (P1 = NULL)
       REPEAT WHILE (P2 != NULL)
               ADD(P3,DEGREE(P2),COEF(P2))
               P2 := NEXT(P2)
       [END OF LOOP]
       [END OF IF]
```

STEP-3 : IF (P2 = NULL)
      REPEAT WHILE (P1 != NULL)
          ADD(P3,DEGREE(P1),COEF(P1))
          P1 := NEXT(P1)
      [END OF LOOP]
      [END OF IF]
STEP – 4: RETURN

ADD(P3,COEF,EXP)

STEP-1 : ALLOCATE A MEMORY TO P3->NEXT
STEP-2 : P3 : = NEXT[P3]
STEP-3 : COEF[P3] := COEF
      EXP[P3] := EXP
STEP-4 : NEXT[P3] := NULL
STEP-5 : RETURN

7.9.2   /* Polynomial With Help of Linked List */

```c
# include <stdio.h>
# include <alloc.h>
struct link
{
        int coef;
        int expo;
        struct link *next;
};
int i;
int number;
struct link start, *previous, *new;

void create(struct link *node)
{
        char ch='y';
        start.next = NULL;   /* Empty list */
        node = &start;       /* Point to the start of the list */
        i = 0;
        while(ch == 'y' || ch=='Y')
        {
                node->next = (struct link* )
malloc(sizeof(struct link));
                node = node->next;
                printf("\nENTER THE COEFFICIENT VALUE:");
                fflush(stdin);
                scanf("%d", &node->coef);
                printf("\nENTER THE EXPONENT VALUE:");
```

```
            fflush(stdin);
            scanf("%d", &node->expo);
            node->next = NULL;
            fflush(stdin);
            printf("\nDO YOU WANT TO CREATE MORE
NODES[Y/N]");
            scanf("%c",&ch);
            i++;
     }
     printf("\nNUMBER OF NODES = %d\n", i);
}
void display(struct link *node)
{
     node = &start;
     node = node->next;
      printf(" %d", node->coef);   // PRINTING THE FIRST
ELEMENT
      printf("X^%d", node->expo);
      node=node->next;
     while (node)
     {
            printf("+ %d", node->coef);
            printf("X^%d", node->expo);
            node = node->next;
     }
}
```

```
void main()
{
     struct link *node;
     create(node);
     display(node);
}
```

7.9.3 Program for Linked Queue

```
#include<stdio.h>
#include<iostream>
using namespace std;
struct Q
 {
  int info;
  struct Q *next;
 };
 struct Q *front,*rear,*New;
```

```c
void insert()
  {
   New = (struct Q *)malloc(sizeof(struct Q));
      printf("\n Enter a number");
      scanf("%d",&New->info);
 New ->next = NULL;
  if(front == NULL)
   {
      front = New;
      rear = New;
      }

else
      {
       rear->next = New;
       rear = rear ->next;
      }
  }

void delet()
  {
  if(front == NULL)
   {
      printf("\n QUEUE IS EMPTY");
      return;
   }
    New = front;
      if(New != NULL)
        {
         printf("%d IS DELETED",New->info);
         front = front-> next;
         free(New);
        }
   }

void display()
  {
   New = front;
     if(New == NULL)
       {
           printf("\n QUEUE IS EMPTY");
           return;
       }
  printf("\n THE QUEUE IS ");
   while(New != NULL)
     {
      printf("%5d",New->info);
      New = New->next;
     }
 }
```

```
int main()
 {
   int opt;
    while(1)
       {
         cout<<"\n 1. INSERT 2. DELETE  0. EXIT";
         cin>>opt;
         if(opt==1)
           {
            insert();
            cout<<"\n AFTER INSERTION THE QUEUE IS :";
            display();
           }
```

```
else
       if(opt==2)
           {
               delet();
               printf("\n AFTER DELETE THE QUEUE IS: ");
               display();
               }
               else
                if(opt==0)
                  exit(0);
       }
   }
```

7.9.4   Program for Linked Stack

```
#include<stdio.h>
#include<dos.h>
struct stack
 {
   int info;
   struct stack *next;
 };
 struct stack *start=NULL,*node, *first,*New;

void push()
   {
    New = (struct stack *)malloc(sizeof(struct stack));
      printf("\n Enter a number");
      scanf("%d",&New->info);
        if(start == NULL)
        {
         start = New;
         New->next = NULL;
        }
```

```
        else
          {
           New->next = start;
           start = New;
          }
    }

void pop()
  {
     first = start;
     if(start == NULL)
       printf("\n STACK IS EMPTY");
         else
         {
          start = start->next;
          printf("\n %d IS POPPED",first->info);
          free(first);
         }
  }




void traverse()
 {
    if(start == NULL)
      printf("\n EMPTY STACK");
        else
         {
          first = start;
            while(first)
              {
               printf("   %d",first->info);
               first = first->next;
              }
         }
  }

int main()
 {
 int opt;
  while(1)
    {
      printf("\n 1. PUSH 2. POP 0.EXIT");
      scanf("%d",&opt);
        if(opt==1)
          {
             push();
```

```
printf("\n AFTER PUSH THE STACK IS ");
  traverse();
  }
  else
    if(opt==2)
      {
       pop();
       printf("\n AFTER DELETE THE STACK IS ");
        traverse();
      }
  else
   if(opt==0)
     exit(0);
   }
}
```

7.10   Garbage Collection and Compaction

After use of any memory it must be reusable, and its the work of the operating system to find out those memory which are allocated but not used anywhere so the operating system will perform a task as a result these unused memory spaces will added into the free memory space.

The technique which does this collection is called garbage collection.

The garbage collection may take place when there is only some minimum amount of space or no space at all left in the free storage list, or when the CPU is idle and has time to do the collection. The garbage collectionis invisible to the programmer.

Memory management system uses the concept called compaction, which collects all free space blocks and places them at one location in a single free block. So the request for memory allocation will be from this free block. Memory management system uses some technique for tis. Different methods for assigning the requested memory from free block such as

- FIRST FIT METHOD
- BEST FIT METHOD
- WORST FIT METHOD

In *first fit* method of memory allocation, the first entry which has free block equal to or more than required one is taken.

For example

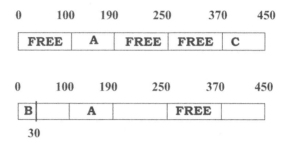

Now to allocate a memory of 30 Byte for B the system will choose the memory area of 0–100.

In **best fit** method of memory allocation, the entry which is smallest among all the entries which are equal or bigger than the required one is choosen.

For example

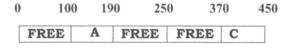

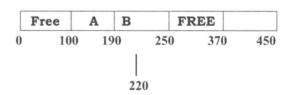

Now to allocate a memory of 30 Byte for B the system will choose the memory area of 190–250.

In **worst fit** method of memory allocation, the system always allocates a portion of the largest free block in memory.

For example

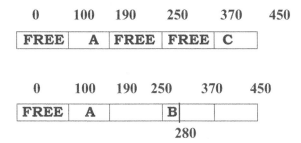

Now to allocate a memory of 30 Byte for B the system will choose the memory area of 250-370.

7.11 Questions

1. What is the benefit of linked list over array?
2. What are the types of linked list?
3. What is garbage collection?
4. What is compaction?
5. What are the types of memory allocation?
6. What is header linked list?
7. Write a program to implement employee data base using double-linked list.
8. Write a program to implement a phone directory system using header linked list.
9. What is the use of linked list?
10. Write a program to add, subtract, and multiply two polynomials using linked list.

A tree is a nonlinear data structure in which the elements are arranged in the parent and child relationship manner. We can also say that in the tree data structure the elements can also be stored in a sorted order, and is used to represent the hierarchical relationship.

> A TREE is a dynamic data structure that represents the hierarchical relationships between individual data items.
> In a tree, nodes are organized in a hierarchical way in such a way that
>
> ➤ There is a specially designated node called the root, at the beginning of the structure except when the tree is empty
> ➤ Lines connecting the nodes are called branches and every node except the root is joined to just one node at the next higher level(parent)
> ➤ Nodes that have no children are called as leaf nodes or terminal nodes.

8.1 Tree Terminologies

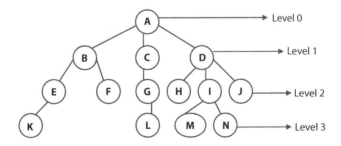

Sachi Nandan Mohanty and Pabitra Kumar Tripathy. *Data Structure and Algorithms Using C++: A Practical Implementation*, (249–294) © 2021 Scrivener Publishing LLC

NODE: Each element of a tree is called as node. It is the basic structure in a tree. It specifies the information and links(branches) to other data items. In the above diagram 14 nodes are there.

ROOT: It is specially designated node in a tree. It is the first node in the hierarchial arrangement of data items. In the diagram A is the root node.

PARENT: Parent of a node is the immediate predecessor of an node. Here B is the parent of E and F.

CHILD:

Each immediate successor of a node is known as child. In the above diagram B, C, D are children of A.

SIBLINGS:

The child nodes of a given parent node are called siblings. In the figure H, I, J are siblings.

DEGREE OF A NODE:

The number of sub-trees of a node in a given tree is called degree of that node. In the figure

The degree of node A is 3
The degree of node B is 2
The degree of node G is 1
The degree of node F is 0

DEGREE OF TREE:

The maximum degree of nodes in a given tree is called the degree of the tree. In the figure the maximum degree of nodes A and D is 3. So the degree of Tree is 3.

TERMINAL NODE:

A node with degree zero is called terminal node or a leaf. In the figure K, F, L, H, M, N, J are terminal nodes.

NON-TERMINAL NODE:

Any node (except the root node) whose degree is not zero is called as non-terminal node. In the above tree B, E, C, G, D, I are non-terminal nodes.

LEVEL:

The entire tree structured is leveled in such a way that the root is always at the level 0, then its immediate children are at level 1, and their immediate children are at level 2 and so on up to the leaf node. The above tree has four levels.

EDGE:

Edge is the connecting line of 2 nodes. CG is an edge of the above tree.

PATH:

Path is the sequence of consecutive edges from the source node to the destination node. In the above tree the path between A and M is (A,D),(D,I),(I,M)

DEPTH:

The depth of node n is the length of the unique path from the root to n. The depth of E is 2 and B is 1.

HEIGHT:

The height of node n is the length of the longest path from n to leaf. The height of B is 2 and F is 0.

BINARY TREE

> A binary tree is a special form of a tree in which every node of the tree can have at most two children.
> ### OR
> In a binary tree the degree of each node is less than or equal to 2.

EXAMPLE

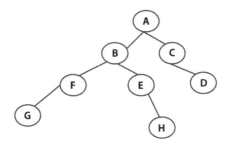

8.2   Binary Tree

The BINARY TREE are of THREE types such as

- Complete Binary Tree
- Almost Complete Binary Tree
- **Strictly Binary Tree**
- **Extended Binary Tree**

COMPLETE BINARY TREE

A binary tree with **n** nodes and of depth **d** is a strictly binary tree all of whose terminal nodes are at level **d.** In a complete Binary Tree the out degree of every node is either 2 or Nil.

EXAMPLE:

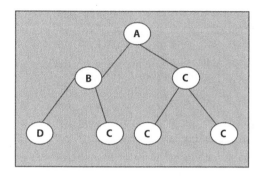

ALMOST COMPLETE BINARY TREE

An almost complete binary TREE IS A BINARY TREE in which the following conditions must hold:

1. All the leaves are at the bottom level or the bottom 2 levels
2. All the leaves are in the leftmost possible positions and all levels are completely filled with nodes.

STRICTLY BINARY TREE

If every non-terminal node in a binary tree consists of non empty left subtree and right subtree , then such a tree is called as the STRICTLY binary tree.

EXAMPLE

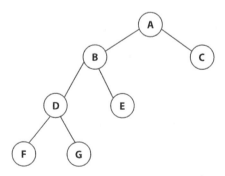

EXTENDED BINARY TREE

A binary tree is called as extended binary tree or 2-TREE if every node of tree has zero or two children.

In this case the nodes with 2-children are called as Internal nodes and the nodes with 0 children are called as External nodes.

EXAMPLE

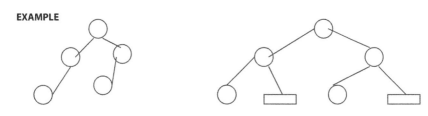

It is not a 2-TREE but Binary Tree

It is the extended form of the previous binary tree and it is 2-TREE

8.3 Representation of Binary Tree

A binary tree can be represented by using

- Array
- Linked List

8.3.1 Array Representation of a Tree

An array can be used to represent the BINARY tree. The total number of elements in the array depends on the total number of nodes in the TREE.

The ROOT node is always kept as the FIRST element of the array i.e/ in the 0-Index the root node will be store. Then, in the successive memory locations the left child and right child are stored.

Ex.

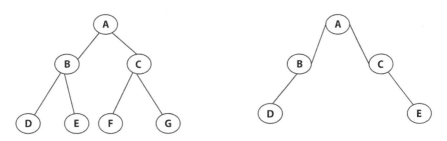

ARRAY REPRESENTATION

A
B
C
D
E
F
G

A
B
C
D
–
–
E

8.3.2 Linked List Representation of a Tree

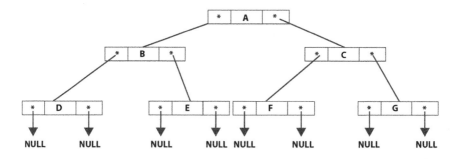

While representing the Binary tree we will have to use the Concept of Double Linked List.

8.4 Operations Performed With the Binary Tree

The most commonly implemented operations with the Binary Tree are

- ➢ Creation
- ➢ Insertion
- ➢ Deletion
- ➢ Searching
- ➢ Some other operations are
- ➢ Copying
- ➢ Merging
- ➢ Updating

ALGORITHM FOR CREATION OF BINARY TREE

CREATE (NODE, INFO) [NODE is the Structure type Variable having both left and right pointer. INFO is the
information]

STEP-1 : IF (NODE = NULL) THEN:
ALLOCATE A MEMORY TO NODE
INFO[NODE] := INFO
LEFT[NODE] := NULL
RIGHT[NODE] := NULL
RETURN
[END OF IF]
STEP-2 : IF INFO[NODE] >= INFO THEN:
CREATE(LEFT[NODE],INFO)
ELSE:
CREATE(RIGHT[NODE],INFO)
[END OF IF]
STEP3 : RETURN(NODE)

8.4.1 /*Creation of a Tree*/

```
#include<stdio.h>
# include<alloc.h>
struct node
{
      int info;
      struct node *left;
      struct node *right;
};


struct node *create(int , struct node *);
void display(struct node *, int );
void main()
{
      int info ;
      char ch='y';
      struct node *tree ;
      tree = NULL;
      while(ch == 'y' || ch=='Y')
      {
            printf("\n Input information of the node: ");
            scanf("%d", &info);
            tree = create(info, tree);
            printf("\n Tree is ");
```

```
                display(tree, 1);
                printf("\nDO YOU WANT TO CREATE MORE
CHILDS[Y/N]");
                scanf("%c",&ch);
        }
}
struct node * create(int info, struct node *n)
{
        if (n == NULL)
        {
                n = (struct node *) malloc( sizeof(struct node ));
                n->info = info;
                n->left = NULL;
                n->right= NULL;
                return (n);
        }

                if (n->info >= info )
                n->left = create(info, n->left);
else
                n->right = create(info, n->right); return(n);
}
void   display(struct node *tree, int no)
{
        int i;
        if (tree)
        {
                display(tree->right, no+1);
                printf("\n ");
                for (i = 0; i < no; i++)
                        printf("    ");
                printf("%d", tree->info);
                printf("\n");
                display(tree->left, no+1);
                }
        }
}
```

8.5   Traversing With Tree

The tree traversing is the way to visit all the nodes of the tree on a specific order. The Tree traversal can be accomplished in three different ways such as

- ➢ **INORDER traversal**
- ➢ **POST ORDER traversal**
- ➢ **PRE ORDER traversal.**
- ➢ Level Order Traversal

Tree traversal can be performed in two different ways such as
> BY USING RECURSION
> WITHOUT USING RECURSION

RECURSIVELY

Inorder traversal
> Traverse the Left Subtree in **INORDER(Left)**
> Visit the Root node
> Traverse the Right Subtree in **INORDER(Right)**

Preorder traversal
> Visit the Root Node
> Traverse the Right Subtree in **PREORDER(Left)**
> Traverse the Right Subtree in **PREORDER(Right)**

Postorder traversal
> Traverse the Right Subtree in **POSTORDER(Left)**
> Traverse the Right Subtree in **POSTORDER(Right)**
> Visit the Root Node

WITHOUT USING RECURSION

Nonrecursive Inorder Traversal Algorithm

```
STEP-1  NODE = root;
STEP -2 Repeat  while(node or stack is nonempty)
        if(node != NULL) then
        stack=node->info
        node=node->link
        else
        pop stack into node;
        visit the node
        node = node->right
        [end of if]
                    OR
```

STEP1: Repeat Step 2,3 while STACK is not empty or Ptr is not Equal to NULL
STEP2: If Ptr is not Equal to NULL
    PUSH ptr on STACK
    Ptr = ptr -> left_child
STEP3: If ptr is equal to NULL
    POP an address from STACK
    Traverse the node at that address
    Ptr = ptr->right_child

Nonrecursive Preorder Traversal Algorithm

Step - 1 node = root; //start the traversal at the root node
Step-2 while(node or stack is nonempty)
    if(node)
    visit node
    stack=node->info
    node = node->left
    else
    pop stack into node
    node = node->right
    [end of if]
                          OR
STEP1: Push the Address of Root node on the STACK
STEP2: POP an address from the STACK
STEP3: IF the popped address is NOT NULL
    TRAVERSE THE NODE
    PUSH RIGHT CHILD OF NODE ON STACK
    PUSH LEFT CHILD OF NODE ON STACK
    [END OF IF]
STEP4: Repeat Steps 2,3 until the STACK is not Empty

Nonrecursive Postorder Traversal Algorithm

STEP1: First PUSH NULL to STACK
Step2: Repeat Step 3,4,5 while ptr != NULL
STEP3: Move on the leftmost path rooted at ptr, and all the nodes which come on this path are to be pushed on STACK and the value of flag is

made1 for these nodes. Besides putting these nodeson the STACK we also check whether the node has right child or not, if the node has right child then that right child is also pushed on STACK and the value of flag is made -1 for these types of nodes.

STEP4: Save the value of top_prev , and then pop an address from the STACK and assign that address to ptr.

STEP5: Repeat following steps while flag[top_prev]= 1

Traverse the node whose address is ptr.

POP another node from the STACK.

LEVEL ORDER TRAVERSAL

In this type of traversal the elements will be visited according to level wise but it is not so far used.

EXAMPLES

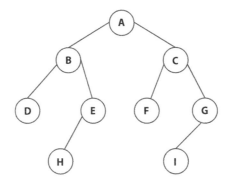

INORDER   : D B H E A F C I G
PREORDER   : A B D E H C F G I
POST ORDER : D H E B F I G C A
LEVEL ORDER : A B C D E F G H I

8.5.1   /* Binary Tree Traversal */

```
# include<stdio.h>
struct link
{
        int info;
        struct link *left;
        struct link *right;
};
```

```
struct link *binary(int *list, int lower, int upper)
{
        struct node *node;
        int mid = (lower + upper)/2;
        node = (struct link *) malloc(sizeof(struct link));
        node->info = list [mid];
        if ( lower>= upper)
        {
                node->left = NULL;
                node->right = NULL;
                return (node);
        }

        if (lower <= mid - 1)
                node->left=binary(list, lower, mid - 1);
        else
                node->left = NULL;
        if (mid + 1 <= upper)
                node->right = binary(list,  mid + 1, upper);
        else
                node->right = NULL;
        return(node);
}
void output(struct link *t, int level)
{
        int i;
        if (t)
        {
                output(t->right, level+1);
                printf("\n");
                for (i = 0; i < level; i++)
                        printf(«   «);
                printf(« %d», t->info);
                output(t->left, level+1);
        }
}
void preorder (struct link *node)
{
        if (node)
        {
                printf(" %d", node->info);
                preorder(node->left);
                preorder(node->right);
        }
}
void inorder (struct link *node)
{
        if (node)
```

```
        {
                inorder(node->left);
                printf(" %d", node->info);
                inorder(node->right);
        }
}
void postorder (struct link *node)
{
        if (node)
        {
                postorder(node->left);
                postorder(node->right);
                printf(" %d", node->info);
        }
}
void main()
{
        int list[100];
        int number = 0;
        int info;
        char ch='y';
        struct link *t ;
        t = NULL;
        while(ch == 'y' || ch=='Y')
        {
                printf("\n Enter the value of the node");
                scanf("%d", &info);
                list[number++] = info;
                printf("\nDO YOU WANT TO CREATE MORE
NODES[Y/N]");
                scanf("%c",&ch);
        }
        number --;
        printf("\n Number of elements in the list is %d",
number);
        t = binary(list, 0, number);
output(t,1);
        printf("\n Pre-order traversal\n");
        preorder (t);
        printf("\n In-order traversal\n");
        inorder (t);
        printf(«\n Post-order traversal\n»);
        postorder (t);
}
```

8.6 Conversion of a Tree From Inorder and Preorder

INORDER : D B H E A F C I G
PREORDER : A B D E H C F G I

Choose the ROOT from the preorder and from inorder find the nodes in left and right and this process will continue up to all the elements are chosen from the preorder/inorder.

STEP1: From preorder A is the root and from inorder we will find that in the left of A (**D,B,H,E**) and in the right (**F,C,I,G**)

STEP2: Again from Preorder 'B' will be chosen as PARENT and from Inorder in the left of B (**D**) and in the right (**H,E**).

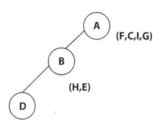

STEP3: From Preorder 'E' will chosen as the PARENT and from inorder on its left 'H' is present.

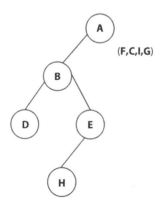

STEP4: From Preorder we will choose 'C' as the PARENT and from inorder we observe that in the left of 'C' (**F**) will placed and in the right (**I,G**)

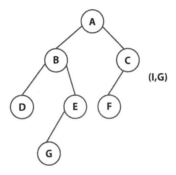

STEP5: From the PREORDR we observe that 'G' is the parent and from the INORDER **I** will be used as the Left child of 'G'.

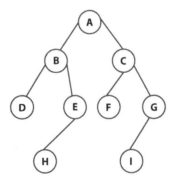

CONVERSION OF A TREE FROM INORDER AND POSTORDER
INORDER   : D B H E A F C I G
POST ORDER : D H E B F I G C A
Choose the **ROOT** from the postorder **(from the right)** and from inorder find the nodes in left and right and this process will continue up to all the elements are chosen from the postorder/inorder.

STEP1 : From the right of POSTORDER 'A' will be chosen as the ROOT and from INORDER we observe that in the left of A (**D,B,H,E,A**) and in the right (**F,C,I,G**) will be there.

(D,B,H,E,A)   (F,C,I,G)

STEP2: From the POSTFIX 'C' will be chosen as the PARENT and from INORDER we observe that in the right of 'C' **(I,G)** and to the left **(F)** will be used.

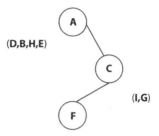

STEP3: From the right of POSTORDER 'G' will be chosen as the PARENT and from inorder to the left of 'G' **(I)** will be used.

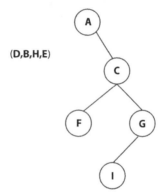

STEP4: From the right to postorder 'B' will be chosen as the PARENT and from the INORDER to we observe that to the right of 'B' **(H,E,A)** and to the left **(D)** will be used.

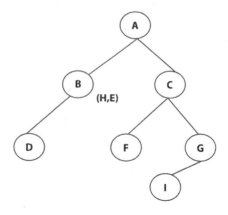

STEP5: From the right to postorder we will choose 'E' as PARENT and from the Inorder to the left of 'E' (**H**) will be used.

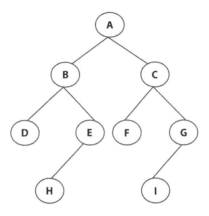

8.7 Types of Binary Tree

There are different types of BINARY trees are found but some of them which are frequently used are

- ➢ Expression Tree
- ➢ Binary Search Tree
- ➢ Height Balanced Tree (**AVL** Tree)
- ➢ Threaded Binary Tree
- ➢ Heap Tree
- ➢ Huffman Tree
- ➢ Decision Tree
- ➢ Red Black Tree

8.8 Expression Tree

An expression tree is a Binary Tree which stores/represents the mathematical (arithmetic) expressions.

The leaves of an expression tree are operands, such as constants or variable names and all the internal nodes are the operators. An expression tree will be always a binary tree because an arithmetic expression contains either binary operators or unary operators.

Formally we can define an expression Tree as a special kind of binary tree in which:

- Each leaf is an operand. Examples: a, b, c, 6, 100
- The root and internal nodes are operators. Examples: +, -, *, /, ^
- Subtrees are subexpressions with the root being an operator.

Construction of Expression Tree:
Now For constructing expression tree we use a stack. We loop through input expression and do following for every character.

1) If character is operand push that into stack.
2) If character is operator pop two values from stack make them its child and push current node again.

At the end only element of stack will be root of expression tree.

EXAMPLE
Represent an Expression Tree

$$A + (B*C) - (D^\wedge E) / F + G * H$$

While constructing the TREE choose an operator in such a way that the terms in parenthesis will be in a side (for better construction) and choose a operator having higher precedence.

STEP1:

A + (B*C) – (D^E)   /   F + G * H

STEP2:

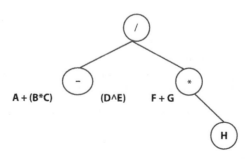

Step3:

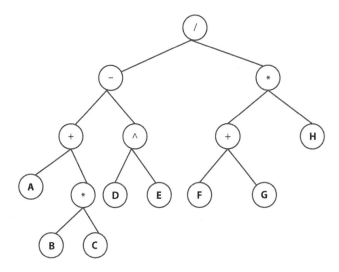

Depending on the expression used we have different types of expressions:

- Prefix expression
- Infix expression
- Postfix expression

Example

Construct an expression tree for 5 7 - 3 /

Scan the symbols from left and since 5 and 7 are operands so push them into stack.

5	7				

Next read '-', since – is an operator so pop the stack and make these as chile of the operator.

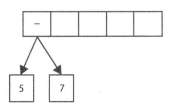

Next, '**3**' will read then push it into stack.

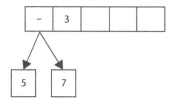

Last read the character '/' since it is an operator so pop the symbols from stack and add them into '/' as its child.

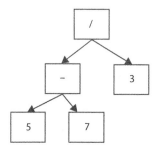

8.9   Binary Search Tree

A binary Search Tree is a Binary Tree that is either empty or in which each node possesses a key that satisfy the properties like

- The element in the left subtree are smaller than the key in the root
- The element in the right subtree are greater than or equal to the root
- The left and right subtrees are also the Binary Search Tree.

OPERATIONS PERFORMED WITH A BST

The most commonly used operations with BST are
    Insertion   Deletion   Searching

EXAMPLE

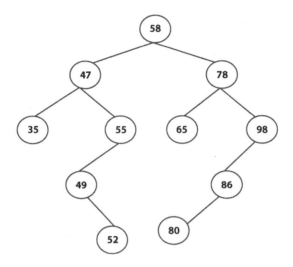

SEARCHING

To search any node in a Binary tree, initially the data item that is to be searched is compared with the data of the root node. If the data is equal to the data of the root node then the search is successful.

If the data is found to be greater than the data of the root node then the searching process proceeds in the right sub-tree, otherwise searching process proceeds in the left sub-tree.

Repeat the same process till the element is found and while searching if Leaf node is found than print that the number is not found.

INSERTION

To insert any node into a binary search tree, initially data item that is to be inserted is compared with the data of the root node.

If the data item is found to be greater than or equal to the data item of root node then the new node is inserted in the right sub tree of the root node, other wise the new node is inserted in the left sub tree of the root node.

Now the root node of the right or left sub tree is taken and its data is compared with the data that is to be inserted and the same procedure is repeated. This is done till the left or right sub tree where the new node to be inserted is found to be empty. Finally the new node is made the appropriate child of this current node.

DELETION

While deletion if the deleted node has only one sub tree, in this case simply link the parent of the deleted node to its sub tree.

When the deleted node has both left and right sub tree then the process is too complicated and there we have to follow the following four cases such as

CASE1: No node in the tree contains the specified data item.

CASE2: The node containing the data item has no children

CASE3: The node containing the data item has exactly one child

CASE4: The node containing the data item has two children.

CASE1

In first case we have to check the condition whether tree is empty or not.
Condition is

IF (ROOT = NULL)
WRITE : "TREE IS EMPTY"
[END OF IF]

CASE2

In this case where the node to be deleted is a leaf node i.e/ its left and right node is not there then just delete it by assigning NULL to its parent node.
Condition is

IF ([left]item = NULL AND [RIGHT]ITEM = NULL)

Ex: If we want to delete 52 than add NULL to 49.

CASE3

In this case where the node having either left sub tree or right sub tree.
Condition is

IF ([left]item != NULL AND [RIGHT]ITEM = NULL)
IF ([left]item = NULL AND [RIGHT]ITEM != NULL)

Ex: If we want to delete 49 , which has only one child , so we can delete it simply by giving address of right child to its parent left pointer. Here 55 is the parent of 49 and 52 is the right child of 49. So after delete of 49 52 will be added to left of 55.

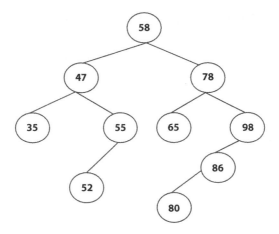

CASE4

In this case the node to be deleted has two children. Now we have to consider the condition when the node has both left and right child. This can be checked as

If(left[item] !=NULL AND right[item]!=NULL)

For example Let we want to delete 78, which has left and right children, for this we have to first delete the item which is inorder successor of 78. Here 80 is the inorder successor of 78. We delete the 80 by simply giving NULL value to its parents left pointer.

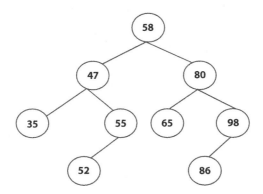

8.10 Height Balanced Tree (AVL Tree)

A height balanced tree is a binary tree in which the difference in heights between the left and the right subtree is not more than one for every node.

The height of a tree is the number of nodes in the longest path from the root to any leaf.

The property of this tree is described by two Russian Mathematicians G.M. Adel'son – vel'skii and E.M. Landis. There fore this tree is so called for their honour.

> A Binary Search Tree in which the difference of heights of the right and left sub trees of any node is less than or equal to one is known as AVL tree.

While insertion of any node to the tree we have to find out the Balancing Factor which is the difference between the left height–right height.

the Balancing Factor is 1 than the tree is Left heavy

If the Balancing Factor is   -1 than the tree is Right Heavy

If the Balancing Factor is   0 than the tree is Balanced

INSERTION WITH AN AVL TREE

We can insert a new node into an AVL tree by first using the usual binary tree insertion technique, comparing the key of the new node with that in the root and inserting the new node into the left or right subtrees accurately.

But AVL tree has a property that the height of left and right subtree will be with maximum difference 1. Suppose after inserting new node, this difference becomes more than 1, i.e/ the value of the balance factor has some value other than -1,0,1. So now our work is to restore the property of AVL tree again.

To convert an unbalanced tree to AVL tree some rotations are needed such as

- LR rotation
- RL Rotation
- LL rotation
- RR notation

For simplification just observe the follwing rotations carefully.

TRICK1

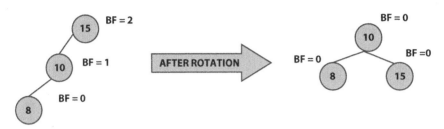

TRICK2

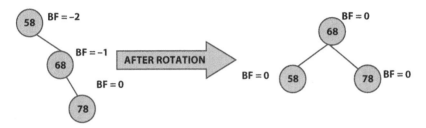

TRICK3

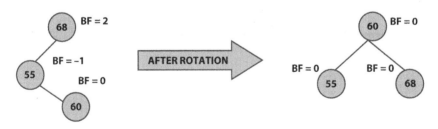

TRICK4

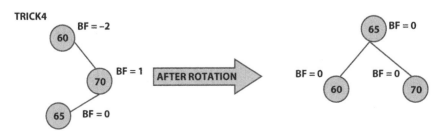

TRICK5:

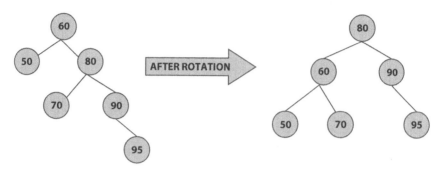

TRICK6:

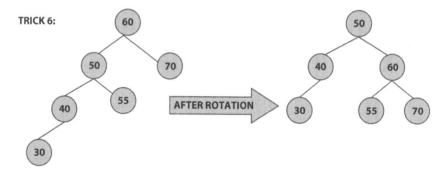

CONSTRUCT AN AVL TREE BY CONSIDERING THE NUMBERS 12, 25, 32, 65, 74, 26, 13, 08, 45

STEP1:

STEP2 :

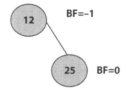

STEP3:

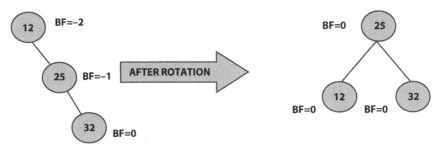

STEP4:

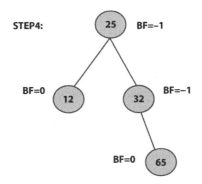

STEP5:

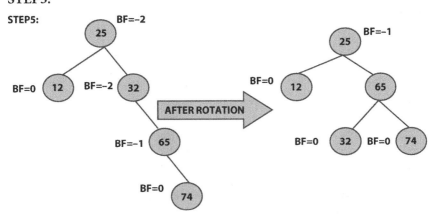

STEP6 :

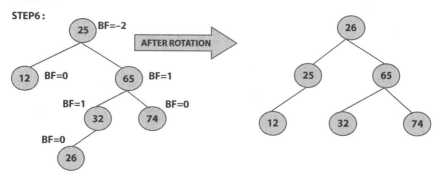

STEP7:

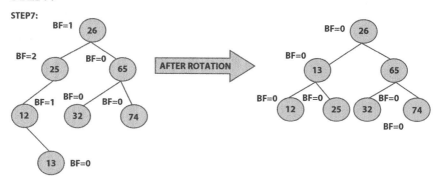

STEP8:

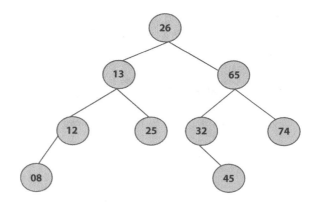

DELETION: The deletion from an AVL tree is the same as the Binary Search Tree.

8.11   Threaded Binary Tree

When a binary tree is represented using pointers then the pointers to empty subtrees are set to NULL. That is the left pointer of a node whose left child is an empty subtree is normally set to NULL simillarily the right pointer of a node whose right child is an empty subtree is also set to NULL. Thus a large number of pointers are set to NULL. It will be useful to use these pointers fields to keep some other information for operations in binary tree. The most common operation in Binary tree is traversing. We can use these pointer fields to contain the address pointer which points to the nodes higher in the tree. Such pointer which keeps the address of the nodes higher in the tree is called as **Thread**. A binary tree which implements these pointers is called Threaded Binary Tree.

In the context of Data structure the threaded binary tree are of three types such as

- Left threaded Binary tree
- Right threaded binary tree
- Complete threaded binary tree

ADVANTAGE

Thread mechanism is used to avoid recursive function call and also it saves stacks and memory.

LEFT-THREADED BINARY TREE

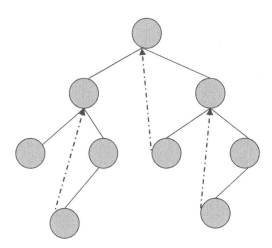

Here all the left pointers are attached with its inorder predecessor.

RIGHT-THREADED BINARY TREE

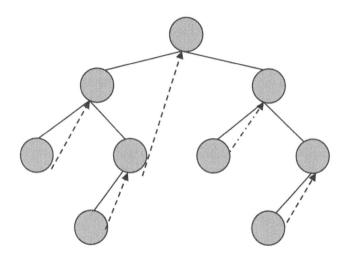

Here all the right pointers are attached with its inorder predecessor.

COMPLETE-THREADED BINARY TREE

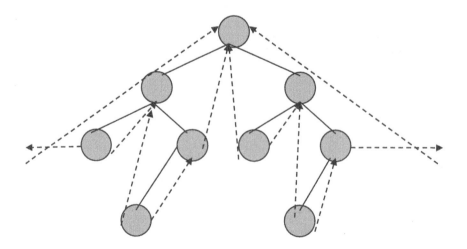

8.12 Heap Tree

A heap is a complete binary tree and is implemented in an array as sequential representation rather than the linked representation. A heap can be constructed in two different ways such as MAX – HEAP or MIN – HEAP.

A heap is called as Max – Heap or Descending Heap is every node of a heap has a value greater than or equal to the value of every child of that node. In max heap the value of the root will be the biggest number.

A heap is called as min heap or ascending heap if every node of heap has a value less than or equal to the value of every child of that node.

CREATION OF HEAP TREE

When we want to create an heap it must be filled up in a sequential order i.e/ either from left or from right side. After fill up one level then the next level insrtion will start.

Ex:

Create a MAX-HEAP by considering the numbers

14, 52, 2, 65, 84, 44, 35

STEP1:

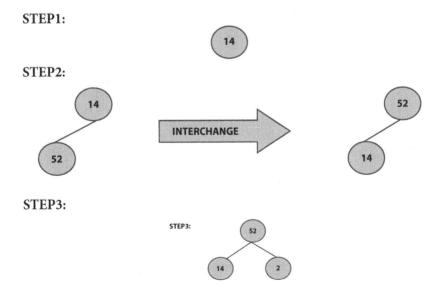

STEP2:

STEP3:

STEP4:

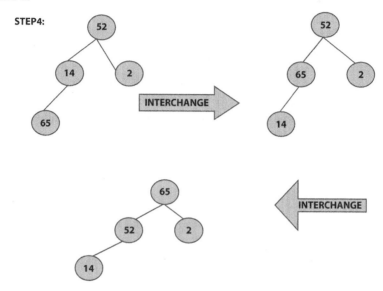

STEP5:

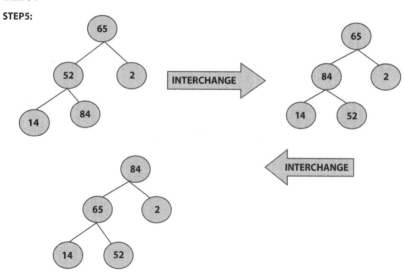

STEP6:

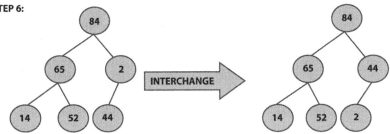

STEP 6:

INTERCHANGE

STEP7:

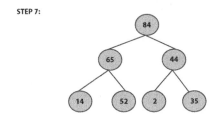

STEP 7:

Like the MAX-HEAP we can also create a MIN-HEAP by following the same procedure but the main aim should that the root node must be the smallest element.

INSERTION WITH HEAP

When we want to insert an element into an heap it must have to satisfy the property of HEAP if not then make some interchange with that tree.

DELETION FROM THE HEAP

The delete operation can be as

- Find the index number of the number to be deleted
- Take the last node of the tree at the place of deleted node
- Keep the node at the appropriate place.

To keep the node at right place the steps would be

- Compare it with its parent, if the parent is less than the node then interchange with its parent. Compare it again with it's new parent until the parent is greater than the inserted item.
- If the parent is greater than the node then compare it with left and right child, if it is smaller then replace it with greater value child. Compare it again until it is greater than or equal to both the left and right child.

8.13   Huffman Tree

Generally the HUFFMAN TREE concept is implemented based upon the concepts of extended binary tree. In extended binary tree we known that every node has zero or two children. The nodes which have two children that is called as internal nodes and the node which have no children that is called as external node.

In every extended binary tree the number of external nodes is more than the number of internal nodes.

Mathematically

External node = internal node + 1

i.e/ E = I+1

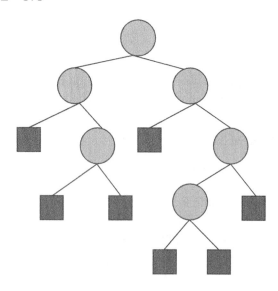

The external nodes are represented by the square brackets and the internal nodes are represented by the Circles.

The path length for any node is the number of minimum nodes traversed from root to that node.

In the above figure the total length for internal and external nodes are :-

Path(I) = 0 + 1 + 2 + 1 + 2 + 3 = 9

Path(E) = 2 + 3 + 3 + 2 + 4 + 4 + 3 = 21

We can also get the total path length of external node as

PATH(E) = PATH(I) + 2N Where N is the number of internal nodes.

Suppose each node having some weights then the weighted path length will be

P = W1P1 + W2P2 + ... + WNPN

W is the weight and P is the path length of an external node.

FOR EXAMPLE

Let we will create different trees with 5, 8, 10, 6

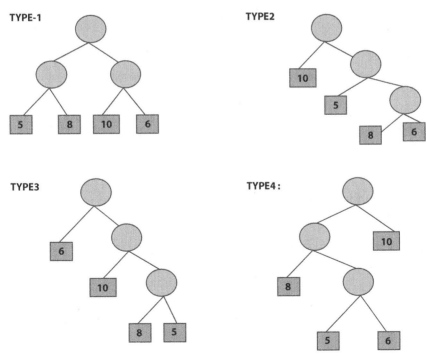

Programming in Data Structure

TYPE-1

TYPE2

TYPE3

TYPE4 :

FOR TYPE1 :
$$P = 5*2 + 8*2 + 10*2 + 6*2 = 10 + 16 + 20 + 12 = 58$$
FOR TYPE2 :
$$P = 10*1 + 5*2 + 8*3 + 6*3 = 10 + 10 + 24 + 18 = 62$$
FOR TYPE3 :
$$P = 6*1 + 10*2 + 8*3 + 5*3 = 6+20+24+15 = 65$$
FOR TYPE4 :
$$P = 8*2 + 10*1 + 5*3 + 6*3 = 16+10+15+18 = 59$$

From the above we observe that different trees have different path lengths even if same type of trees. So problem arises to find the minimum weighted path length. This type of extended binary tree can be obtained by the Huffmann algorithm.

HUFFMAN ALGORITHM

STEP1 : Lets Consider there are N numbers of weights as W1,W2,.....,WN
STEP2 : Take two minimum weights and create a sub tree. Suppose W1 and W2 are first two minimum weights then sub tree will be of the form

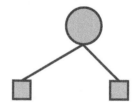

STEP3 : Now the remaining weights will be W1 + W2 , W3,....WN
STEP4 : Create all subtrees at the last weight

Example
Create a Huffman Tree by considering the numbers as
   15, 18, 25, 7, 8, 11, 5

STEP1: Taking Two nodes with minimum weights as 5 and 7

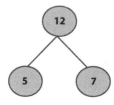

Now the elements in the list are : 15, 18, 25, 12, 8, 11
STEP2: Taking two nodes with minimum weights as 8 and 11

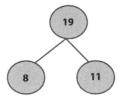

Now the remaining nodes are 15, 18, 25, 12, 19
STEP3: Taking two nodes with minimum weights as 12 and 15

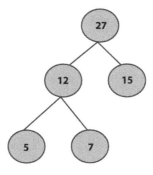

Now the remaining elements are 18, 25, 27, 19

STEP4: Taking two nodes with minimum weights as 18 and 19

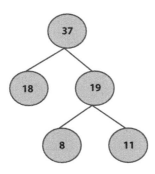

Now the remaining elements are 37, 25, 27

STEP5: Taking two nodes with minimum weights as 25 and 27

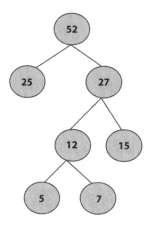

Now the remaining elements are 37 and 52

STEP6: Taking the two remaining elements as 37 and 52 the tree will be

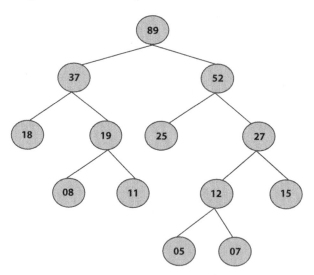

8.14   Decision Tree

A decision tree is a binary tree where a node represents some decision and edges emanating from a node represent the outcome of the decision. External nodes represent the ultimate decisions.

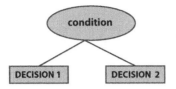

EXAMPLE

Find the Greatest among 3 numbers

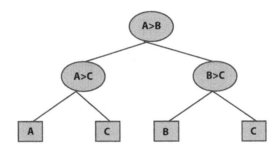

8.15   B-Tree

B-TREE is a balanced multi way tree.

- It is also known as balanced sort tree.
- It is not a binary tree.
- All the leaves of the tree must be at same level and height of the tree must be kept minimum.

B-Tree of order N can be defined as

- All the non-leaf nodes (except the root node) have at least (n/2) children and at most (n) children.
- All leaf nodes will be at same level
- All leaf nodes can contain maximum (n-1) keys.
- All non leaf nodes can contain (m-1) keys where m is the number of children for that node.
- All the values that appear on the left most child of a node are smaller than the first value of that node. All the values that appear on the right most child of a node are greater than the last value of that node.

INSERTION IN B-TREE

While insertion process we have to use the traversing. Through traversal it will find that key to be inserted is already existing or not. Suppose key does not exist in tree then through traversal it will reach the leaf node. Now we have to focus on two cases such as

- Node is not FULL
- Node is already FULL

In the first case we can simply add the key at that node. But in the second case we will need to split the node into two nodes and median key will go to the parent of that node. If parent is also full then same thing will be repeated until it will get non full parent node. Suppose root is full then it will split into two nodes and median key will be the root.

EXAMPLE
Create an B-TREE of order 5
12, 15, 33, 66, 55, 24, 22, 11, 85, 102, 105, 210, 153, 653, 38, 308, 350, 450

STEP1: Insert 12

```
12
```

STEP2: Insert 15

```
12  15
```

STEP3: Insert 33

```
12  15  33
```

STEP4: Insert 66

```
12  15  33  66
```

STEP5: Insert 55

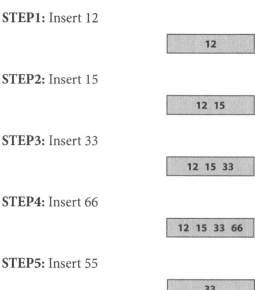

STEP6: Insert 24

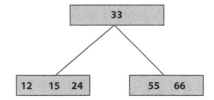

STEP7: Insert 22

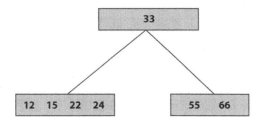

STEP8: Insert 11

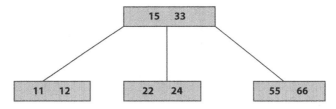

STEP9: Insert 85

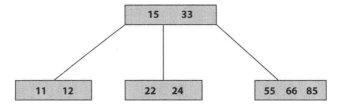

STEP10: Insert 102

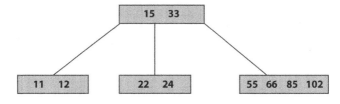

STEP11: Insert 105

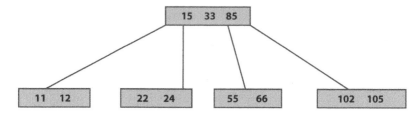

STEP12: Insert 210

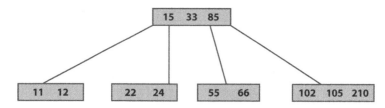

STEP13: Insert 153

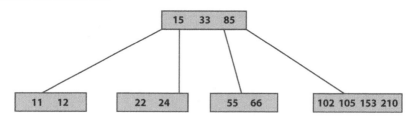

STEP14: Insert 653

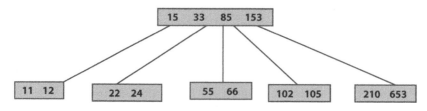

STEP15: Insert 38

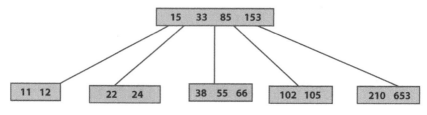

STEP16: Insert 308

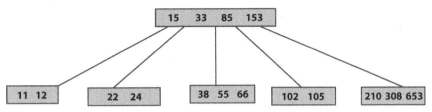

STEP17: Insert 350

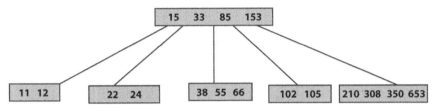

STEP18: Insert 450

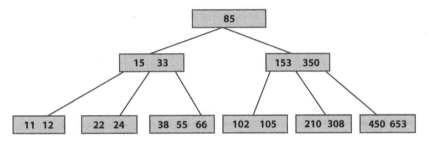

DELETION FROM THE B-TREE

Deletion from a B-Tree is similar to the insertion. Initially we need to find the node from which the value is to be deleted. After the deletion of the value we need to check, whether the tree still maintains the property of B-TREE or not.

Like insertion here also two situations will occur as

- Node is leaf node
- Node is non leaf node

For example: **Delete 55**

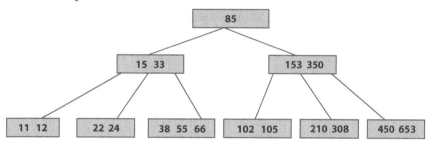

Delete 33

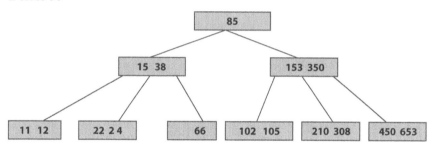

8.16   B + Tree

In B-TREE we can access records randomly but sequential traversal is not provided by it. B+ TREE is a special tree which provides the random access as well as sequential traversal.

In B+ tree all the non leaf nodes are interconnected i.e/ a leaf node will point to next leaf node.

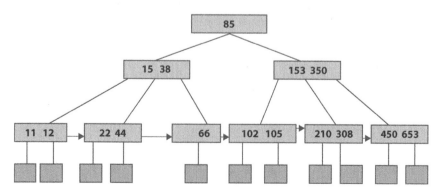

8.17 General Tree

A general tree is such a tree where there is no rules or restrictions such as

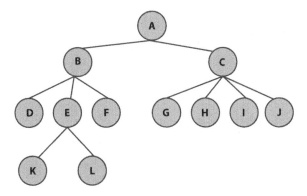

To convert a general tree to Binary tree just create a link in between like

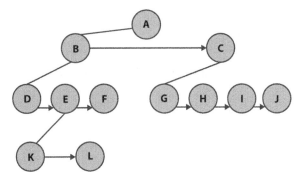

FOREST

Forest is the collection of number of trees which are not linked with each other. A forest can be obtained by removing the root from a rooted tree.

8.18 Red–Black Tree

A *red-black tree* is a binary search tree with one extra attribute for each node: the *colour*, which is either red or black. We also need to keep track of the parent of each node, so that a red-black tree's node structure would be:

```
struct TREE {
    enum { red, black } colour;
    void *item;
    struct t_red_black_node *left,
                            *right,
                            *parent;
}
```

For the purpose of this discussion, the NULL nodes which terminate the tree are considered to be the leaves and are coloured black.

Definition of a red-black tree

A red-black tree is a binary search tree which has the following *red-black properties*:

1. Every node is either red or black.
2. Every leaf (NULL) is black.
3. If a node is red, then both its children are black.
4. Every simple path from a node to a descendant leaf contains the same number of black nodes.

A red-black tree with n internal nodes has height at most $2\log(n+1)$.

8.19 Questions

1. What is TREE data structure and how can it be used in a computer system?
2. What are the different types of tree traversals?
3. Provide nonrecursive algorithms for TREE traversal.
4. What is an expression and how can it be formed? Explain with a suitable example.
5. What is Height balanced tree? Construct by using 12,45, 65,7,87,98,6,54,22,23.
6. How to find the Lowest Common Ancestor of two nodes in a Binary Tree?
7. What is the difference between B Tree and B+ Tree?
8. What is a Heap Tree? What is its use?
9. What is a 2-3 TREE?
10. What is RED-BLACK tree.

9

Graph

GRAPH is a non linear data structure in which the elements are arranged randomly in side the memory and are interconnected with each other like TREE. The GRAPH having a wide range of application in general life implementation like road map, electrical circuit designs etc...

A graph G is an ordered pair of sets (V,E) where V is the set of vertices and E is the edges which connect the vertices.

A graph can be of two types such as

- Directed Graph
- Undirected Graph

DIRECTED GRAPH

A graph in which every edge is directed is called undirected graph.

UNDIRECTED GRAPH

A graph in which every edge is undirected is called undirected graph.

If in a graph some edges are directed and some are undirected then that graph will be called as mixed graph.

9.1 Graph Terminologies

DIRECTED GRAPH

A graph in which every edge is directed is called undirected graph.

UNDIRECTED GRAPH

A graph in which every edge is undirected is called undirected graph.

Sachi Nandan Mohanty and Pabitra Kumar Tripathy. Data Structure and Algorithms Using C++: A Practical Implementation, (295–348) © 2021 Scrivener Publishing LLC

WEIGHTED GRAPH

A graph is said to be weighted if its edges have been assigned some non negative value as weight.

ADJACENT NODES

A node N_0 is adjacent to another node or is a neighbor of another node N_1 if there is an edge from node N_0 to N_1.

In undirected graph if (N_0, N_1) is an edge than N_0 is adjacent to N_1 and N_1 is adjacent to N_0.

In Digraph $< N_0, N_1>$ is an edge then N_0 is adjacent to N_1 and N_1 is adjacent from N_0.

INCIDENCE

In an undirected graph the edge (V_0, V_1) is incident on nodes V_0 and V_1.

In a digraph the edge $<V_0, V_1>$ is incident from node V_0 and is incident to node V_1

PATH

A path from a node U_0 to node U_n is a sequence of nodes $U_1, U_2, U_{3,........}, U_n$ such that U_0 is adjacent to U_1, U_1 is adjacent to U_2, ..., U_{n-1} is adjacent to Un,.

In other words we can say that $(U_0, U_1), (U_1, U_2),(U_2, U_3)$ .... are the edges.

LENGTH OF PATH

It is the total number of edges included in the path.

CLOSED PATH

A path is said to be closed if first and last nodes of the path are same.

SIMPLE PATH

Simple path is a path in which all the nodes are distinct with an exception that the first and last nodes of the path can be same.

GRAPH   297

CYCLE

Cycle is a simple path in which first and last nodes are the same or we can say that a closed simple path is a cycle.

In a digraph a path is called a cycle if it has one or more nodes and the start node is connected to the last node.

In an undirected graph a path is called a cycle if it has at least three nodes and the start node is connected to the last node. In undirected graph if (u,v) is an edge then u-v-u should not be considered as a path since (u,v) and (v,u) are the same edges. So for a path to be a cycle in an undirected graph there should be at least three nodes.

CYCLIC GRAPH

A graph that has cycles is called as cyclic graph

ACYCLIC GRAPH

A graph that has no cycle is known as acyclic graph.

DAG

A directed acyclic graph is named as dag after its acronym. Graph-5 is a dag.

DEGREE

In an undirected graph the number of edges connected to a node is called the degree of that node, or we can say that degree of a node is the number of edges incident on it. In graph-2 degree of the node A is 1, degree of node B is 0. In graph-3 the degree of the node A is 3 and the degree of the node B is 2.

In digraph there are two degrees for every node known as indegree and outdegree.

INDEGREE

The indegree of a node is the number of edges coming to that node or in other words edges incident to it. In graph-8 the indegree of nodes A, B, D, and G are 0, 2, 6, and 1, respectively.

OUTDEGREE

The outdegree of node is the number of edges going outside from that node, or in other words the edges incident from it. In graph-8 outdegrees of nodes A, B, D, F, and G are 3, 1, 6, 3, and 2, respectively.

SOURCE

A node which has no incoming edges, but has outgoing edges, is called a source. The indegree of source is zero. In graph-8 nodes A and F are sources.

SINK

A node, which has no outgoing edges but has incoming edges, is called as sink. The outdegree of a sink is zero. In graph-8 node D is a sink.

PENDANT NODE

A node is said to be pendant if its indegree is equal to 1 and outdegree is equal to 0.

REACHABLE

If there is a path from a node to any other node then it will be called as reachable from that node.

ISOLATED NODE

If a node has no edges connected with any other node then its degree will be 0 and it will be called isolated node. In graph-2 node B is an isolated node.

SUCCESSOR AND PREDECESSOR

In graph is a node u is adjacent to node v, then u is the predecessor of v and v is the successor of u.

CONNECTED GRAPH

An undirected graph is connected if there is a path from any node of graph to any other node, or any node is reachable from any other node. Graph-2 is not a connected graph.

GRAPH   299

STRONGLY CONNECTED

A digraph is strongly connected if there is a directed path from any node of graph to any other node. We can also say that a digraph is strongly connected if for any pair of node u and v, there is a path from u and v and also a path from v to u. Graph-7 is strongly connected.

WEAKLY CONNECTED

A digraph is weakly connected or unilaterally connected if for any pair of node u and v, there is a path from u to v or a path from v to u. If from the digraph we remove the directions and the resulting undirected graph is connected then that digraph is weakly connected. Graph-6 is weakly connected graph.

MAXIMUM EDGES IN GRAPH

In an undirected graph there can be $n(n - 1)/2$ maximum edges and in a digraph there can be $n(n - 1)$ maximum edges, where n is the total number of nodes in the graph.

COMPLETE GRAPH

A graph is complete if any node in the graph is adjacent to all the nodes of the graph or we can say that there is an edge between any pair of nodes in the graph. An undirected complete graph will contain $n(n - 1)/2$ edges.

MULTIPLE EDGE

If between a pair of nodes there is more than one edge then they are known as multiple edges or parallel edges. In graph-3 there are multiple edges between nodes A and C.

LOOP

An edge will be called loop or self edge if it starts and ends on the same node. Graph-4 has a loop at node B.

MULTIGRAPH

A graph which has loop or multiple edges can be described as multigraph. Graph-3 and Graph-4 are multigraphs.

REGULAR GRAPH

A graph is regular if every node is adjacent to the same number of nodes, Graph-1 is regular since every node is adjacent to other three nodes.

PLANAR GRAPH

A graph is called planar if it can be drawn in a plane without any two edges intersecting. Graph-1 is not a planar graph, while graphs Graph-2, graph-3, and graph-4 are planar graphs.

ARTICULATION POINT

If on removing a node from the graph the graph becomes disconnected then that node is called as the articulation point.

BRIDGE

If on removing an edge from the graph the graph becomes disconnected then that edge is called the bridge.

TREE

An undirected connected graph will be called tree if there is no cycle in it.

BICONNECTED GRAPH

A graph with no articulation points is called as a biconnected graph.

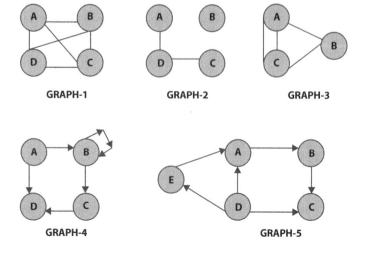

GRAPH-1   GRAPH-2   GRAPH-3

GRAPH-4   GRAPH-5

GRAPH 301

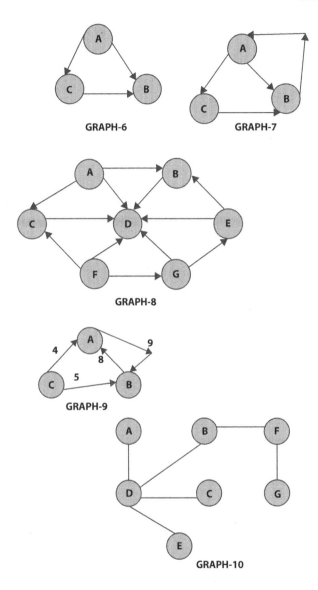

GRAPH-6

GRAPH-7

GRAPH-8

GRAPH-9

GRAPH-10

9.2 Representation of Graph

The major components of the graph are node and edges. Like tree the graph can also be represented in two different ways such as

- ARRAY REPRESENTATION
- LINKED REPRESENTATION

But Ovarall there are four major approaches to represent the graph as

- Adjacency Matrix
- Adjacency Lists
- Adjacency Multilists
- Incedince Matrix

ADJACENCY MATRIX

The nodes that are adjacent to one another are represented as matrix. Thus adjacency matrix is the matrix, which keeps the information of adjacent or nearby nodes. In other words we can say that this matrix keeps the information whether the node is adjacent to any other node or not.

The adjacency matrix is a sequence matrix with one row and one column for each vertex. The values in the matrix are either 0 or 1. The adjancy matrix of the graph G is a two dimensional array of size n * n(Where n is the number of vertices in the graph) with the property that A[I][J] = 1, if the edge (V_I, V_J) is in the set of edges and A[I][J] = 0 if there is no such edge.

EXAMPLE:

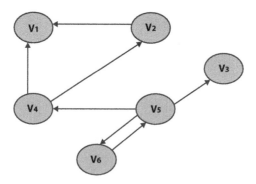

ADJACENCY MATRIX IS

	V1	V2	V3	V4	V5	V6
V1	0	0	0	0	0	0
V2	1	0	0	0	0	0
V3	0	0	0	0	0	0

GRAPH   303

	V1	V2	V3	V4	V5	V6
V4	1	1	0	0	0	0
V5	0	0	1	1	0	1
V6	0	0	0	0	1	0

If the above is Undirected then the matrix will be

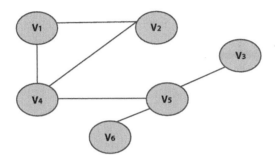

	V1	V2	V3	V4	V5	V6
V1	0	1	0	1	0	0
V2	1	0	0	1	0	0
V3	0	0	0	0	1	0
V4	1	1	0	0	1	0
V5	0	0	1	1	0	1
V6	0	0	0	0	1	0

ADJACENCY LIST

The use of adjacency matrix to represent a graph is inadequate because of the static implementation. The solution to this problem is by using a linked list structure, which represents graph using adjacency list. If the graph is not dense, that is if the graph is sparse, a better solution lies in an adjacency list representation.

For each vertex we keep a list of all adjacent vertices. In adjacent list representation of graph, we will maintain two lists. First list will keep the track of all nodes in the graph and in the second list we will maintain a list of adjacent adjacent nodes for every node. Each list has a header node which will be the corresponding node in the first list. The header nodes are sequential providing easy random access to the adjacency list for any particular vertex.

EXAMPLE :

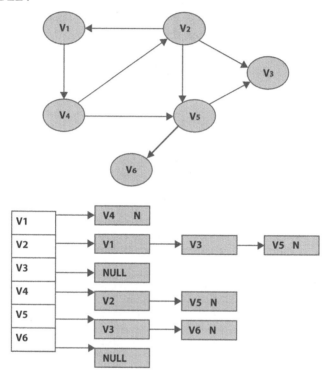

INCEDENCE MATRIX

Consider the Graph as

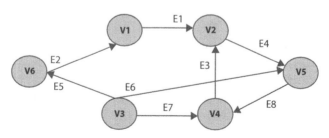

GRAPH 305

In this type of representation the major part is the edges of the graphs it clearly signifies that to which vertices the edges are connected. The vertex from where the edge start that represented as 1 and the end at which it ends that is represented by −1

	V1	V2	V3	V4	V5	V6
E1	1	-1	0	0	0	0
E2	-1	0	0	0	0	1
E3	0	-1	0	1	0	0
E4	0	1	0	0	-1	0
E5	0	0	1	0	0	-1
E6	0	0	1	0	-1	0
E7	0	0	1	-1	0	0
E8	0	0	0	-1	1	0

9.3 Traversal of Graph

The Graph Traversal is of two types such as

- Breadth First Search (BFS)
- Depth First Search (DFS)

9.3.1 Breadth First Search (BFS)

BFS starts at a given vertex, which is at level '0'. In the first stage we visit all vertices at level 1. In the second stage we visit all vertices at second level.

These new vertices, which are adjacent to level 1 vertices and so on.

The BFS terminates when every vertex has been visited.

BFS used to solve

1. Testing whether graph is connected or not.
2. Computing a spanning forest of Graph.
3. Computing a cycle in graph or reporting that no such cycle exists.

4. Computing for every vertex in graph, a path with the minimum number of edges between start vertex and current vertex or reporting that no such path exists.

Analysis: Total Running time of BFS = O(V + E)

ALGORITHM BFS(G,S)

1. for each vertex u ∈V[G]- {S}
2. do color[u] ←white
3. d[u] ← ∞ i.e/ distance from S
4. P[u] ← NIL i.e/ Parent in the BFS tree
5. color[S] ← gray
6. d[S] ← 0
7. Q ← {S}
8. while Q ≠ φ do
9. u ← head[Q]
10. for each v ∈ Adj[u] do
11. if color[v] = white then
12. color[v] ← gray
13. d[v] ← d[u] + 1
14. p[v] ← u
15. ENQUEUE(Q,v)
16. DEQUEUE(Q)
17. color[u] ← black

Example :

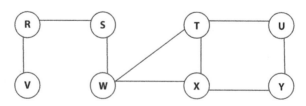

BFS(G,S)
for each vertex u ∈V[G]- {S}
        do color[u] ←white
                so color[S] = white
                color[S] = gray
        d[S] = 0
        Q = {S}

GRAPH   307

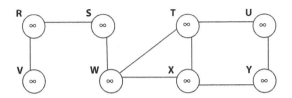

STEP-2 While Q ≠ φ

      Since Q is not empty so S = Head[Q]

for each v ∈ Adj[u]

i.e/ for each v ∈ Adj[S]

find Adj[S] = [R,W]

if color[v] = white i.e/ color[R] = WHITE and color[W] = white

so color[R] = gray and color[W] = gray

  d[v] = d[u] + 1 i.e/ d[R] = d[S] + 1 = 0 + 1 = 1

                  d[W] = d[S] + 1 = 0 + 1 = 1

ENQUE(Q,v)

i.e/ ENQUE(Q,R) and ENQUE(Q,W)

DEQUEUE(Q) and color[S] = BLACK

      So DEQUEUE(S) and color[S] = black.

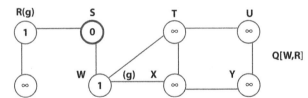

STEP-3

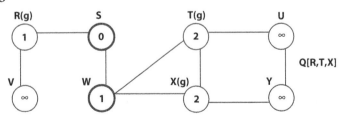

STEP-4

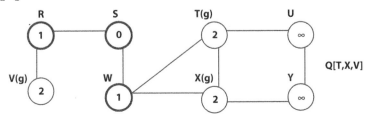

STEP-5

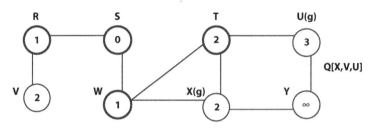

STEP-6

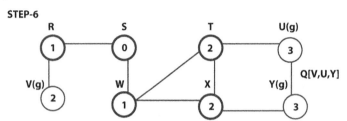

STEP-7

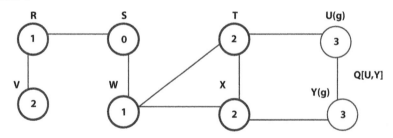

STEP-8

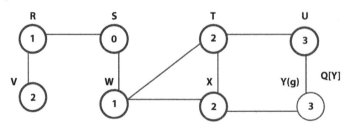

GRAPH 309

STEP- 9

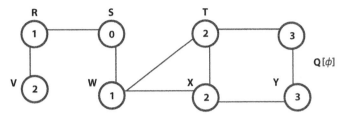

Final result of BFS is **S,W,R,T,X,V,U,Y**

Final result of BFS is **S,W,R,T,X,V,U,Y**
Simplest Way for BFS

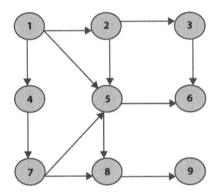

BREADTH FIRST SEARCH

The BFS uses QUEUE for the traversal of Graph.
PROCEDURE

1. Insert Starting Node into the QUEUE
2. Delete front element from the queue and insert all its unvisited neighbors into the queue at the end and traverse them. Also make the value of visited array true for these nodes.
3. Repeat Step-2 until the queue is empty

STEP-1

Insert starting node 1 into the QUEUE

Traverse nodes = 1

Visited[1] = T

Front = 0 Rear = 0 queue = 1

Traversal = 1

STEP-2

Delete the element from the queue and insert all the unvisited neighbors into the queue i.e/

Traverse node = 2,4,5

Visited[2] = T Visited[4] = T visited [5] = T

Front = 0 Rear = 2 queue = 2,4,5

Traversal = 1,2,4,5

STEP–3

Delete front element node 2 from queue, traverse its unvisited neighbors 3 and insert it into the queue

Traverse node = 3

Visited [3] = T

Front = 1 Rear = 3 queue = 4,5,3

Traversal = 1,2,4,5,3

STEP-4

Delete 4 and insert 7

Traverse nodes = 7

Visited[7] = T

Front = 2 Rear = 4 queue = 5,3,7

Traversal = 1,2,4,5,3,7

STEP-5

Delete 5 and insert 6,8

Traverse nodes – 6,8

Visited[6]= T visited[8] = T

Front = 3 Rear = 6 queue = 3,7,6,8

Traversal = 1,2,4,5,3,7,6,8

STEP-6

Delete 3 and since it has no unvisited neighbors so insert operation will not perform

Front = 4 Rear = 6 queue = 7,6, 8

Traversal = 1,2,4,5,3,7,6,8

STEP-7

Delete 7 and since it has no unvisited neighbors so insert operation will not perform

Front = 5 Rear = 6 queue = 6, 8

Traversal = 1,2,4,5,3,7,6,8

GRAPH 311

STEP-8

Delete 6 and since it has no unvisited neighbors so insert operation will not perform

Front = 6 Rear = 6 queue = 8

Traversal = 1,2,4,5,3,7,6,8

STEP-9

Delete 8 and insert 9

Front = 0 Rear = 0 queue = 9

Traversal = 1,2,4,5,3,7,6,8,9

STEP-10

Delete 9 and since it has no unvisited neighbors so insert operation will not perform

Front = -1 Rear = -1 queue = EMPTY

Traversal = 1,2,4,5,3,7,6,8,9

9.3.2 Depth First Search

Depth First Search is another way of traversing of graph. It uses STACK data structure for traversing.

ALGORITHM DFS(G)

1. for each vertex u $\in$ V[G]
2. do color[u] $\leftarrow$ white
3. π (u) $\leftarrow$ NIL
4. time $\leftarrow$ 0
5. for each vertex u $\in$ V[G]
6. do if color[u] $\leftarrow$ white
7. DFS-VISIT(u)

ALGORITHM DFS-VISIT(u)

1. color[u] $\leftarrow$ gray
2. time $\leftarrow$ time + 1
3. d[u] $\leftarrow$ time
4. for each v $\in$ Adj[u]
5. if color[v] $\leftarrow$ white
6. then π (v) $\leftarrow$ u
7. DFS-VISIT(v)
8. color(u) $\leftarrow$ black
9. finish[u] $\leftarrow$ time $\leftarrow$ time+1

EXAMPLE

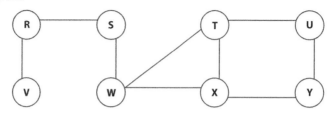

STEP-1 u=R

Color[R] = gray, time = 0+1 = 1 d[R] = 1

$v \in Adj[u] \Rightarrow v = (S,V)$

if color(S) = white and Since color(S) = white

$\pi(V) = u \Rightarrow \pi(S) = R$

COLOR

PARENT (π)

R	S	T	U	V	W	X	Y
Nil	Nil	Nil	Nil	Nil	Nil	Nil	Nil
	R	W	Y	R	S	T	X

TIME

R	S	T	U	V	W	X	Y
1	2	4	7	14	3	5	6
16	13	11	8	15	12	10	9

R	S	T	U	V	W	X	Y
White	White	White	White	White	White	White	White
Gray	Gray	Gray	Gray	Gray	Gray	Gray	Gray
Black	Black	Black	Black	Black	Black	Black	Black
8	6	4	1	7	5	3	2

GRAPH   313

Simplest Way for DFS

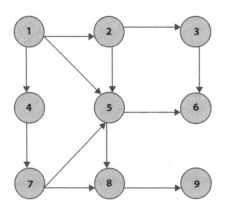

DEPTH FIRST SEARCH

The DFS uses STACK for the traversal of Graph.
PROCEDURE

1. PUSH starting node into the STACK
2. Pop an element from the STACK, if it has not traversed then traverse it, if it has already been traversed then just ignore it. After traversing make the value of visited array true for this node.
3. Now PUSH all the unvisited adjacent nodes of the popped element on STACK. PUSH the element even if it is already on the stack.
4. Repeat Step-3 and step-4 until stack is empty.

STEP-1
   PUSH 1 into STACK
   Top = 0 stack =1
STEP-2
   Pop 1 and traverse it and add all the unvisited adjacent node as 5,4,2
   Traverse Node = 1
   Visited[1] = T
   Top = 2 stack = 5,4,2
   Traversal = 1

STEP-3

Pop 2 and traverse it and insert 5,3 into STACK

Traverse node = 2

Visited[2] = T

Top = 3 stack = 5,4,5,3

Traversal = 1,2

STEP-4

Pop 3 , traverse it and insert 6 into the STACK

Traverse node = 3

Visited [3] = T

Top = 3 stack = 5,4,5,6

Traversal = 1,2,3

STEP-5

Pop 6 , traverse it and nothing is to PUSH into the STACK

Traverse node = 6

Visited [6] = T

Top = 2 stack = 5,4,5

Traversal = 1,2,3,6

STEP-6

Pop 5 , traverse it and PUSH 8 into the STACK and 6 is also adjacent but since it is visited so it will not PUSH.

Traverse node = 5

Visited [5] = T

Top = 2 stack = 5,4,8

Traversal = 1,2,3,6,5

STEP-7

Pop 8 , traverse it and PUSH 9 into the STACK.

Traverse node = 8

Visited [8] = T

Top = 2 stack = 5,4,9

Traversal = 1,2,3,6,5,8

STEP-8

Pop 9 , traverse it and nothing is to PUSH into the STACK.

Traverse node = 9

Visited [9] = T

Top = 1 stack = 5,4

Traversal = 1,2,3,6,5,8,9

STEP-9

Pop 4 , traverse it and   PUSH 7 into the STACK.

Traverse node = 4

Visited [4] = T

GRAPH   315

Top = 1 stack = 5,7
Traversal = 1,2,3,6,5,8,9,4

STEP-10

Pop 7 , traverse it and nothing is to PUSH into the STACK.
Traverse node = 7
Visited [7] = T
Top = 0 stack = 5
Traversal = 1,2,3,6,5,8,9,4,7

STEP-11

Pop 5 , traverse it but since Visited[5] = T so just ignore it.
Top = 0 stack =EMPTY

9.4   Spanning Tree

Let a graph G = (V,E) , if T is a sub graph of G and contains all the vertices
but no cycles/circuit, then T may be called as Spanning Tree.

MINIMUM SPANNING TREE

If a weighted graph is considered, than the weight of the spanning tree (T)
of graph G can be calculated by summing all the individual weights, in the
spanning tree T. But we observe that for a graph a number of spanning tree
are available but minimum spanning tree means the spanning tree with
minimum weight.

A tree is a connected Graph with no cycles

1. A graph is a tree if and only if there is one and only one path
   joining any two of its vertices.
2. A connected graph is a tree if and only if every one of its
   edges is a bridge.
3. A connected graph is a tree if and only if it has N vertices
   and N-1 edges.

One practical implementation of MST would be in the design of network.
Another useful application of MST is to finding airline routes.

9.4.1   Kruskal Algorithm

The Kruskal Algorithm is used to build the minimum spanning tree in
forest. Initially each vertex is in its own tree in forest. Then algorithm

considers each edge in turn, order by increasing weight. If an edge (u,v) connects two different trees then (u,v) is added to the set of edges of MST , and two trees connected by an edge(u,v) are merged into a single tree.

On the other hand if an edge(u,v) connects two vertices in the same tree, then edge(u,v) is discarded. It uses a disjoint set data structure to maintain several disjoint sets of elements.

Each set contains the vertices in a tree of current forest.

ALGORITHM KRUSKAL(G,W)

1. A = { ϕ}
2. for each vertex v $\in$V[G]
3. do MAKE-SET(v)
4. Sort edges E by increasing order of weight W
5. for each edge(u,v) in E(G)
6. do if FIND-SET(u) $\neq$ FIND-SET(v)
7. then A = A $\cup${(u,v)}
8. UNION(u,v)
9. return A

Example :

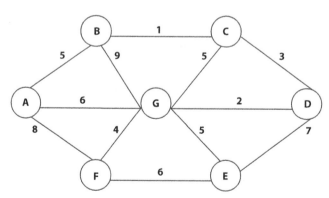

First sort the edges according to their weights in ascending order.

EDGES	WEIGHT
(B,C)	1
(G,D)	2
(C,D)	3
(F,G)	4
(A,B)	5

GRAPH 317

(C,G)	5
(G,E)	5
(A,G)	6
(F,E)	6
(E,D)	7
(A,F)	8
(B,G)	9

Now connect each and every edge from the beginning of the above list and if a closed path is found then discard that edge.

(B,C)

(G,D)

(C,D)

(F,G)

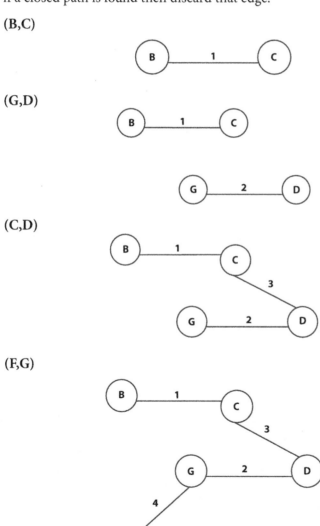

(A,B)

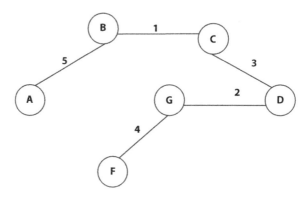

Since (C,G) forms a closed path so discard it.

(G,E)

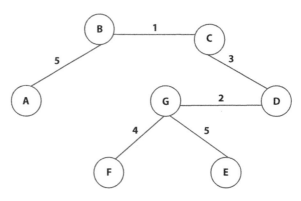

Since (A,G), (F,E), (E,D), (A,F), (B,G) forms closed paths so discard them and the above graph is the minimum spanning tree.

The Kruskal Algorithm is a greedy algorithm because at each step it adds to the forest an edge at least possible.

9.4.2   Prim's Algorithm

The key to implementing Prim's algorithm efficiently is to make it easy to select a new edge to be added to the tree formed by the edges in A in the pseudo code below, the connected graph G and the root R of the minimum spanning tree to be grown are inputs to the algorithm. During execution of the algorithm all vertices that are not in the tree reside in a min priority queue Q based in a key field. For each vertex V, Key[V] is the minimum weight of any edge connecting V to a vertex in the tree, by conversion key[V]= ∞ if there is no such edge. The field π (V) names the parent of V in the tree.

GRAPH   319

ALGORITHM PRIM(G,W,R)

1. for each u ∈ V(G)
2. do key[u] ←∞
3. π(u) ← Nil
4. Key[R] ← 0
5. Q ← V(G)
6. While Q ≠ φ
7. do u ← EXTRACT-MIN(Q)
8. for each v ∈ Q and w(u,v) < key(v)
9. then π(v) ← u
10. key[R] ← w(u,v)

Example:

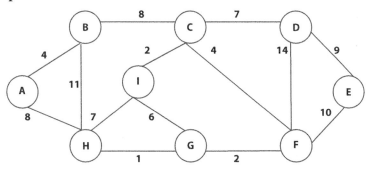

Queue :

A	B	C	D	E	F	G	H	I

KEY

Steps	A	B	C	D	E	F	G	H	I
	∞	∞	∞	∞	∞	∞	∞	∞	∞
0	0								
1		4						8	
2			8						
3				7		4			2
4							6	7	
5					10		2		
6								1	
7					9				

PARENT (π)

Steps	A	B	C	D	E	F	G	H	I
	Nil	Nil	Nil	Nil	Nil	Nil	Nil	Nil	Nil
1		A						A	
2			B						
3				C		C			C
4							I	I	
5						F	F		
6								G	
7				D					

Step-1: u = Extract_min(Q) i.e/ A and Key[A] = 0

 V = {B,H} [Adjacent of A]
 W(A,B) < Key[B]   i.e/ 4 < ∞ so **Key[B] = 4**   **π(B) = A**
 W(A,H) < Key[H]   i.e/ 8 < ∞ so **Key[H] = 8**   **π(H) = A Delete A**

Step-2: u = Extract_min(Q) i.e/ B because the Minimum of [4,8] so 4 i.e/ B

 V = {C,H} [Adjacent of B]
 W(B,C) < Key[C]   i.e/ 8 < ∞ so **Key[C] = 8**   **π(C) = B**
 W(B,H) < Key[H]   i.e/ 8 < 8 Since condition is false so no action will
take   **Delete : B**

Step-3: u = Extract_min(Q) i.e/ Min of (8,8) so C

 V = {B,I,F,D} [Adjacent of C] Since **B** is not in Q so **B** will not be
considered.

 W(C,I) < Key[I]   i.e/ 2 < ∞ so **Key[I] = 2**   **π(I) = C**
 W(C,F) < Key[F]   i.e/ 4 < ∞ so **Key[F] = 4**   **π(F) = C**
 W(C,D) < Key[D]   i.e/ 7 < ∞ so **Key[D] = 7**   **π(D) = C Delete C**

Step-4: u = Extract_min(Q) i.e/ Min of (7,4,8,2) so I

 V = {C,H,G} [Adjacent of I] Since **C** is not in Q so **C** will not be considered

 W(I,H) < Key[H]   i.e/ 7 < 8 so **Key[H] = 7**   **π(H) = I**
 W(I,G) < Key[G]   i.e/ 6 < ∞ so **Key[G] = 6**   **π(G) = I Delete I**

GRAPH 321

Step-5: u = Extract_min(Q) i.e/ Min of (7,4,6,7) so F

V = {E,C,D,G} [Adjacent of F] Since C is not in Q so C will not be considered
W(F,G) < Key[G] i.e/ 2 < 6 so **Key[G] = 2** **π(G) = F**
W(F,E) < Key[E] i.e/ 10 < ∞ so **Key[E] = 10** **π(E) = F Delete F**
W(F,D) < Key[D] i.e/ 14 < 7 (False)

Step-6: u = Extract_min(Q) i.e/ Min of (D,E,G,H)(7,10,2,7) so G

V = {H,I,F} [Adjacent of G] **I,F** will not be considered (Not In Queue)

W(G,H) < Key[H] i.e/ 1 < 7 so **Key[H] = 1** **π(H) = G Delete G**

Step-7: u = Extract_min(Q) i.e/ Min of (D,E,H)(7,10,1) so H
V = {A,B,I,G} [Adjacent of H]
Since all are not in Queue so all will be discarded
Delete H

Step-8: u = Extract_min(Q) i.e/ Min of (D,E)(7,10) so D
V = {C,F,E} [Adjacent of D] **C,F** will not be considered (Not In Queue)

W(D,E) < Key[E] i.e/ 9 < 10 so **Key[E] = 9** **π(E) = D Delete D**

Step-9: u = Extract_min(Q) i.e/ Min of (E)(9) so E
V = {D,F} [Adjacent of H]
Since all are not in Queue so all will be discarded
                                                    Delete E

Finally all the vertices are deleted from the Q. Now plot the graph according to the parent table.

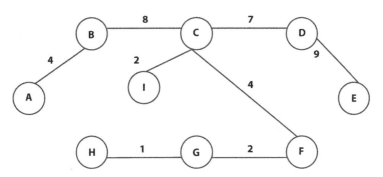

9.5   Single Source Shortest Path

The shortest path weight from a vertex u $\in$ V to a vertex v $\in$ V in the weighted graph is the minimum cost of all paths from u to v if there exists no such path from vertex u to vertex v then the weight of the shortest path is ∞

We can also define as

$$\delta(u, v) = \begin{cases} Min\{w(p) : u \bullet\!\!-\!\!\stackrel{p}{-}\!\!-\!\!\rightarrow\!\bullet v \text{ if there is a path from u to v }\} \\ \infty \qquad\qquad\qquad\qquad\text{otherwise} \end{cases}$$

NEGATIVE WEIGHTED EDGES

The negative weight cycle is a cycle whose total weight is −ve. No path from starting vertex S to a vertex on the cycle can be a shortest path.

Since a path can run around the cycle many many times so it may get any -ve costing other word we can say that a negative cycle invalidates the notion of distance based on edge weights.

If some path from S to v contains a negative cost sysle , there does not exist a shortest path otherwise there exist one that is simple.

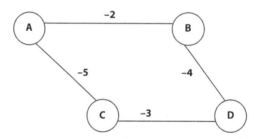

RELAXATION TECHNIQUE

This technique consists of testing whether we can improve the shortest path found so far, if so update the shortest path. A relaxation step may or may not decrease the value of the shortest path estimate.

ALGORITHM RELAX(u,v,w)

1. if d[u] + w(u,v) <d[v]
2. then d[v] ←d[u] + w(u,v)
3. π [v] ← u

GRAPH 323

Example :

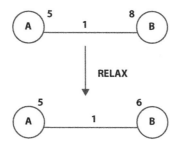

ALGORITHM INITIALIZE_SINGLE_SOURCE(G,S)

1. for each vertex v ∈ V[G]
2. do d[v] ← ∞
3. π (v) ← Nil
4. d[s] ← 0

9.5.1 Bellman–Ford Algorithm

Bellman ford algorithm solves the single source shortest path problem in the general case in which edges of a given digraph can have –ve weight as long as G contains no negative cycles.

It uses d[u] as an upper bound on the distance d[u,v] from u to v. The algorithm progressively decreases an estimate d[v] on the weight of the shortest path from the source vertex S the each vertex v in V until it achieves the actual shortest path.

This algorithm returns TRUE if the given digraph contains no –ve cycle that are reachable from source vertex S otherwise FALSE.

ALGORITHM BELLMAN-FORD(G,W,S)

1. INITIALIZE-SINGLE-SOURCE(G,S)
2. for each vertex i = 1 to V[G] – 1 do
3. for each edge(u,v) ∈ E(G) do
4. RELAX(u,v,w)
5. for each edge(u,v) in E(G)
6. do if d[u] + w(u,v) < d[v]
7. then return FALSE

8. Return TRUE

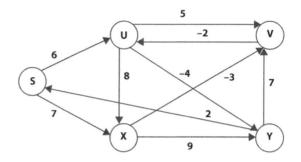

Distance

Steps	S	U	V	Y	X
		∞	∞	∞	∞	∞
	0				
1		6			7
2			11	2	
3			9		
4			4		
5		2			
6				-2	
7	No effect				

Parent (π)

Steps	S	U	V	Y	X
	Nil	Nil	Nil	Nil	Nil
1		S			S
2			U	U	
3			Y		
4			X		
5		V			
6				U	
7	No effect				

GRAPH   325

STEPS

For i=1   Consider the vertex S

Now Since the Adj(S) = (U,X) now implement Relax with (S,U) and (S,X)

Relax(s,u,w)

$d[s] + w(s,u) < d[u] = 0 + 6 < \infty$ so $d[u] = 6$ and $\pi(u) = S$

Relax(s,x,w)

$d[s] + w(s,x) < d[x] = 0 + 7 < \infty$ so $d[x] = 7$ and $\pi(x) = S$

For i=2   Consider the vertex U (min(u,x))

Now Since the Adj(U) = (V,X,Y) now implement Relax with (U,V),(U,X) and (U,Y)

Relax(u,v,w)

$d[u] + w(u,v) < d[v] = 6 + 5 < \infty$ so $d[v] = 11$ and $\pi(v) = u$

Relax(u,x,w)

$d[u] + w(u,x) < d[x] = 6 + 8 < 7$ (False)

Relax(u,y,w)

$d[u] + w(u,y) < d[y] = 6 + -4 < \infty$ so $d[y] = 2$ and $\pi(y) = u$

For i=3   Consider the vertex Y (minimum)

Now Since the Adj(Y) = (V,S) now implement Relax with (Y,V) and (Y,S)

Relax(y,v,w)

$d[y] + w(y,v) < d[v] = 2 + 7 < 11$ so $d[v] = 9$ and $\pi(v) = y$

Relax(y,s,w)

$d[y] + w(y,s) < d[s] = 2 + 2 < 0$ (False)

For i=4   Consider the vertex X (minimum)

Now Since the Adj(X) = (V,Y) now implement Relax with (X,V) and (X,Y)

Relax(x,v,w)

$d[x] + w(x,v) < d[v] = 7 + -3 < 9$ so $d[v] = 4$ and $\pi(v) = x$

Relax(x,y,w)

   d[x] + w(x,y) < d[y] = 7 + 9 < 2 (False)

For i=5   Consider the vertex V (minimum)

   Now Since the Adj(V) = (U) now implement Relax with (V,U)

Relax(v,u,w)

   d[v] + w(v,u) < d[u] = 4 + -2 < 6 so d[u] = 2 and π(u) = v

For i=6   Consider the vertex U (minimum)

   Now Since the Adj(U) = (V,Y,X) now implement Relax with (U,V),(U,Y),(U,X)

Relax(u,v,w)

   d[u] + w(u,v) < d[v] = 2 + 5 < 4 (False)

Relax(u,y,w)

   d[u] + w(u,y) < d[y] = 2 + -4 < 2 so d[y] = -2 and π(y) = u

Relax(u,x,w)

   d[u] + w(u,x) < d[x] = 2 + 8 < 7 (False)

For i=7   Consider the vertex Y (minimum)

   Now Since the Adj(Y) = (V,S) now implement Relax with (Y,V),(Y,S)

Relax(y,v,w)

   d[y] + w(y,v) < d[v] = -2 + 7 < 4 (False)

Relax(y,s,w)

   d[y] + w(y,s) < d[s] = -2 + 2 < 0 (False)

So the shortest path graph is

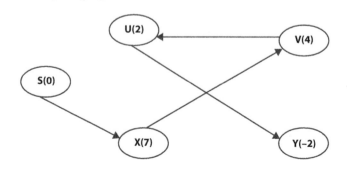

GRAPH   327

9.5.2   Dijkstra's Algorithm

Dijkstra's algorithm solves the single source shortest path problem when all edges have non –ve weights. It is a greedy algorithm and similar to prim's algorithm. Algorithm starts at the source vertex S it grows a tree T that ultimately spans all vertices rechable from S. Vertices are added to T in order of distance i.e/ first S, then the vertex closest to S, then the next closest and so on.

ALGORITHM DIJKSTRA(G,W,S)

1. INITIALIZE-SINGLE-SOURCE(G,S)
2. S ←{ }
3. Initialize Priority Queue i.e/ Q ←V[G]
4. While Q ≠ φ
5. do u ← Extract_min(Q)
6. S ← S ∪{u}
7. for each vertex v ∈Adj[u]
8. do RELAX(u,v,w)

Example:

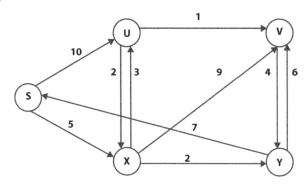

Distance

Steps	S	U	V	Y	X
	∞	∞	∞	∞	∞
	0				
1		10			5
2		8	14	7	
3			13		
4			9		

Parent (π)

Steps	S	U	V	Y	X
	Nil	Nil	Nil	Nil	Nil
1		S			S
2		X	X	X	
3				Y	
4			U		

STEP-1   Consider the vertex S
       Now Since the Adj(S) = (X,U) now implement Relax with (S,U) and (S,X)

Relax(s,u,w)
       $d[s] + w(s,u) < d[u] = 0 + 10 < \infty$ so $d[u] = 10$ and $\pi(u) = S$
Relax(s,x,w)
       $d[s] + w(s,x) < d[x] = 0 + 5 < \infty$ so $d[x] = 5$ and $\pi(x) = S$ **delete S**
STEP-2   Consider the vertex X (minimum)
       Now Since the Adj(X) = (U,V,Y) now implement Relax with (X,U) (X,Y)and (X,V)

Relax(x,u,w)
       $d[x] + w(x,u) < d[u] = 5 + 3 < 10$ so $d[u] = 8$ and $\pi(u) = X$
Relax(x,v,w)
       $d[x] + w(x,v) < d[v] = 5 + 9 < \infty$ so $d[v] = 14$ and $\pi(v) = X$
Relax(x,y,w)
       $d[x] + w(x,y) < d[y] = 5 + 2 < \infty$ so $d[y] = 7$ and $\pi(y) = X$ **delete X**

STEP-3   Consider the vertex Y (minimum)
       Now Since the Adj(Y) = (S,V) now implement Relax with (Y,S) (Y,V)
Relax(y,s,w)
       $d[y] + w(y,s) < d[s] = 7 + 7 < 0$ (False)
Relax(y,v,w)
       $d[y] + w(y,v) < d[v] = 7 + 6 < 14$ so $d[v] = 13$ and $\pi(v) = Y$
delete Y

GRAPH   329

STEP-4   Consider the vertex U (minimum)
          Now Since the Adj(U) = (V,X) now implement Relax with (U,V)
(U,X)
Relax(u,v,w)
          d[u] + w(u,v) < d[v] = 8 + 1 < 13 so d[v] = 9 and π(v) = U

Relax(u,x,w)
          d[u] + w(u,x) < d[x] = 8 + 2 < 5 (False)   **delete U**
So final shortest path matrix is

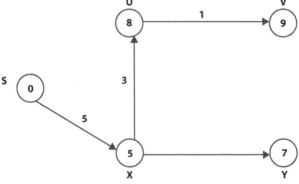

Dsv = Dsx + Dxu + Duv = 5 + 3+ 1 = 9

PROGRAM USING DIJKSTRA ALGORITHM

```
#include<stdio.h>
#include<conio.h>
#define INFINITY 9999
#define MAX 10
void createGraph(int G[MAX][MAX],int n) ;
void dijkstra(int G[MAX][MAX],int n,int startnode);

int main()
{
      int G[MAX][MAX],i,j,n,u;
      char ch;
//input the number of vertices
      printf("Enter no. of vertices:");
      scanf("%d",&n);

      createGraph(G,n);
      printf("\nEnter the starting node:");
```

```
        fflush(stdin);
        scanf("%c",&ch);//read the starting vertex
        u= toupper(ch)-65;//convert to its equivalent numeric
value i.e/ a=0,b=1,c=2 and so on....
        dijkstra(G,n,u);

        return 0;
}

//create the graph by using the concepts of adjacency
matrix.
 void createGraph(int G[MAX][MAX],int n)
 {
        int i,j;
 //read the adjacency matrix
        printf("\nEnter the adjacency matrix:\n");

        for(i=0;i<n;i++)
              for(j=0;j<n;j++)
                    scanf("%d",&G[i][j]);

 }

void dijkstra(int G[MAX][MAX],int n,int startnode)
{

        int cost[MAX][MAX],distance[MAX],pred[MAX];
        int visited[MAX],count,mindistance,nextnode,i,j;
        char ver='A';

        //pred[] stores the predecessor of each node
        //count gives the number of nodes seen so far
        //create the cost matrix
        for(i=0;i<n;i++)
              for(j=0;j<n;j++)
                    if(G[i][j]==0)
                          cost[i][j]=INFINITY;
                    else
                          cost[i][j]=G[i][j];

        //initialize pred[],distance[] and visited[]
        for(i=0;i<n;i++)
        {
              distance[i]=cost[startnode][i];
              pred[i]=startnode;
              visited[i]=0;
        }

        distance[startnode]=0;
```

GRAPH   331

```
        visited[startnode]=1;
        count=1;

        while(count<n-1)
        {
                mindistance=INFINITY;

                //nextnode gives the node with minimum
distance
                for(i=0;i<n;i++)
                        if(distance[i]<mindistance&&!visited[i])
                        {
                                mindistance=distance[i];
                                nextnode=i;
                        }

                //check if a better path exists through
nextnode or not
                        visited[nextnode]=1;
                        for(i=0;i<n;i++)
                                if(!visited[i])

if(mindistance+cost[nextnode][i]<distance[i])
                                        {

distance[i]=mindistance+cost[nextnode][i];
                                                pred[i]=nextnode;
                                        }
                count++;
        }

        //print the path and distance of each node from
strating node
        for(i=0;i<n;i++)
                if(i!=startnode)
                {
                        printf("\nDistance of node from %c to %c
= %d",ver, ver+i,distance[i]);

                        printf("\nPath=%c",ver+i);
                        j=i;
                        do
                        {
                                j=pred[j];

                                printf("<-%c",ver+j);
                        }while(j!=startnode);
                }
}
```

OUTPUT

```
Enter no. of vertices:6
Enter the adjacency matrix:
0
2
7
4
0
0
2
0
0
0
4
5
7
0
0
3
8
0
4
0
3
0
6
3
0
4
8
6
0
0
0
5
0
3
0
0

Enter the starting node:a
Distance of node from A to B = 2
Path=B<-A
Distance of node from A to C = 7
Path=C<-A
Distance of node from A to D = 4
Path=D<-A
Distance of node from A to E = 6
Path=E<-B<-A
Distance of node from A to F = 7
Path=F<-B<-A
----------------------------------------
Process exited after 39.95 seconds with return value 0
Press any key to continue . . .
```

BY USING ADJACENCY MATRIX

```cpp
#include<iostream.h>

#define INFINITY 9999

void dijkstra(int gra[50][50],int n,int startnode,int last);

int main()
{
    int gra[50][50],i,j,n,u,v;
    cout<<"Enter no. of vertices:";
    cin>>n;          // ask about the number of vertices
    cout<<"\nEnter the adjacency matrix:\n";
```

GRAPH   333

```
                      // enter the graph
   for(i=1;i<=n;i++)
      for(j=1;j<=n;j++)
         cin>>gra[i][j];
   cout<<endl<<"GRAPH IS \n";
   for(i=1;i<=n;i++)
     {
       for(j=1;j<=n;j++)
          cout<<"      "<<gra[i][j];
          cout<<endl;
     }

   cout<<"\nEnter the starting node:";
   cin>>u;                  // input the starting vertex
   cout<<"\n Enter the last vertex";
   cin>>v;                  //enter the last vertex
   dijkstra(gra,n,u,v);

   return 0;
}
                      //find the shortest path
void dijkstra(int gra[50][50],int n,int startnode,int last)
{

   int cost[50][50],distance[50],pred[50];
   int visited[50],count,mindistance,nextnode,i,j;

   //pred[] stores the predecessor of each node
   //count gives the number of nodes seen so far
   //create the cost matrix
   for(i=1;i<=n;i++)
      for(j=1;j<=n;j++)
         if(gra[i][j]==0)
            cost[i][j]=INFINITY;
         else
            cost[i][j]=gra[i][j];

   //initialize pred[],distance[] and visited[]
   for(i=1;i<=n;i++)
   {
      distance[i]=cost[startnode][i];
      pred[i]=startnode;
      visited[i]=0;
   }

   distance[startnode]=0;
   visited[startnode]=1;
   count=1;
```

```
while(count<n-1)
{
    mindistance=INFINITY;

    //nextnode gives the node at minimum distance
    for(i=1;i<=n;i++)
        if(distance[i]<mindistance&&!visited[i])
        {
            mindistance=distance[i];
            nextnode=i;
        }

        //check if a better path exists through nextnode
        visited[nextnode]=1;
        for(i=1;i<=n;i++)
            if(!visited[i])
                if(mindistance+cost[nextnode]
[i]<distance[i])
                {
                    distance[i]=mindistance+cost[nextnode]
[i];
                    pred[i]=nextnode;
                }
    count++;
}

//print the path and distance of each node
for(i=1;i<=n;i++)
    if(i!=startnode && i==last)
    {
        cout<<"\nShortest Distance "<<startnode<<" to
"<<i<<" = "<<distance[i];
        cout<<"\nShortest Path = "<<i;

        j=i;
        do
        {
            j=pred[j];
            cout<<"<-"<<j;
        }while(j!=startnode);
    }
}
```

GRAPH   335

OUTPUT

```
GRAPH IS
    0    12     7     0     0     0     0     0     0     0
   12     0     0     4    14     0     0     0     0     0
    7     0     0     6     0     0    12     0     0     0
    0     4     6     0     2     0     0     0     0     0
    0    14     0     2     0     7     0     4     0     0
    0     0     0     0     7     0     5    14     1     0
    0     0    12     0     0     5     0     0     4     0
    0     0     0     0     4    14     0     0     0     2
    0     0     0     0     0     1     4     0     0     2
    0     0     0     0     0     0     0     2     2     0

Enter the starting node:1

 Enter the last vertex4

Shortest Distance 1 to 4 = 13
Shortest Path = 4<-3<-1
```

9.6   All Pair Shortest Path

Given a directed, connected weighted graph G(V,E), for each edge ⟨u,v⟩∈E, a weight w(u,v) is associated with the edge. The all pairs of shortest paths problem (APSP) is to find a shortest path from u to v for every pair of vertices u and v in V.

The representation of G
The input is an n×n matrix W=(wij).

$$
w(i,j) = \begin{cases}
0 & \text{if } i = j \\
\text{the weight of the directed edge}\langle i,j\rangle & \text{if } i \neq j \text{ and} \langle i,j\rangle \in E \\
\infty & \text{if } i \neq j \text{ and} \langle i,j\rangle \notin E
\end{cases}
$$

The all-pairs-shortest-path problem is generalization of the single-source-shortest-path problem, so we can use Floyd's algorithm, or Dijkstra's algorithm (varying the source node over all nodes).

- Floyd's algorithm is $O(N^3)$
- Dijkstra's algorithm with an adjacency matrix is $O(N^2)$, so varying over N source nodes is $O(N^3)$

- Dijkstra's algorithm with adjacency lists is O(E log N), so varying over N source nodes is O(N E log N)

For large sparse graphs, Dijkstra's algorithm is preferable.

Floyd–Warshall Algorithm

Floyd–Warshall's algorithm is based upon the observation that a path linking any two vertices u and v may have zero or more intermediate vertices. The algorithm begins by disallowing all intermediate vertices. In this case, the partial solution is simply the initial weights of the graph or infinity if there is no edge.

The algorithm proceeds by allowing an additional intermediate vertex at each step. For each introduction of a new intermediate vertex x, the shortest path between any pair of vertices u and v, x,u,v∈V, is the minimum of the previous best estimate of δ(u,v), or the combination of the paths from u→x and x→v.

The Floyd–Warshall algorithm compares all possible paths through the graph between each pair of vertices. It is able to do this with only $\Theta(|V|^3)$ comparisons in a graph. This is remarkable considering that there may be up to $\Omega(|V|^2)$ edges in the graph, and every combination of edges is tested. It does so by incrementally improving an estimate on the shortest path between two vertices, until the estimate is optimal.

$$\delta(u,v)\leftarrow\min(\delta(u,v),\delta(u,x)+\delta(x,v))$$

Let the directed graph be represented by a weighted matrix W.

FLOYD–WARSHALL (W)

```
1    n ← rows [W]
2    D(0) ← W
3    for k ← 1 to n
4        do for i ← 1 to n
5            do for j ← 1 to n
6                do d_{ij}^{(k)} ← MIN(d_{ij}^{(k-1)}, d_{ik}^{(k-1)} + d_{kj}^{(k-1)})
7    return  D(n)
```

The time complexity of the algorithm above is O(n3).

GRAPH 337

Example

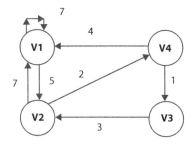

The path matrix is

$$
D^0 = \begin{matrix}
7 & 5 & \infty & \infty \\
7 & \infty & \infty & 2 \\
\infty & 3 & \infty & \infty \\
4 & \infty & 1 & \infty
\end{matrix}
$$

According to the algorithm k = 4, i= 4 and j= 4.
So the total number of repetition will be $O(4^3) = 64$

We have to compute D1,D2,D3,D4.

For k =1 & I = 1
J=1 : $D^1[1][1] = \min(D^0[1][1], D^0[1][1] + D^0[1][1]) = (7,7+7) = 7$
J=2 : $D^1[1][2] = \min(D^0[1][2], D^0[1][1] + D^0[1][2]) = (5,7+5) = 5$
J=3 : $D^1[1][3] = \min(D^0[1][3], D^0[1][1] + D^0[1][3]) = (\infty,7+\infty) = \infty$
J=4 : $D^1[1][4] = \min(D^0[1][4], D^0[1][1] + D^0[1][4]) = (\infty,7+\infty) = \infty$

For k =1 & I = 2
J=1 : $D^1[2][1] = \min(D^0[2][1], D^0[2][1] + D^0[1][1]) = (7,7+7) = 7$
J=2 : $D^1[2][2] = \min(D^0[2][2], D^0[2][1] + D^0[1][2]) = (\infty,7+5) = \mathbf{12}$
J=3 : $D^1[2][3] = \min(D^0[2][3], D^0[2][1] + D^0[1][3]) = (\infty,7+\infty) = \infty$
J=4 : $D^1[2][4] = \min(D^0[2][4], D^0[2][1] + D^0[1][4]) = (2,7+\infty) = 2$

For k =1 & I = 3
J=1 : $D^1[3][1] = \min(D^0[3][1], D^0[3][1] + D^0[1][1]) = (\infty,\infty+7) = \infty$
J=2 : $D^1[3][2] = \min(D^0[3][2], D^0[3][1] + D^0[1][2]) = (3, \infty+5) = \mathbf{3}$
J=3 : $D^1[3][3] = \min(D^0[3][3], D^0[3][1] + D^0[1][3]) = (\infty,\infty+\infty) = \infty$
J=4 : $D^1[3][4] = \min(D^0[3][4], D^0[3][1] + D^0[1][4]) = (\infty,\infty+\infty) = \infty$

For k =1 & I = 4

J=1 : $D^1[4][1] = min(D^0[4][1], D^0[4][1] + D^0[1][1]) = (4,4+7) = 4$

J=2 : $D^1[4][2] = min(D^0[4][2], D^0[4][1] + D^0[1][2]) = (\infty,4+5) = 9$

J=3 : $D^1[4][3] = min(D^0[4][3], D^0[4][1] + D^0[1][3]) = (1,4+\infty) = 1$

J=4 : $D^1[4][4] = min(D^0[4][4], D^0[4][1] + D^0[1][4]) = (\infty,4+\infty) = \infty$

$$D^1 = \begin{matrix} 7 & 5 & \infty & \infty \\ 7 & 12 & \infty & 2 \\ \infty & 3 & \infty & \infty \\ 4 & 9 & 1 & \infty \end{matrix}$$

For k =2 & I = 1

J=1 : $D^2[1][1] = min(D^1[1][1], D^1[1][2] + D^1[2][1]) = (7,5+7) = 7$

J=2 : $D^2[1][2] = min(D^1[1][2], D^1[1][2] + D^1[2][2]) = (5,5+12) = 5$

J=3 : $D^2[1][3] = min(D^1[1][3], D^1[1][2] + D^1[2][3]) = (\infty,5+\infty) = \infty$

J=4 : $D^2[1][4] = min(D^1[1][4], D^1[1][2] + D^1[2][4]) = (\infty,5+2) = 7$

For k =2 & I = 2

J=1 : $D^2[2][1] = min(D^1[2][1], D^1[2][2] + D^1[2][1]) = (7,12+7) = 7$

J=2 : $D^2[2][2] = min(D^1[2][2], D^1[2][2] + D^1[2][2]) = (12,12+12) = 12$

J=3 : $D^2[2][3] = min(D^1[2][3], D^1[2][2] + D^1[2][3]) = (\infty,12+\infty) = \infty$

J=4 : $D^2[2][4] = min(D^1[2][4], D^1[2][2] + D^1[2][4]) = (2,12+2) = 2$

For k = 2 & I = 3

J=1 : $D^2[3][1] = min(D^1[3][1], D^1[3][2] + D^1[2][1]) = (\infty,3+7) = 10$

J=2 : $D^2[3][2] = min(D^1[3][2], D^1[3][2] + D^1[2][2]) = (3, 3+12) = 3$

J=3 : $D^2[3][3] = min(D^1[3][3], D^1[3][2] + D^1[2][3]) = (\infty,3+\infty) = \infty$

J=4 : $D^2[3][4] = min(D^1[3][4], D^1[3][2] + D^1[2][4]) = (\infty,3+2) = 5$

For k =2 & I = 4

J=1 : $D^2[4][1] = min(D^1[4][1], D^1[4][2] + D^1[2][1]) = (4,9+7) = 4$

J=2 : $D^2[4][2] = min(D^1[4][2], D^1[4][2] + D^1[2][2]) = (9,9+12) = 9$

J=3 : $D^2[4][3] = min(D^1[4][3], D^1[4][2] + D^1[2][3]) = (1,9+\infty) = 1$

J=4 : $D^2[4][4] = min(D^1[4][4], D^1[4][2] + D^1[2][4]) = (\infty,9+2) = 11$

$$D^2 = \begin{matrix} 7 & 5 & \infty & 7 \\ 7 & 12 & \infty & 2 \\ 10 & 3 & \infty & 5 \\ 4 & 9 & 1 & 11 \end{matrix}$$

GRAPH 339

For k =3 & I = 1

J=1 : $D^3[1][1] = \min(D^2[1][1], D^2[1][3] + D^2[3][1]) = (7, \infty+10) = 7$
J=2 : $D^3[1][2] = \min(D^2[1][2], D^2[1][3] + D^2[3][2]) = (5, \infty+3) = 5$
J=3 : $D^3[1][3] = \min(D^2[1][3], D^2[1][3] + D^2[3][3]) = (\infty, \infty+\infty) = \infty$
J=4 : $D^3[1][4] = \min(D^2[1][4], D^2[1][3] + D^2[3][4]) = (7, \infty+5) = 7$

For k =3 & I = 2

J=1 : $D^3[2][1] = \min(D^2[2][1], D^2[2][3] + D^2[3][1]) = (7, \infty+10) = 7$
J=2 : $D^3[2][2] = \min(D^2[2][2], D^2[2][3] + D^2[3][2]) = (12, \infty+3) = 12$
J=3 : $D^3[2][3] = \min(D^2[2][3], D^2[2][3] + D^2[3][3]) = (\infty, \infty+\infty) = \infty$
J=4 : $D^3[2][4] = \min(D^2[2][4], D^2[2][3] + D^2[3][4]) = (2, \infty+5) = 2$

For k = 3 & I = 3

J=1 : $D^3[3][1] = \min(D^2[3][1], D^2[3][3] + D^2[3][1]) = (10, \infty+10) = 10$
J=2 : $D^3[3][2] = \min(D^2[3][2], D^2[3][3] + D^2[3][2]) = (3, \infty+3) = 3$
J=3 : $D^3[3][3] = \min(D^2[3][3], D^2[3][3] + D^2[3][3]) = (\infty, \infty+\infty) = \infty$
J=4 : $D^3[3][4] = \min(D^2[3][4], D^2[3][3] + D^2[3][4]) = (5, \infty+5) = 5$

For k =3 & I = 4

J=1 : $D^3[4][1] = \min(D^2[4][1], D^2[4][3] + D^2[3][1]) = (4, 1+10) = 4$
J=2 : $D^3[4][2] = \min(D^2[4][2], D^2[4][3] + D^2[3][2]) = (9, 1+3) = \mathbf{4}$
J=3 : $D^3[4][3] = \min(D^2[4][3], D^2[4][3] + D^2[3][3]) = (1, 1+\infty) = 1$
J=4 : $D^3[4][4] = \min(D^2[4][4], D^2[4][3] + D^2[3][4]) = (11, 1+5) = \mathbf{6}$

$$D^3 = \begin{matrix} 7 & 5 & \infty & 7 \\ 7 & 12 & \infty & 2 \\ 10 & 3 & \infty & 5 \\ 4 & 4 & 1 & 6 \end{matrix}$$

For k =4 & I = 1

J=1 : $D^4[1][1] = \min(D^3[1][1], D^3[1][4] + D^3[4][1]) = (7, 7+4) = 7$
J=2 : $D^4[1][2] = \min(D^3[1][2], D^3[1][4] + D^3[4][2]) = (5, 7+4) = 5$
J=3 : $D^4[1][3] = \min(D^3[1][3], D^3[1][4] + D^3[4][3]) = (\infty, 7+1) = \mathbf{8}$
J=4 : $D^4[1][4] = \min(D^3[1][4], D^3[1][4] + D^3[4][4]) = (7, 7+6) = 7$

For k =4 & I = 2

J=1 : $D^4[2][1] = \min(D^3[2][1], D^3[2][4] + D^3[4][1]) = (7, 2+4) = \mathbf{6}$
J=2 : $D^4[2][2] = \min(D^3[2][2], D^3[2][4] + D^3[4][2]) = (12, 2+4) = \mathbf{6}$
J=3 : $D^4[2][3] = \min(D^3[2][3], D^3[2][4] + D^3[4][3]) = (\infty, 2+1) = \mathbf{3}$
J=4 : $D^4[2][4] = \min(D^3[2][4], D^3[2][4] + D^3[4][4]) = (2, 2+6) = 2$

For k = 4 & I = 3
J=1 : $D^4[3][1] = min(D^3[3][1], D^3[3][4] + D^3[4][1]) = (10, 5+4) = \mathbf{9}$
J=2 : $D^4[3][2] = min(D^3[3][2], D^3[3][4] + D^3[4][2]) = (3, 5+4) = 3$
J=3 : $D^4[3][3] = min(D^3[3][3], D^3[3][4] + D^3[4][3]) = (\infty, 5+1) = \mathbf{6}$
J=4 : $D^4[3][4] = min(D^3[3][4], D^3[3][4] + D^3[4][4]) = (5, 5+6) = 5$

For k =4 & I = 4
J=1 : $D^4[4][1] = min(D^3[4][1], D^3[4][4] + D^3[4][1]) = (4,6+4) = 4$
J=2 : $D^4[4][2] = min(D^3[4][2], D^3[4][4] + D^3[4][2]) = (4,6+4) = 4$
J=3 : $D^4[4][3] = min(D^3[4][3], D^3[4][4] + D^3[4][3]) = (1,6+1) = 1$
J=4 : $D^4[4][4] = min(D^3[4][4], D^3[4][4] + D^3[4][4]) = (6,6+6) = 6$

$$
D^3 = \begin{matrix}
7 & 5 & 8 & 7 \\
6 & 6 & 3 & 2 \\
9 & 3 & 6 & 5 \\
4 & 4 & 1 & 6
\end{matrix}
$$

From the above matrix we can plot the graph with All pair shortest path.

Example
The path matrix is

$$
D^0 = \begin{matrix}
0 & 8 & \infty & 1 \\
\infty & 0 & 1 & \infty \\
4 & \infty & 0 & \infty \\
\infty & 2 & 9 & 0
\end{matrix}
$$

According to the algorithm k = 4, i= 4 and j= 4.
So the total number of repetition will be $O(4^3) = 64$
We have to compute D1,D2,D3,D4.

For k =1 & I = 1
J=1 : $D^1[1][1] = min(D^0[1][1], D^0[1][1] + D^0[1][1]) = (0,0+0) = 0$
J=2 : $D^1[1][2] = min(D^0[1][2], D^0[1][1] + D^0[1][2]) = (8,0+8) = 8$
J=3 : $D^1[1][3] = min(D^0[1][3], D^0[1][1] + D^0[1][3]) = (\infty,0+\infty) = \infty$
J=4 : $D^1[1][4] = min(D^0[1][4], D^0[1][1] + D^0[1][4]) = (1,0+\infty) = 1$

For k =1 & I = 2
J=1 : $D^1[2][1] = min(D^0[2][1], D^0[2][1] + D^0[1][1]) = (\infty,\infty+0) = \infty$
J=2 : $D^1[2][2] = min(D^0[2][2], D^0[2][1] + D^0[1][2]) = (0, \infty+8) = 0$

GRAPH 341

J=3 : $D^1[2][3] = \min(D^0[2][3], D^0[2][1] + D^0[1][3]) = (1, \infty+\infty) = 1$
J=4 : $D^1[2][4] = \min(D^0[2][4], D^0[2][1] + D^0[1][4]) = (\infty,\infty+1) = \infty$

For k =1 & I = 3

J=1 : $D^1[3][1] = \min(D^0[3][1], D^0[3][1] + D^0[1][1]) = (4,4+0) = 4$
J=2 : $D^1[3][2] = \min(D^0[3][2], D^0[3][1] + D^0[1][2]) = (\infty, 4+8) = \mathbf{12}$
J=3 : $D^1[3][3] = \min(D^0[3][3], D^0[3][1] + D^0[1][3]) = (0,4+\infty) = 0$
J=4 : $D^1[3][4] = \min(D^0[3][4], D^0[3][1] + D^0[1][4]) = (\infty,4+1) = \mathbf{5}$

For k =1 & I = 4

J=1 : $D^1[4][1] = \min(D^0[4][1], D^0[4][1] + D^0[1][1]) = (\infty,\infty+0) = \infty$
J=2 : $D^1[4][2] = \min(D^0[4][2], D^0[4][1] + D^0[1][2]) = (2, \infty+8) = \mathbf{2}$
J=3 : $D^1[4][3] = \min(D^0[4][3], D^0[4][1] + D^0[1][3]) = (9, \infty+\infty) = \mathbf{9}$
J=4 : $D^1[4][4] = \min(D^0[4][4], D^0[4][1] + D^0[1][4]) = (0, \infty+1) = 0$

$$D^1 = \begin{matrix} 0 & 8 & \infty & 1 \\ \infty & 0 & 1 & \infty \\ 4 & 12 & 0 & 5 \\ \infty & 2 & 9 & 0 \end{matrix}$$

For k =2 & I = 1

J=1 : $D^2[1][1] = \min(D^1[1][1], D^1[1][2] + D^1[2][1]) = (0,8+\infty) = 0$
J=2 : $D^2[1][2] = \min(D^1[1][2], D^1[1][2] + D^1[2][2]) = (8,8+0) = 8$
J=3 : $D^2[1][3] = \min(D^1[1][3], D^1[1][2] + D^1[2][3]) = (\infty,8+1) = \mathbf{9}$
J=4 : $D^2[1][4] = \min(D^1[1][4], D^1[1][2] + D^1[2][4]) = (1,8+\infty) = 1$

For k =2 & I = 2

J=1 : $D^2[2][1] = \min(D^1[2][1], D^1[2][2] + D^1[2][1]) = (\infty,0+\infty) = \infty$
J=2 : $D^2[2][2] = \min(D^1[2][2], D^1[2][2] + D^1[2][2]) = (0,0+0) = 0$
J=3 : $D^2[2][3] = \min(D^1[2][3], D^1[2][2] + D^1[2][3]) = (1,0+1) = 1$
J=4 : $D^2[2][4] = \min(D^1[2][4], D^1[2][2] + D^1[2][4]) = (\infty,0+\infty) = \infty$

For k = 2 & I = 3

J=1 : $D^2[3][1] = \min(D^1[3][1], D^1[3][2] + D^1[2][1]) = (4,12+\infty) = 4$
J=2 : $D^2[3][2] = \min(D^1[3][2], D^1[3][2] + D^1[2][2]) = (12, 12+0) = 12$
J=3 : $D^2[3][3] = \min(D^1[3][3], D^1[3][2] + D^1[2][3]) = (0,12+1) = 0$
J=4 : $D^2[3][4] = \min(D^1[3][4], D^1[3][2] + D^1[2][4]) = (5,12+\infty) = 5$

For k =2 & I = 4

J=1 : $D^2[4][1] = \min(D^1[4][1], D^1[4][2] + D^1[2][1]) = (\infty,2+\infty) = \infty$
J=2 : $D^2[4][2] = \min(D^1[4][2], D^1[4][2] + D^1[2][2]) = (2,2+0) = 2$

J=3 : $D^2[4][3] = \min(D^1[4][3], D^1[4][2] + D^1[2][3]) = (9,2+1) = $ **3**
J=4 : $D^2[4][4] = \min(D^1[4][4], D^1[4][2] + D^1[2][4]) = (0,2+\infty) = 0$

$$D^2 = \begin{matrix} 0 & 8 & 9 & 1 \\ \infty & 0 & 1 & \infty \\ 4 & 12 & 0 & 5 \\ \infty & 2 & 3 & 0 \end{matrix}$$

For k =3 & I = 1
J=1 : $D^3[1][1] = \min(D^2[1][1], D^2[1][3] + D^2[3][1]) = (0, 9+4) = 0$
J=2 : $D^3[1][2] = \min(D^2[1][2], D^2[1][3] + D^2[3][2]) = (8, 9+12) = 8$
J=3 : $D^3[1][3] = \min(D^2[1][3], D^2[1][3] + D^2[3][3]) = (9,9+0) = 9$
J=4 : $D^3[1][4] = \min(D^2[1][4], D^2[1][3] + D^2[3][4]) = (1,9+5) = 1$

For k =3 & I = 2
J=1 : $D^3[2][1] = \min(D^2[2][1], D^2[2][3] + D^2[3][1]) = (\infty, 1+4) = $ **5**
J=2 : $D^3[2][2] = \min(D^2[2][2], D^2[2][3] + D^2[3][2]) = (0, 1+12) = 0$
J=3 : $D^3[2][3] = \min(D^2[2][3], D^2[2][3] + D^2[3][3]) = (1,1+0) = 1$
J=4 : $D^3[2][4] = \min(D^2[2][4], D^2[2][3] + D^2[3][4]) = (\infty,1+5) = $ **6**

For k = 3 & I = 3
J=1 : $D^3[3][1] = \min(D^2[3][1], D^2[3][3] + D^2[3][1]) = (4, 0+4) = 4$
J=2 : $D^3[3][2] = \min(D^2[3][2], D^2[3][3] + D^2[3][2]) = (12, 0+12) = 12$
J=3 : $D^3[3][3] = \min(D^2[3][3], D^2[3][3] + D^2[3][3]) = (0,0+0) = 0$
J=4 : $D^3[3][4] = \min(D^2[3][4], D^2[3][3] + D^2[3][4]) = (5, 0+5) = 5$

For k =3 & I = 4
J=1 : $D^3[4][1] = \min(D^2[4][1], D^2[4][3] + D^2[3][1]) = (\infty,3+4) = 7$
J=2 : $D^3[4][2] = \min(D^2[4][2], D^2[4][3] + D^2[3][2]) = (2,3+12) = 2$
J=3 : $D^3[4][3] = \min(D^2[4][3], D^2[4][3] + D^2[3][3]) = (3,3+0) = 3$
J=4 : $D^3[4][4] = \min(D^2[4][4], D^2[4][3] + D^2[3][4]) = (0,3+5) = 0$

$$D^3 = \begin{matrix} 0 & 8 & 9 & 1 \\ 5 & 0 & 1 & 6 \\ 4 & 12 & 0 & 5 \\ 7 & 2 & 3 & 0 \end{matrix}$$

For k =4 & I = 1
J=1 : $D^4[1][1] = \min(D^3[1][1], D^3[1][4] + D^3[4][1]) = (0, 1+7) = 0$
J=2 : $D^4[1][2] = \min(D^3[1][2], D^3[1][4] + D^3[4][2]) = (8, 1+2) = 3$
J=3 : $D^4[1][3] = \min(D^3[1][3], D^3[1][4] + D^3[4][3]) = (9,1+3) = $ **4**
J=4 : $D^4[1][4] = \min(D^3[1][4], D^3[1][4] + D^3[4][4]) = (1, 1+0) = 1$

GRAPH 343

For k =4 & I = 2

$J=1$: $D^4[2][1] = \min(D^3[2][1], D^3[2][4] + D^3[4][1]) = (5,6+7) = 5$

$J=2$: $D^4[2][2] = \min(D^3[2][2], D^3[2][4] + D^3[4][2]) = (0, 6+2) = 0$

$J=3$: $D^4[2][3] = \min(D^3[2][3], D^3[2][4] + D^3[4][3]) = (1,6+3) = 1$

$J=4$: $D^4[2][4] = \min(D^3[2][4], D^3[2][4] + D^3[4][4]) = (6, 6+0) = 6$

For k = 4 & I = 3

$J=1$: $D^4[3][1] = \min(D^3[3][1], D^3[3][4] + D^3[4][1]) = (4, 5+7) = 4$

$J=2$: $D^4[3][2] = \min(D^3[3][2], D^3[3][4] + D^3[4][2]) = (12, 5+2) = \mathbf{7}$

$J=3$: $D^4[3][3] = \min(D^3[3][3], D^3[3][4] + D^3[4][3]) = (0,5+3) = 0$

$J=4$: $D^4[3][4] = \min(D^3[3][4], D^3[3][4] + D^3[4][4]) = (5, 5+0) = 5$

For k =4 & I = 4

$J=1$: $D^4[4][1] = \min(D^3[4][1], D^3[4][4] + D^3[4][1]) = (7,0+7) = 7$

$J=2$: $D^4[4][2] = \min(D^3[4][2], D^3[4][4] + D^3[4][2]) = (2,0+2) = 2$

$J=3$: $D^4[4][3] = \min(D^3[4][3], D^3[4][4] + D^3[4][3]) = (3,0+3) = 3$

$J=4$: $D^4[4][4] = \min(D^3[4][4], D^3[4][4] + D^3[4][4]) = (0,0+0) = 0$

The all pair shortest path matrix is

$$D^4 = \begin{matrix} 0 & 3 & 4 & 1 \\ 5 & 0 & 1 & 6 \\ 4 & 7 & 0 & 5 \\ 7 & 2 & 3 & 0 \end{matrix}$$

PROGRAM FOR FLOYD–WARSHALL

```c
#include<stdio.h>
int i, j, k,n,x,y,dist[10][10];
void floydWarshell ()
{
 for (k = 0; k < n; k++)
  {
      printf("\n For K = %d",k);
      for (i = 0; i < n; i++)
      {
            for (j = 0; j < n; j++)
            {
            if (dist[i][k] + dist[k][j] < dist[i][j])
            {
                    printf("\nFor i=%d, j= %d,dist[%d]
[%d]+dist[%d][%d] < dist[%d][%d], %d + %d < %d (T), dist[%d]
[%d] = %d",i,j,i,k,k,j,i,j,dist[i][k] ,dist[k][j],dist[i]
[j],i,j,dist[i][k] + dist[k][j]);
```

```
                         dist[i][j] = dist[i][k] + dist[k][j];
                    }
                    else
                    {
                         printf("\n For i=%d, j= %d,dist[%d][%d]
+ dist[%d][%d] < dist[%d][%d] i.e/ %d + %d < %d
(False)",i,j,i,k,k,j,i,j,dist[i][k] ,dist[k][j],dist[i][j]);
                    }


               }


          }
        printf("\n\n PATH MATRIX - %d\n",k+1) ;
           for (x = 0; x < n; x++)
               {
                      for (y = 0; y < n; y++)
                            printf ("%d\t", dist[x][y]);
                      printf("\n");
               }
     getch();

     }


}


int main()
{
  int i,j;
  printf("enter no of vertices :");
  scanf("%d",&n);
  printf("\n");
  for(i=0;i<n;i++)
  for(j=0;j<n;j++)
    {
      printf("dist[%d][%d]:",i,j);
      scanf("%d",&dist[i][j]);
    }
 floydWarshell();
 printf (" \n\n shortest distances between every pair of
vertices \n");
 for (i = 0; i < n; i++)
 {
  for (j = 0; j < n; j++)
   printf ("%d\t", dist[i][j]);
  printf("\n");
 }
 return 0;
}
```

GRAPH   345

9.7   Topological Sorting

In any directed graph which has no cycle, topological sort gives the sequential order of all the nodes x,y and x comes before y in sequential order if a path exists from x to y. So this sequential order will indicate the depedency of one task on another.a

For topological sorting the steps are

- Take all the nodes which have zero indegree.
- Delete those nodes and edges going from those nodes.
- Do the same process again until all the nodes are deleted.

Ex :

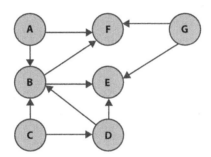

The Adjacency List of the above graph is
A -> B,F
B -> E,F
C -> B,D
D -> B,E
E ->
F ->
G-> E,F

STEP-1:
Indegree of the Nodes are
A=0, B=3, C=0, D=1, E=3, F=3, G=0

STEP-2:
    1) Taking all the nodes, which have zero indegree
        A,C,G
    2) Add all zero indegree nodes to queue
        QUEUE : A,C,G   front = 1 Rear = 3

3) Delete the node A and edges going from A
    QUEUE : C,G   front = 2 Rear = 3 SORT : A

4) Now the indegree of nodes will be
    B=2, D=1, E=3, F=2

STEP-3:

1) Delete the node C and edges going from C
    QUEUE :G   front = 3 Rear = 3 SORT :A,C

2) Now the indegree of nodes will be
    B=1, D=0, E=3, F=2

STEP-4:

1) Add the node D to the Queue
    QUEUE : G,D   front = 3, rear = 4   SORT : A,C

2) Delete the node G and edges going from G
    QUEUE :D   front = 4 Rear = 4 SORT :A,C,G

3) Now the indegree of nodes will be
    B=1, E=2, F=1

STEP-5:

1) Delete the node D and edges going from D
    QUEUE :   front = 0 Rear = 0 SORT :A,C,G,D

2) Now the indegree of nodes will be
    B=0, E=1, F=1

STEP-6:

1) Add the node B to the Queue
    QUEUE : B   front = 1, rear = 1   SORT : A,C,G,D

2) Delete the node B and edges going from B
    QUEUE :   front = 0 Rear = 0 SORT :A,C,G,D,B

3) Now the indegree of nodes will be
    E=0, F=0

STEP-7:

1) Add the node E,F to the Queue
    QUEUE : E,F   front = 1, rear = 2 SORT : A,C,G,D,B

2) Delete the node E and edges going from E
    QUEUE :F   front = 2 Rear = 2 SORT :A,C,G,D,B,E

GRAPH   347

STEP-8:
1) Delete the node F and edges going from F
QUEUE :   front = 0 Rear = 0 SORT :A,C,G,D,B,E,F

Now the topological sorting graph will be A,C ,G,D,B,E,F

9.8   Questions

1. What is graph data structure?
2. Draw the Minimum spanning tree of

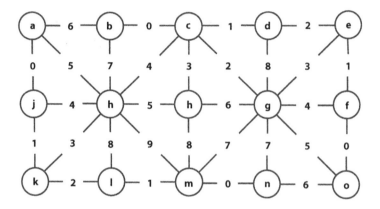

3. Write a program to implement PRIM'S algorithm.
4. What are the types of graph traversing?
5. What is the difference between Dijkstra and Bellman–Ford algorithm?
6. What is topological sorting?

Searching and Sorting

Searching is the process of finding out the position of an element in an list. If the element is found inside the list then the searching process is successful otherwise the searching process is failure.

Searching is of two types such as

Linear Search
Binary Search

10.1 Linear Search

This is the simplest method of searching .In this method the element to be found is sequentially searched in the list.

This method can be applied to a sorted or an un-sorted list.Searching is case of sorted list starts from 0th element and continues until the element is found or an element whose value is greater (Assuming the list is sorted in ascending order) than the value being searched is reached.

As against this,searching in case of unsorted list starts from 0th element and continues until the element is found or the end of list is reached.

Algorithm

N → Boundary of the list
Item → Searching number
Data → Linear array

Step-1   I=0
Step-2 Repeat while I<=n
   If (item = data[i])
      Print "Searching is successful"
      Exit

Sachi Nandan Mohanty and Pabitra Kumar Tripathy. *Data Structure and Algorithms Using C++: A Practical Implementation*, (349–390) © 2021 Scrivener Publishing LLC

Else
    Print "Searching is Unsuccessful"
Step-3 exit
Analysis of the Sequential Search

The number of comparisons for a successful search is depends upon the position where the key value is present. If the searched value is present at the 1st place then m 1 comparison is required. So in general mth comparisons are required to search the mth element.

Best Case Complexity

If the key value is present at first position on the array then $T(n) = O(1)$

Worst Case Complexity

If the value is present at the end of the array then $T(n) = O(n)$
Average Case Complexity
(Best case + Worst Case)/2 $= (1+n)/2$
$T(n) = O(n)$

Program on Linear Search

```
#include<iostream>
using namespace std;
int main()
{
int *a,no,n,i;
//ask user to input the number of elements to store in the
array
cout<<"\nENTER HOW MANY ELEMENTS TO BE STORED IN THE LIST";
cin>>n; //read the number
a = new int[n]; //dynamically allocate memory for array
//loop to input the elements into the array
for(i=0;i<n;i++)
   {
      cout<<"\nENTER A NUMBER";
      cin>>a[i];
   }
cout<<"\nENTER THE NUMBER TO SEARCH";
cin>>no; //ask user to input the number to search
//loop to search the number in the list
for(i=0;i<n;i++)
```

```
    {
      if(a[i]==no)
        {
            cout<<"\nTHE NUMBER IS FOUND IN THE LIST";
            break;
        }
        else
          if(i==n-1)
            cout<<"\nTHE NUMBER IS NOT FOUND IN THE LIST";
    }
}
```

OUTPUT

```
ENTER HOW MANY ELEMENTS TO BE STORED IN THE LIST10
ENTER A NUMBER36
ENTER A NUMBER56
ENTER A NUMBER58
ENTER A NUMBER9
ENTER A NUMBER23
ENTER A NUMBER54
ENTER A NUMBER74
ENTER A NUMBER8
ENTER A NUMBER95
ENTER A NUMBER6
ENTER THE NUMBER TO SEARCH6
THE NUMBER IS FOUND IN THE LIST

Process exited after 18.59 seconds with return value 0
Press any key to continue . . .
```

10.2   Binary Search

Binary search method is very fast and efficient. This method requires that the list of element is to be sorted.

In this method to search an element we compare it with the element present at the center of the list..I f it matches then the search is successful. Otherwise,the list is devided into two halfs.One from the 0th position to center position(1st half) and another from center to last element (2nd half).

As a result all the element in the 1st half are smaller than the center element, whereas all the elements in the 2nd half are greater than the center element.

The searching will now proceed in either of the two halves depending upon whether the element is greater or smaller than the center element .If the element is smaller than the center element then searching will be done in the 1st half otherwise in the 2nd half. Same process of comparing the required element with the center element and if not found then deviding the elements into two halves is repeated for the 1st half or 2nd half. This procedure is repeated till ther element is found, or the division of half parts gives one element.

For eg

1 2 3 9 11 13   17 25 57 80

Suppose the array consists of 10 sorted numbers and 57 is the number that is to be searched. Then the binary search method when applied to this array work as follows.

57 is compared with the element present at the center of the list i.e/11 since 57 is greater than it, the searching is applied only to the 2nd half of the array.

Now 57 ios compared with the center element of the 2nd half of the array i.e/25. Here again 57 is greater than 25,so searching is now proceed ion the elements present between the 25 and the last element 90.

This process is repeated till 57 is found or no further division of array is possible.

Algorithm

STEP-1   low=0,up=n-1
Step-2   Repeat while low<=up
                     mid = int(low+up)/2
               if(no=arr[mid])
                     print "Searched element is found"
                     exit
                     else
               if(no < arr[mid]) then
                          up = mid-1
                     else
                          low = mid+1
step-3   print "searched element is not found"
step-4   exit

Best Case Complexity

If the searched value is found at the middle of the list then the comparison required $T(n) = O(1)$

Worst Case Complexity

Let K, be the smallest integer such that $n <= 2^k$ and c is one constant time required for one comparison so,

$T(n) = T(n/2) + c$
$t(2^k) = T(2^K/2) + c \Rightarrow T(2^k) = T(2^{k-1}) + c$

By the method of induction we have
$\quad T(2^k) = T(2^{k-1}) + c$
$\quad T(2^{k-1}) = T(2^{k-2}) + c$
$\quad \ldots\ldots\ldots\ldots\ldots$
$\quad \ldots\ldots\ldots\ldots\ldots$
$\quad \ldots\ldots\ldots\ldots\ldots$
$\quad \ldots\ldots\ldots\ldots\ldots$
$\quad T(2^l) = T(2^{k-l(k-l)}) + c$

$\rule{4cm}{0.4pt}$

$\quad T(2^k) = T(l) + kc$
$T(n) <= kc \qquad T(1)$ as constant
$T(n) <= c* \log_2 n \ (\ n = 2^k \Rightarrow k = \log_2 n)$
$T(n) = O(\log n)$

Program for Binary Search

```
//input the elements in ascending order

#include<iostream>
using namespace std;
int main()
{
int *a,no,up,i,low=0,f=0;

cout<<"\nENTER HOW MANY ELEMENTS TO BE STORED IN THE LIST";
cin>>up;
a = new int[up];
//loop to input the elements into the array
for(i=0;i<up;i++)
```

```
  {
     cout<<"\nENTER A NUMBER";
     cin>>a[i];
  }
cout<<"\nENTER THE NUMBER TO SEARCH";
cin>>no;
for(i=(low+up)/2;low<=up;i=(low+up)/2)
  {
     if(a[i]==no)
     {
        f=1;
        break;
     }
else
   if(a[i]>no)
     up=i-1;
       else
        low = i+1;
       }
   if(f==1)
     cout<<"\nTHE SEARCHING ELEMENT IS FOUND";
       else
        cout<<"\nTHE SEARCHING ELEMENT IS NOT FOUND";
       }
```

OUTPUT

```
ENTER HOW MANY ELEMENTS TO BE STORED IN THE LIST8
ENTER A NUMBER32
ENTER A NUMBER65
ENTER A NUMBER47
ENTER A NUMBER55
ENTER A NUMBER59
ENTER A NUMBER64
ENTER A NUMBER75
ENTER A NUMBER85
ENTER THE NUMBER TO SEARCH25
THE SEARCHING ELEMENT IS NOT FOUND
Process exited after 20.34 seconds with return value 0
Press any key to continue . . .
```

SORTING

Sorting means arranging the data in a particular order. i.e. either ascending or descending.

There are different methods for sorting. These methods can be divided into two categories such as

Internal Sorting
External Sorting

INTERNAL SORTING

If all the data that is to be sorted can be accommodated at a time in memory then internal sorting method can be used.

EXTERNAL SORTING

When the data is to be sorted is so large that some of the data is present in the memory and some is kept in auxiliary memory(Hard disk, floppy disk, tape etc.) then the external sorting methods are used.

INTERNAL SORTING

There are different types of internal sorting methods are used out of them some of are discussed. All the methods below are discussed for the ascending order.

10.3   Bubble Sort

> *Bubble sort is a reasonable sort to use for sorting a fairly small number of items and is easy to implement.*

But for the smaller list this sorting procedure works fine.

In this method to arrange elements in ascending order, begin with the 0th element, and is compared with the 1st element. If it is found to be greater than the 1st element then they are interchanged. Then the 1st element is compared with the 2nd element. If it is found to be greater then they are interchanged. In the same way all the elements (Excluding the last) are compared with their next element and are interchanged if required.

This is the 1st iteration and on completing this iteration the largest element gets placed at the last position. Similarily, in the second iteration the comparisons are made till the last but one element and this time the second largest element gets placed at the second last position in the list. As a result, after all the iterations the list becomes a sorted list.

For ex.
Let an array having five numbers.

8	12	10	78	5

Step-1: In the 1st iteration the 0th element 8 is compared with 1st element 12 and since 8 is less than 12 then there is nothing to do.

Step-2: Now the 1st element 12 is compared with the 2nd element 10 and here the swapping will be performed.

Step-3: This process is repeated until $(n - 2)$th element is compared with the $(n - 1)$th element and during comparison if the 1st element other wise no intercheange.

Step-4: If there are n number of elements then n-1 iterations are required.

ALGORITHM

n->Number of elements of the array
Step-1 I=0
    Repeat through step 3 while (I<n)
Step-2 j=0
    Repeat through step 3 while j<n-I
Step-3 if arr[j]<arr[j+1]
       Temp = arr[j]
       arr[j+1] = arr[j]
       arr[j]=temp
Step-4 exit

Program for Bubble Sort

```
#include <iostream>
#include<iomanip>
using namespace std;
void sort(int a[], int size)
```

```
{
    int i, j,temp;
    for (i = 0; i < size-1; i++)

    // Last i elements are already in place
    for (j = 0; j < size-i-1; j++)
        if (a[j] > a[j+1])
           {
             {
                              temp = a[j];
                              a[j] = a[j+1];
                              a[j+1] = temp;

             }
           }
}

//method to display the array elements
void display(int a[], int size)
{
    int i;
    for (i = 0; i < size; i++)
        cout << a[i] << " ";
    cout << endl;
}
//driver program

int main()
{
      int *arr,i,j,temp,no;
      cout<<"\nHOW MANY ELEMENTS TO BE INSERTED INTO THE
LIST";
      cin>>no;
arr = new int[no];
      for (i = 0; i < no; i++)
      {
        cout<<"\nENTER A NUMBER";
        cin>>arr[i];
      }

      sort(arr,no);

      cout<<"\n Sorted list is as follows\n";
      display(arr,no);
}
```

Output

```
HOW MANY ELEMENTS TO BE INSERTED INTO THE LIST5
ENTER A NUMBER25
ENTER A NUMBER95
ENTER A NUMBER2
ENTER A NUMBER35
ENTER A NUMBER4
 Sorted list is as follows
2 4 25 35 95
_____
Process exited after 5.939 seconds with return value 0
Press any key to continue . . .
```

By using functions

```c
#include<stdio.h>
#include<math.h>
#define SIZE 20
//function prototypes
void FillArray(int *array,int size);
void PrintArray(int *array,int size);
void BubbleSort(int *array,int size);
void swap(int *x,int *y);
//driver program
int main()
 {
 int NumList[SIZE],i;
 FillArray(&NumList,SIZE);
  printf("\n Before sort array elements are :\n");
 PrintArray(&NumList,SIZE);
 BubbleSort(&NumList,SIZE);
 printf("\n After sort array elements are :\n");
  PrintArray(&NumList,SIZE);
 }
 //code for fillarray()
void FillArray(int *array,int size)
{
      int i;
      for(i=0;i<SIZE;i++)
       *(array+i)= rand() % 100 ; //generate 20 random
numbers and assigned to array
}
//logic for printing the array elements
void PrintArray(int *array,int size)
```

```
{
      int i;
      for(i=0;i<SIZE;i++)  //loop to print the array
elements
      printf("%5d",*(array+i));
}
//logic for bubble sort
void BubbleSort(int *array,int size)
{
      int i,j;
      //logic for bubble sort
      for(i=0;i<SIZE-1;i++)
        {
              for(j=0;j<SIZE-1-i;j++)
                { //condition for descending order sorting
                    if(*(array+j) <= *(array+(j+1)))
                    swap((array+j),(array+(j+1))); //
invoke swap()
                }
        }
}
//logic for swappingof two numbers
void swap(int *x,int *y)
  {
      int z;
      z=*x;
      *x=*y;
      *y=z;
  }
```

```
Before sort array elements are :
   41   67   34    0   69   24   78   58   62   64    5   45   81   27   61   91
   95   42   27   36
After sort array elements are :
   95   91   81   78   69   67   64   62   61   58   45   42   41   36   34   27
   27   24    5    0
----------------------------------------------------------------
Process exited after 0.05759 seconds with return value 5
Press any key to continue . . .
```

10.4   Selection Sort

This is the simplest method of sorting. The selection sort starts from 1st element and searches the entire list until it finds the minimum value. The sort places the minimum value in the first place,select the second element and searches for the second smallest element. This process will continue until the complete list is sorted.

ALGORITHM

Step-1 Repeat through step-3 while I < n
Step-2 Repeat through step-3 while k= I+1 to n
Step-3 If arr[i] >arr[k]
      Temp = arr[k]
      arr[k] = arr[i]
      arr[i] = temp
Step-4 exit

Program for selection sort

```cpp
#include<iostream>
#include<iomanip>
using namespace std;
int main()
{
        int n,*arr;
        int i,k,temp;

        cout<<endl<<"Input the number of elements in the list:";
        cin>>n;
        arr = new int[n];
        for(i = 0 ; i < n ; i++)
          {
                cout<<endl<<"Enter a number";
                cin>>arr[i];
          }
        cout<<"\nLIST BEFORE SORTING :\n";
            for(i=0;i<n;i++)
                cout<<setw(5)<<arr[i];

        for(i=0; i<n-1 ;i++)
          for(k = i+1; k<n;k++)
                {
                        if(arr[i] > arr[k])

          {
                        temp = arr[k];
                        arr[k] = arr[i];
                        arr[i]=temp ;


                }
                }
        cout<<"\n LIST AFTER SORTING :\n";
        for(i=0;i<n;i++)
                cout<<setw(5)<<arr[i];
}
```

OUTPUT

```
Input the number of elements in the list:5

Enter a number12

Enter a number32

Enter a number52

Enter a number9

Enter a number85

LIST BEFORE SORTING :
   12   32   52    9   85
 LIST AFTER SORTING :
    9   12   32   52   85
--------------------------------------------
Process exited after 5.546 seconds with return value 0
Press any key to continue . . .
```

10.5   Insertion Sort

Insertion sort is implemented by inserting a particular element at the appropriate position.In this method, the first iteration starts with the comparison of 1st element with the 0th element. In the second iteration 2nd element is compared with the 0th element and 1st element.

In general, in every iteration an element is compared with all the elements before it.During comparison if it is found that the element in question can be inserted at a suitable position then a space is created for it by shifting the other elements one position to the right and inserting the element at a suitable position.This procedure is repeated for all the elements in the array.

For Ex.
    Consider the array

76	52	66	45	33

Step-1 : In the first loop the 1st element 52 is compared with the 0th element 76. Since 52<76, 52 is inserted at 0th place. The 0th element 76 is shifted one position to the right.

Step-2 : In the second loop, the 2nd element 66 and the 0th element 52 are compared since 66>52, then no change will be performed. Then the second element is compared with the 1st element and same procedue will be continued.

Step-3 : In the third loop ,the 3rd element is compared with the 0th element 52, since 45 is smaller than 52 then 45 is inserted in the 0th place in the array and all the elements fom 0th to 2nd are shifted to right by one position.

Step-4 : In the fourth loop the fourth element 33 is compared with the 0th element 45,since 33<45 then 4th element is inserted into the 0th place and all the elements from 0th to 3rd are shifted by one position and as a result we will got the sorted array.

Algorithm

Step-1   Repeat through step-4 while (I<no)
Step-2   Repeat while j<I
Step-3   If arr[j]>arr[i]
                    Temp = arr[j]
                 Arr[j] = arr[i]
             Repeat while k= I to j
                 Arr[k]=arr[k-1]
Step-4   Arr[k+1]=temp

Program for Insertion Sort

```
#include<iostream>
#include<iomanip>
using namespace std;
int  main()
{
      int *arr,i,j,k,temp,no;
      cout<<"\nHOW MANY ELEMENTS TO BE INSERTED INTO THE
LIST";
      cin>>no;
      arr = new int[no];

for (i = 0; i < no; i++)
      {
         cout<<"\nENTER A NUMBER";
         cin>>arr[i];
      }
      for (i = 1; i < no; i++)
            for (j = 0; j < i; j++)
                  if (arr[j] > arr[i])
                  {
                        temp = arr[j];
                        arr[j] = arr[i];
```

```
            for(k=i;k>j;k--)
                arr[k] = arr[k-1];
                arr[k+1]=temp;
        }
    cout<<"\n Sorted list is as follows\n";
    for (i=0;i<no;i++)
            cout<<setw(5)<<arr[i];
}
```

OUTPUT

```
HOW MANY ELEMENTS TO BE INSERTED INTO THE LIST5

ENTER A NUMBER32

ENTER A NUMBER5

ENTER A NUMBER64

ENTER A NUMBER6

ENTER A NUMBER1

 Sorted list is as follows
     1     5     6    32    64

Process exited after 5.527 seconds with return value 0
Press any key to continue . . .
```

10.6   Merge Sort

Merging means combining two sorted lists into one sorted list. For this the elements from both the sorted lists are compared .The smaller of both the elements is then stored in the third array .The sorting is complete when all the elements from both the lists are placed in the third list.

ALGORITHM

step-1 I=0
    J=0
    K=0
Step-2 repeat step-3 while I<n and j<m
Step-3 if(lista[i] < listb[j])
      List[k] = lista[i]
      I = I+1

K=k+1
　Else
　　If(lista[i] > listb[j])
　　List[k] = listb[j]
　j = j+1
　K=k+1
　Else
　　List[k] = lista[I]
　　I=I+1
　　J=j+1
　　K=k+1
Step-4　　　　if I<n
Step-5　for l= I to n-1
　　List[k] = lista[I]
　　I=I+1
　　K=k+1
Step-6　　　　else
　　If j<m
Step-7　　　for l = j to m-1
　　List[k] = listb[j]
　　J=j+1
　　K=k+1
Step-8 stop

PROGRAM

```
#include<iostream>
#include<iomanip>
using namespace std;
int main( )
{
        int a[5];
        int b[5];
        int c[10] ;
        int i, j, k, temp ;
        cout<<endl<<"Enter 5 elements for first array";
        for(i=0;i<5;i++)
            {
              cout<<"\nENTER A NUMBER";
              cin>>a[i];
            }
            cout<<endl<<"Enter 5 elements for second
array";
            for(i=0;i<5;i++)
```

```
                    {
                     cout<<"\nENTER A NUMBER";
                     cin>>b[i];
                    }
            cout<<"\nFirst array:\n";
            for ( i = 0 ; i <= 4 ; i++ )
                    cout<<setw(5)<<a[i];

            cout<<"\n\nSecond array:\n";
            for ( i = 0 ; i <= 4 ; i++ )
                    cout<<setw(5)<<b[i];
            for ( i = 0 ; i <= 3 ; i++ )
            {
                    for ( j = i + 1 ; j <= 4 ; j++ )
                    {
                            if ( a[i] > a[j] )
                            {
                                    temp = a[i] ;
                                    a[i] = a[j] ;
                                    a[j] = temp ;
                            }



if ( b[i] > b[j] )
                            {
                                    temp = b[i] ;
                                    b[i] = b[j] ;
                                    b[j] = temp ;
                            }
                    }
            }

            for (i=j=k=0;i<=9;)
            {
                    if ( a[j] <  b[k] )
                            c[i++] = a[j++] ;


                else
                    if(a[j]>b[k])
                            c[i++] = b[k++] ;
                    else
                        { c[i++]=a[j++];  ++k; }  //c[i++]=b[k++],
j++
                    if ( j == 5 || k == 5 )
                            break ;
            }
```

```
for ( ; j <= 4 ; )
            c[i++] = a[j++] ;

    for ( ; k <= 4 ; )
            c[i++] = b[k++] ;

    cout<<"\n\nArray after sorting:\n";
    for ( i = 0 ; i <= 9 ; i++ )
            cout<<setw(5)<<c[i] ;
}
```

OUTPUT

```
Enter 5 elements for first array
ENTER A NUMBER12

ENTER A NUMBER32

ENTER A NUMBER52

ENTER A NUMBER6

ENTER A NUMBER58

Enter 5 elements for second array
ENTER A NUMBER2

ENTER A NUMBER5

ENTER A NUMBER8

ENTER A NUMBER1

ENTER A NUMBER25

First array:
    12    32    52     6    58

Second array:
     2     5     8     1    25

Array after sorting:
     1     2     5     6     8    12    25    32    52    58
Process exited after 8.971 seconds with return value 0
Press any key to continue . . .
```

10.7   Quick Sort

Quick sort uses the concepts of divide and conquer method. It is also known as partition exchange sort. To Partion the list, we first choose some key from the list for which about half the keys will come before and half after. This selected key is called as pivot. We next partition the entries so that all the keys which are less than the pivot come in one sublist and all the keys which are greater than the pivot come in another sublist. We will repeat the same process until all elements of the list are at proper position in the list.

Ex.

20 55 46 37 9 89 82 32

From the above list choose first number as pivot i.e/20 and the list is partitioned into two sublists

(9) and (55 46 37 89 82 32)

At this point 20 is in its proper position in the array $x[1]$, each element below that position (9) is less than or equals to 20 and each element above that position (55 46 37 89 82 32) is greater than or equals to 20.

The problem is broken into two sub problems that are to sort the two sub arrays. Since the first sub array contains only a single element, so it is already sorted .To sort the second sub array we choose its first element 55 as the pivot and again get two sub arrays (46 37 32) and (89 82) .

So the entire array can be represented as

9 20 (46 37 32) 55 (89 82)

Repeating the same process we will get the result with the steps

20 55 46 37 9 89 82 32

9 20 (46 37 32) 55 (89 82)

9 20 (37 32) 46 55 (89 82)

9 20 (32) 37 46 55 (89 82)

9 20 32 37 46 55 (82) 89

9 20 32 37 46 55 82 89

The average run time efficiency of the quick sort is $O(n(\log_2 n))$. In the worst case when the array is already sorted, the efficiency of quick sort may drop down to $O(n^2)$

PROGRAM

```
#include<iostream>
#include<iomanip>
using namespace std;
int split ( int*, int, int) ;
void quicksort ( int *, int, int ) ;
```

```cpp
int main()
{
        int arr[10] = { 11, 2, 9, 13, 57, 25, 17, 1, 90, 3 }
;
        int i;
        cout<<»\nTHE GIVEN ARRAY IS\n» ;
        for ( i = 0 ; i <= 9 ; i++ )
                cout<<setw(5)<<arr[i];
        quicksort ( arr, 0, 9 ) ;
        cout<<»\nSORTED ARRAY IS\n»;
        for ( i = 0 ; i <= 9 ; i++ )
                cout<<setw(5)<<arr[i];
}
void quicksort ( int a[ ], int lower, int upper )
{
        int i ;
        if ( upper > lower )
        {
                i = split ( a, lower, upper ) ;
                quicksort ( a, lower, i - 1 ) ;
                quicksort ( a, i + 1, upper ) ;
        }
}
int split ( int a[], int lower, int upper )
{
        int i, p, q, t ;
        p = lower + 1 ;
        q = upper ;
        i = a[lower] ;
        while ( q >= p )
        {
                while ( a[p] < i )
                        p++ ;

                while ( a[q] > i )
                        q-- ;
          if ( q > p )
                {
                        t = a[p] ;
                        a[p] = a[q] ;
                        a[q] = t ;
                }
        }
        t = a[lower] ;
        a[lower] = a[q] ;
        a[q] = t ;
        return q ;
}
```

OUTPUT

```
THE GIVEN ARRAY IS
   11     2     9    13    57    25    17     1    90     3
SORTED ARRAY IS
    1     2     3     9    11    13    17    25    57    90

Process exited after 0.3055 seconds with return value 0
Press any key to continue . . .
```

10.8   Radix Sort

The radix sort is based upon the positional value of the actual digits of the number being stored. This method was earlier performed on a mechanical card sorter. For Ex. The number 245 in decimal notation written with a 2 in the hundredth position, 4 in the ten's position and 5 in the unit position. This three digits will be sorted in maximum three passes. In the first pass, the unit digit will be sorted, in the second pass the tens digit will be sorted and in the third and final pass the hundreds digit will be sorted.

Radix sort technique is also used when large lists of names are to be sorted alphabetically.

For Ex.
Sort

42	20	64	51	34	70	31	16	15	12	19	33

In the first pass the unit digits are sorted i.e/.

Number	0	1	2	3	4	5	6	7	8	9
42			42							
20	20									
64					64					
51		51								
34					34					
70	70									

Number	0	1	2	3	4	5	6	7	8	9
31		31								
16							16			
15						15				
12			12							
19										19
33				33						

In the second pass the unit digits are sorted i.e/

Number	0	1	2	3	4	5	6	7	8	9
20			20							
70								70		
51						51				
31				31						
42					42					
12		12								
33				33						
64							64			
34				34						
15		15								
16		16								
19		19								

Finally we will get the sorted list as

12	15	16	19	20	31	33	34	42	51	64	70

PROGRAM FOR RADIX SORT

```cpp
#include<iostream>
using namespace std;

//method to find the maximum value in the array
int maximum(int a[], int n)
{
    int max = a[0],i;
    for (i = 1; i < n; i++)
        if (a[i] > max)
            max = a[i];
    return max;
}

void sort(int a[], int n, int exp)
{
    int out[n]; // output array
    int i, count[10] = {0};

    for (i = 0; i < n; i++)
        count[ (a[i]/exp)%10 ]++;


    for (i = 1; i < 10; i++)
        count[i] += count[i - 1];

    //construct the output array
    for (i = n - 1; i >= 0; i--)
    {
        out[count[ (a[i]/exp)%10 ] - 1] = a[i];
        count[ (a[i]/exp)%10 ]--;
    }


    for (i = 0; i < n; i++)
        a[i] = out[i];
}


void radix(int a[], int n)
{
    // Find the maximum number to know number of digits
    int m = maximum(a, n);

    for (int exp = 1; m/exp > 0; exp *= 10)
        sort(a, n, exp);
}
```

```cpp
void print(int a[], int n)
{
    for (int i = 0; i < n; i++)
        cout << a[i] << " ";
}

int main()
{
    int n,*arr,i;
    cout<<endl<<"Input the number of elements in the list:";
    cin>>n;
    arr = new int[n];
    for(i = 0 ; i < n ; i++)
      {
            cout<<endl<<"Enter a number";
            cin>>arr[i];
      }

    radix(arr, n);
    print(arr, n);
    return 0;
}
```

OUTPUT

```
Input the number of elements in the list:5
Enter a number325
Enter a number62
Enter a number59
Enter a number956
Enter a number5
5 59 62 325 956
Process exited after 7.386 seconds with return value 0
Press any key to continue . . .
```

10.9 Heap Sort

Heaps are based on the concept of a complete tree. Formally a binary tree is completely full if it is of height h and has $2^{h+1} - 1$ nodes. A binary tree of height h is complete if

1. it is empty or
2. Its left subtree is complete of height h − 1 and its right sub-tree is completely full of height h − 2 or

3. its left subtree is completely full of height h − 1 and its right subtree is complete of height h − 1.

A binary tree has the heap property if

1. it is empty or
2. The key in the root is larger than that in either child and both subtrees have the heap property.

A heap can be used as priority queue: the highest priority item is at the root and is trivially extracted .But if the root is deleted , we are left with two sub-trees and we must efficiently re-create a single tree with the heap property.The value of the heap structure is that we can both extract the highest priority item and insert a new one in O(logn) time.

A heap is an ordered balanced binary tree (complete binary tree) in which the value of the node at the root of any sub-tree is less than or equals to the value of either of its children.

ALGORITHM

Step-1 Create a heap
Step-2 [do sorting]
        Repeat through step-10 for k = n to 2
Step-3 list[1] = list[k]
Step-4 temp = list[1]
        I=1
        J=2
Step-5 [find the index of largest child of new element]
        If j+1<k then
        If list[j+1] > list[j]
            Then j=j+1
Step-6 Construct the new heap
        Repeat through step-10 while j<=k-1 and list[j]>temp
Step-7 Interchange elements
        List[I] = list[j]
Step-8 Obtain left child
        I=j
        J= 2*I
Step-9 [Obtain the index of next largest child]
        If j+1<k
        If list[j+1] > list[j] then j=j+1

Else
If j>n then j=1

Step-10[Copy elements into its proper place]
        List[j] = temp
Step-11 exit

/*PROGRAM FOR HEAP SORT*/

```cpp
#include<iostream>
#include<iomanip>
using namespace std;
void  heap(int *, int );
void create(int *, int);
void display(int *, int);

int main()
{
        int arr[100];
        int i, size;
        cout<<endl<<"Enter number of elements";
        cin>>size;

        cout<<"\n Size of the list: "<< size;

        for(i = 1 ; i <= size ; ++i)
        {
                cout<<"\n Enter a number";
                cin>>arr[i];
        }
        cout<<"\n Entered list is as follows:\n";
        display(arr, size);
        create(arr, size);
        cout<<"\n Heap tree is \n";
        display(arr, size);
cout<<endl<<endl;

        heap(arr,size);

        cout<<"\n\n Sorted list is as follows :\n\n";
        display(arr,size);
}
void create(int list[], int n )
{

        int k, j, i, temp;
```

```
for(k = 2 ; k <= n;   ++k)
{
        i = k ;
        temp = list[k];
        j = i / 2 ;

        while((i > 1) && (temp > list[j]))
        {
                list[i] = list[j];
                i = j ;
                j = i / 2 ;
                if ( j < 1 )
                        j = 1 ;
        }

        list[i] = temp ;
    }
}


void heap(int arr[], int n)
{
    int k, temp, value, j, i, p;
    int step = 1;
    for(k = n ; k >= 2; --k)
    {
        temp = arr[1] ;
        arr[1] = arr[k];
        arr[k] = temp ;

        i = 1 ;
        value = arr[1];
        j = 2 ;

        if((j+1) < k)
            if(arr[j+1] > arr[j])
                    j ++;
        while((j <= ( k-1)) && (arr[j] > value))
        {
                arr[i] = arr[j];
                i = j ;
                j = 2*i ;
                if((j+1) < k)
                        if(arr[j+1] > arr[j])
                                j++;
                        else
                                if( j > n)
                                        j = n ;
```

```
                              arr[i] = value;
                }

                cout<<"\n Step =  "<<step;
                step++;
                for(p = 1; p <= n; p++)
                        cout<<setw(5)<<arr[p];
        }
}

void display(int arr[], int n)
{
        int i;
        for(i = 1 ; i <= n; ++ i)
        {
                cout<<setw(5)<<arr[i];
        }
}
```

OUTPUT

```
Enter number of elements7

Size of the list: 7
Enter a number25

Enter a number62

Enter a number8

Enter a number93

Enter a number5

Enter a number7

Enter a number45

Entered list is as follows:
   25    62     8    93     5     7    45
Heap tree is
   93    62    45    25     5     7     8


Step =  1    62    25    45     8     5     7    93
Step =  2    45    25     7     8     5    62    93
Step =  3    25     8     7     5    45    62    93
Step =  4     8     5     7    25    45    62    93
Step =  5     7     5     8    25    45    62    93
Step =  6     5     7     8    25    45    62    93

Sorted list is as follows :

    5     7     8    25    45    62    93

Process exited after 9.935 seconds with return value 0
Press any key to continue . . .
```

SORTING TECHNIQUE	BEST CASE	AVERAGE CASE	WROST CASE
Bubble	$O(n)$	$O(n^2)$	$O(n^2)$
Insertion	$O(n)$	$O(n^2)$	$O(n^2)$
Selection	$O(n^2)$	$O(n^2)$	$O(n^2)$
Quick	$O(n^2)$	$O(n \log n)$	$O(n^2)$
Merge	$O(n \log n)$	$O(n \log n)$	$O(n \log n)$
Radix	$O(n^2)$	$O(n \log n)$	$O(n \log n)$
Heap	$O(n \log n)$	$O(n \log n)$	$O(n \log n)$

COMPARISON BETWEEN THE SORTING PROGRAMS

```cpp
#include<iostream>
#include <ctime>
#include <stdlib.h>
void adjust(int);
void heapify(int);
void swap(long int &,long int &);
int partition(int,int);
void quickSort(int,int);
void merge(int l, int m, int r);
void mergesort(int l, int r) ;
using namespace std;
long int *a;
int n;
void swap(long int* a, long int* b)
{
    long int t = *a;
    *a = *b;
    *b = t;
}

//selection sort
void selection(int n)
{
    int i,j;
    long int t;

    //logic to sort the array of elements
    for(i=0;i<n;i++)
    {
        for(j=i+1;j<n;j++)
```

```cpp
            {
                if(a[i]>a[j])
                { //swap the numbers
                    t=a[i];
                    a[i]=a[j];
                    a[j]=t;
                }
            }
        }
    }
}
//method to generate n random numbers and store it into array
void input(int n)
{
    int i;
    int timetaken[5][6];
    a = new long int[n];//allocate memory for n number of
elements
    for(i=0;i<n;i++)
    { //generate the numbers and assign to array
        a[i] = rand() % 10000 + 1;
    }
}


//heapsort() method

void heapsort(int n)
{
int i,t;
heapify(n); //call to heapify method
for (i=n-1;i>0;i--) {
t = a[0];  //perform swap operation
a[0] = a[i];
a[i] = t;
adjust(i);
}
}
//heapify() method
void heapify(int n) {
int k,i,j,item;
for (k=1;k<n;k++) {
item = a[k];
i = k;
j = (i-1)/2;
while((i>0)&&(item>a[j])) {
a[i] = a[j];
i = j;
j = (i-1)/2;
}
```

```
a[i] = item;
}
}
//adjust() methjod
void adjust(int n) {
int i,j,item;
j = 0;
item = a[j];
i = 2*j+1;
while(i<=n-1) {
if(i+1 <= n-1)
   if(a[i] <a[i+1])
   i++;
if(item<a[i]) {
a[j] = a[i];
j = i;
i = 2*j+1;
} else
   break;
}
a[j] = item;
}

//quick sort
int partition(int low, int high)
{
    long int pivot = a[high];    //assign the pivot element
    int i = (low - 1);

    for (int j = low; j <= high- 1; j++)
    {

        if (a[j] <= pivot)
        {
            i++;    // increment index of smaller element
            swap(&a[i], &a[j]);
        }
    }
    swap(&a[i + 1], &a[high]);
    return (i + 1);
}

void quicksort( int low, int high)
{
    if (low < high)
    {

        int pi = partition(low, high);
```

```
        quicksort(low, pi - 1);
        quicksort(pi + 1, high);
    }
}
//merge sort
void mergesort(int l, int r)
{
    if (l < r)
    {
        int m = l+(r-1)/2;

        // Sort first and second halves
        mergesort(l, m);
        mergesort(m+1, r);

        merge(l, m, r);
    }
}

void merge(int l, int m, int r)
{
    int i, j, k;
    int n1 = m - l + 1;
    int n2 =  r - m;


    int L[n1], R[n2];


    for (i = 0; i < n1; i++)
        L[i] = a[l + i];
    for (j = 0; j < n2; j++)
        R[j] = a[m + 1+ j];

    i = 0;
    j = 0;
    k = l; //index for merge array
    while (i < n1 && j < n2)
    {
        if (L[i] <= R[j])
        {
            a[k] = L[i];
            i++;
        }
        else
        {
            a[k] = R[j];
            j++;
        }
```

```
            k++;
    }

//copy the rest elements of left array
    while (i < n1)
    {
        a[k] = L[i];
        i++;
        k++;
    }

//copy the remaining elements of right array
    while (j < n2)
    {
        a[k] = R[j];
        j++;
        k++;
    }
}


//bubble sort
void bubble (int n)
{
        int i, j;
        for (i = 0; i < n; ++i)
        {
                for (j = 0; j < n-i-1; ++j)
                {

                        if (a[j] > a[j+1])
                        {
                                a[j] = a[j]+a[j+1];
                                a[j+1] = a[j]-a[j + 1];
                                a[j] = a[j]-a[j + 1];
                        }
                }
        }
}

//insertion sort
void insertion(int n)
  {
        int k,t,j;
        for(int k=1; k<n; k++)

    {

        t = a[k];
```

```
            j= k-1;

            while(j>=0 && t <= a[j])

            {

                a[j+1] = a[j];

                j = j-1;

            }

            a[j+1] = t;

    }
}


//driver program
int main()
 {
      int timetaken[5][6],i,j;
      clock_t start, finish;
      double duration;
      //selection sort
      //assign 10000 to n
      n = 10000;
              input(n);
start =clock( ); //time in milliseconds
      selection(n);
finish=clock( ); //time in milliseconds
      duration = (double) ( (finish-start) ); //time in secs.
      timetaken[0][0] = duration;
      delete a;
              //assign 20000 to n
              n = 20000;
              input(n);
start =clock( ); //time in milliseconds
      selection(n);
finish=clock( ); //time in milliseconds
      duration = (double) ( (finish-start) ); //time in secs.
      timetaken[1][0] = duration;
              delete a;
      //assign 30000 to n
              n = 30000;
              input(n);
start =clock( ); //time in milliseconds
      selection(n);
```

```
finish=clock( ); //time in milliseconds
  duration = (double) ( (finish-start) ); //time in secs.
      timetaken[2][0] = duration;
            delete a;
      //assign 40000 to n
            n = 40000;
            input(n);
start =clock( ); //time in milliseconds
      selection(n);
finish=clock( ); //time in milliseconds
      duration = (double) ( (finish-start) ); //time in secs.
      timetaken[3][0] = duration;
            delete a;
      //assign 50000 to n
            n = 50000;
            input(n);
start =clock( ); //time in milliseconds
      selection(n);
finish=clock( ); //time in milliseconds
      duration = (double) ( (finish-start) ); //time in secs.
      timetaken[4][0] = duration;
            delete a;


      //heap sort
      //assign 10000 to n
      n = 10000;
            input(n);
start =clock( ); //time in milliseconds
      heapsort(n);
finish=clock( ); //time in milliseconds
      duration = (double) ( (finish-start)); //time in secs.
      timetaken[0][1] = duration;
            delete a;
            //assign 20000 to n
            n = 20000;
            input(n);
start =clock( ); //time in milliseconds
      heapsort(n);
finish=clock( ); //time in milliseconds
        duration = (double) ( (finish-start)); //time in secs.
      timetaken[1][1] = duration;
            delete a;
      //assign 30000 to n
            n = 30000;
            input(n);
start =clock( ); //time in milliseconds
      heapsort(n);
finish=clock( ); //time in milliseconds
      duration = (double) ( (finish-start)); //time in secs.
```

```
        timetaken[2][1] = duration;
            delete a;
        //assign 40000 to n
            n = 40000;
            input(n);
start =clock( ); //time in milliseconds
        heapsort(n);
finish=clock( ); //time in milliseconds
        duration = (double) ( (finish-start) ); //time in secs.
        timetaken[3][1] = duration;
            delete a;
        //assign 50000 to n
            n = 50000;
            input(n);
start =clock( ); //time in milliseconds
  heapsort(n);
finish=clock( ); //time in milliseconds
        duration = (double) ( (finish-start) ); //time in secs.
        timetaken[4][1] = duration;
            delete a;


        //quick sort
        //assign 10000 to n
        n = 10000;
            input(n);
start =clock( ); //time in milliseconds
        quicksort(0,n-1);
finish=clock( ); //time in milliseconds
        duration = (double) ( (finish-start)); //time in secs.
        timetaken[0][2] = duration;
            delete a;
            //assign 20000 to n
            n = 20000;
            input(n);
start =clock( ); //time in milliseconds
        quicksort(0,n-1);
finish=clock( ); //time in milliseconds
        duration = (double) ( (finish-start) ); //time in secs.
        timetaken[1][2] = duration;
            delete a;
        //assign 30000 to n
            n = 30000;
            input(n);
start =clock( ); //time in milliseconds
            quicksort(0,n-1);
finish=clock( ); //time in milliseconds
        duration = (double) ( (finish-start) ); //time in secs.
        timetaken[2][2] = duration;
            delete a;
```

```
        //assign 40000 to n
              n = 40000;
              input(n);
start =clock( ); //time in milliseconds
              quicksort(0,n-1);
finish=clock( ); //time in milliseconds
        duration = (double) ( (finish-start) ); //time in secs.
        timetaken[3][2] = duration;
              delete a;
        //assign 50000 to n
              n = 50000;
              input(n);
start =clock( ); //time in milliseconds
        quicksort(0,n-1);
finish=clock( ); //time in milliseconds
        duration = (double) ( (finish-start)); //time in secs.
        timetaken[4][2] = duration;
              delete a;


  //merge sort
              //assign 10000 to n
        n = 10000;
              input(n);
start =clock( ); //time in milliseconds
        mergesort(0,n-1);
finish=clock( ); //time in milliseconds
  duration = (double) ( (finish-start)); //time in secs.
        timetaken[0][3] = duration;
              delete a;
              //assign 20000 to n
              n = 20000;
              input(n);
start =clock( ); //time in milliseconds
        mergesort(0,n-1);
finish=clock( ); //time in milliseconds
        duration = (double) ( (finish-start) ); //time in secs.
        timetaken[1][3] = duration;
              delete a;
        //assign 30000 to n
              n = 30000;
              input(n);
start =clock( ); //time in milliseconds
        mergesort(0,n-1);
finish=clock( ); //time in milliseconds
        duration = (double) ( (finish-start) ); //time in secs.
        timetaken[2][3] = duration;
              delete a;
        //assign 40000 to n
              n = 40000;
              input(n);
```

```
start =clock( ); //time in milliseconds
            mergesort(0,n-1);
finish=clock( ); //time in milliseconds
        duration = (double) ( (finish-start)); //time in secs.
        timetaken[3][3] = duration;
            delete a;
        //assign 50000 to n
            n = 50000;
            input(n);
start =clock( ); //time in milliseconds
        mergesort(0,n-1);
finish=clock( ); //time in milliseconds
  duration = (double) ( (finish-start) ); //time in secs.
        timetaken[4][3] = duration;
            delete a;


        //bubble sort
        //assign 10000 to n
        n = 10000;
            input(n);
start =clock( ); //time in milliseconds
        bubble(n);
finish=clock( ); //time in milliseconds
        duration = (double) ( (finish-start)); //time in secs.
        timetaken[0][4] = duration;
        delete a;
            //assign 20000 to n
            n = 20000;
            input(n);
start =clock( ); //time in milliseconds
            bubble(n);
finish=clock( ); //time in milliseconds
        duration = (double) ( (finish-start) ); //time in secs.
        timetaken[1][4] = duration;
            delete a;
        //assign 30000 to n
            n = 30000;
            input(n);
start =clock( ); //time in milliseconds
            bubble(n);
finish=clock( ); //time in milliseconds
  duration = (double) ( (finish-start) ); //time in secs.
        timetaken[2][4] = duration;
            delete a;
        //assign 40000 to n
            n = 40000;
            input(n);
start =clock( ); //time in milliseconds
            bubble(n);
```

```
finish=clock( ); //time in milliseconds
  duration = (double) ( (finish-start) ); //time in secs.
      timetaken[3][4] = duration;
            delete a;
      //assign 50000 to n
            n = 50000;
            input(n);
start =clock( ); //time in milliseconds
      selection(n);
finish=clock( ); //time in milliseconds
      duration = (double) ( (finish-start) ); //time in secs.
      timetaken[4][4] = duration;
            delete a;


//insertion sort
      //assign 10000 to n
      n = 10000;
            input(n);
start =clock( ); //time in milliseconds
      insertion(n);
finish=clock( ); //time in milliseconds
      duration = (double) ( (finish-start) ); //time in secs.
      timetaken[0][5] = duration;
      delete a;
            //assign 20000 to n
            n = 20000;
            input(n);
start =clock( ); //time in milliseconds
                  insertion(n);
finish=clock( ); //time in milliseconds
  duration = (double) ( (finish-start)); //time in secs.
      timetaken[1][5] = duration;
            delete a;
      //assign 30000 to n
            n = 30000;
            input(n);
start =clock( ); //time in milliseconds
                  insertion(n);
finish=clock( ); //time in milliseconds
  duration = (double) ( (finish-start)); //time in secs.
      timetaken[2][5] = duration;
            delete a;
      //assign 40000 to n
            n = 40000;
            input(n);
start =clock( ); //time in milliseconds
                  insertion(n);
```

```
finish=clock( ); //time in milliseconds
        duration = (double) ( (finish-start)); //time in secs.
        timetaken[3][5] = duration;
            delete a;
        //assign 50000 to n
            n = 50000;
            input(n);
start =clock( ); //time in milliseconds
            insertion(n);
finish=clock( ); //time in milliseconds
        duration = (double) ( (finish-start)); //time in secs.
        timetaken[4][5] = duration;
            delete a;




        //print the details
 cout<<endl<<"\tSELECTION  HEAP   QUICK   MERGE   BUBBLE
INSERTION\n\n"                ;

for(i=0;i<5;i++)
 {
        cout<< (i+1)*10000<<"\t";
 for(j=0;j<6;j++)
   {
        cout<<timetaken[i][j]<<"   \t  ";
   }
   cout<<endl;
 }


 }
```

OUTPUT

	SELECTION	HEAP	QUICK	MERGE	BUBBLE	INSERTION
10000	293	2	2	2	337	88
20000	1052	3	5	4	1355	351
30000	2150	6	8	6	3107	791
40000	3655	7	10	8	5557	1406
50000	5510	9	14	10	5184	2194

Process exited after 33.76 seconds with return value 0
Press any key to continue . . .

10.10   Questions

1. With detailed steps, sort 12,34,54,6,78,34,2,33,41,87 using heap sort.
2. Write the algorithm for Quick sort.
3. Write a program to implement the merge sort.
4. Write a single program to compare selection sort, insertion sort, and bubble sort by generating 1000 random numbers.
5. Compare all sorting techniques in terms of time taken by them to sort 10,000 randomly generated numbers.
6. When are binary search and linear search implemented? Explain with an example.
7. Sort 123,435,678,.8765,324,23,4,56 using radix sort.

## 11

Hashing

A Hash table is simply an array that is addressed via a function. For Ex. The below hash table is an array with eight elements. Each element is a pointer to a linked list of numeric data. The hash function for this example is simply divides the data key by 8. and uses the remainder as an index into the table. This yields a number from 0 to 7. Since the Range of indices for hash Table is 0 to 7. To insert a new item in the table, we hash the key to determine which list the term goes on and then insert the item at the beginning of the list. Ex to insert 11, we divide 11 by 8 whose remainder is 3. Thus, 11 goes on the list starting at hash table [3]. To find a number we hash the number and chain down the correct list to see if it is in the table. To delete a number we find the number and remove and remove the node from the linked list.

11.1 Hash Functions

The hash functions are chosen to avoid collision and also with simple operations. When we choose a particular hashing method is noted that hash function should not be biased towards any particular slot in the hash table so as to minimize collision. Also a hash function will have the characteristic that each key is likely to hash to anyone of the slots available in the hash table. Some of the hash functions are

Division Method

This method is considered as a simplest method. In this method integer x is divided by M and then by using the remainder. This method is also called as the division method of hashing.

Sachi Nandan Mohanty and Pabitra Kumar Tripathy. *Data Structure and Algorithms Using C++: A Practical Implementation,* (391–396) © 2021 Scrivener Publishing LLC

The format of hash function will be H(x) = x mod m;

This method works fine for just about any value of M. While choosing the value of M some care should be taken and it is better to take an large prime number. A way making M as a large prime number the keys are spreaded out evenly. The advantage of the division hash function is simplicity and drawback of this method is due to the property that conjuctive keys are mapped consecutive hash values.

Middle Square Method

The middle square method employs hashing method that avoids the use of division and the working of this hash method is that a key is multiplied by itself and the address is obtained by choosing an appropriate number of bits or digits from the middle of the square. The selection depends upon the table size and also they should fit into one computer word of memory. The same positions in the square must be used for all keys.

Ex: 56,789 squaring it the number becomes 3,224,990,521. If three digit address is needed then choose 990.

Multiplication Method

We can form this hashing method by making slight variation in middle-square method. In this technique instead of multiplying the value by itself we have to multiply the number by a constant and then extract the middle K bits from the result.

Folding Method

In this technique a key is divided into a number of parts and each part should have equal length. The exception should given to the last part. The splitted parts are then added together and if we get final carry it should be ignored.

Ex : Let us consider 456,123,789. Now this key is divided into three sub parts and adding them we will get 456 + 123 + 789 = 1386.

So by ignoring the final carry of 1 we will have 368 and this method is called as fold-shifting.

A slight variation can also be implemented by reversing the first and last subparts. This process is known as foldboundary method.

11.2 Collisions

It is not guarantee that the hash function will generate the unique hash key value for all the entries. It also happened that two or more entries having a same key value. So in that situation these two records have to place at the same hash table and also in the same position, which does not possible. This situation leads to the collision. So it is work to find out a space for the newly allocated element. The problem of avoiding these collisions is the challenge in designing a good hash function.A good hash function minimizes collisions by spreading the elements uniformly throughout the array. But Minimization of the collision is very difficult.

11.3 Collision Resolution Methods

Linear Probing

A simple approach to resolving collisions is to store the colliding record into the next available space. This technique is known as linear probing. Linear probing resolves hash collision by sequential searching a hash table beginning at the location returned by the hash function. What happens if the key hashes to the last index in the array and that space is in use? We consider the array as circular structure and continue looking for an empty room at the beginning of the array.

Ex: Consider a hash function as $h(x) = x\%7$

Then arrange the numbers 23,50,30,38 in the hash table

0	1	2	3	4	5	6
	50	23	30	38		

Quadratic Probing

In this case, when collision occurs at the hash address h, then this method searches the table at location h+1, h+4, h+9, etc. The hash function is defined as $(h(x) + i^2) \%$ hash size.

Ex : The numbers are 23,81,93,113

The function is $h(x) = x \% 10$

0	1	2	3	4	5	6	7	8	9
	81		23	93			113		

Separate chaining

The hash function is h(x) = x %10
Store the numbers   23,45,56,78,81,38,113

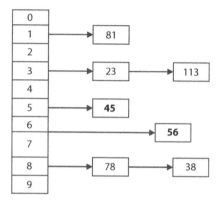

Entries in the hash table are dynamically allocated and entered on a linked list associated with each hash table entry. This technique is known as Chaining. An alternative method, where all entries are stored in the hash table itself, is known as direct or open addressing and may be found in the references.

11.4   Clustering

One problem with the linear probing is that its results in a situation called clustering. A good hash function results in a uniform distribution of indexes throughout the array, each room equally likely to be filled.

Bucket and Chaining

Another alternative way for handling Collisions is to allow multiple element keys to hash to the same location. One solution is to let each computed hash location contain rooms for multiple elements.rather than just a single element. Each of these multi-element locations is called buckets. Using this approach, we can allow collisions to produce duplicate entries at the same hash location, up to a point. When the becomes full we must again deal with handling collisions.

Another solution, which avoids this problem, is to use the hash value not as the actual location of the element., but as the index into an array of pointers. Each pointer accesses a chain of elements that share the same hash location.

Selecting a Good Hash Function

One way to minimize collisions is to use data structure that has more space than is actually needed for the number of elements, inorder to increase the range of the hash function.

11.5 Questions

1. Why is hashing necessary?
2. Discuss the different methods of hashing.
3. What is collision and how to avoid it?
4. Discuss different collision resolution methods with suitable example.
5. How to minimize collision?
6. Given the keys as 3,7,17,33,47,9,26,14,13,23,50,40. Hash function is $H(x) = x\%10$. Explain the hashing process using linear probing and Quadratic probing.
7. Given the elements as 66,47,87,90,126,140,145,153,177,285, 393,395,467,566,620,735. Hash function is $h(X) = x \bmod 20$. Rehash function is $(key+3) \bmod 20$. Allocate the elements in 20-sized heap.

Index

Printed and bound by CPI Group (UK) Ltd, Croydon, CR0 4YY